THE PILGRIM HYPOTHESIS

THE PILGRIM HYPOTHESIS

EXPLORING THE POSSIBLE CONNECTIONS
BETWEEN THE RESTORATION OF THE GOSPEL,
THE GATHERING OF ISRAEL, AND THE
PILGRIMS WHO FOUNDED AMERICA

TIMOTHY BALLARD

Covenant Communications, Inc.

Praise for *The Pilgrim Hypothesis*

If you have ever read the stories of Moses, Lehi, or the Brother of Jared and wondered why miracles like that don't happen today, then this book was written for you. Filled with history and replete with miraculous interventions, The Pilgrim Hypothesis will convince you of the reality of a God whose promised-land miracles aren't only recorded in scripture. The stories in this book will endear you to historical figures such as John Adams, Thomas Jefferson, William Bradford, John Howland, and even Christopher Columbus. More importantly, Tim Ballard will convince you that God's fingerprint can be found woven through the words of modern-day prophets and historical heroes. I will treasure what I learned about the American covenant in reading this book, and my Fourth of July celebrations will never be the same.

—Emily Belle Freeman, Bestselling co-author of *Don't Miss This in the Book of Mormon* and author of *Grace Where You Are*

What Tim Ballard, one of the world's experts in extraction operations, does with this book is extract evidence of God's hand in the discovery, colonization, and faith of the pilgrims. Tim teaches that the pilgrim's self-understanding was based on the biblical notion of "covenant." The covenant was not merely one doctrine among others for them; it was the foundation of a church and the society they hoped to establish.

—Paul Cardall, Internationally Acclaimed,
Dove Award Winning Pianist

A super insightful view of the least likely set of characters and their impact on the Restoration of the Church of Jesus Christ. Tim unfolds a number of sacred scriptures that suddenly come to life as they connect covenants and prophesies with the enduring faith of Columbus, the Pilgrims, the Puritans, Native Americans, the Founding Fathers, and the Prophet Joseph Smith. It will change the way you think of modern-day America and the role you and I must play in the future!

—Tom Holmoe, Athletic Director—Brigham Young University

For Katherine

Cover image: *The Landing of the Pilgrim Fathers, Plymouth, Massachusetts, North America on December 21st 1620*, contributed by Hilary Morgan / Alamy Stock Photo

Cover design copyright © 2020 by Covenant Communications, Inc.

Published by Covenant Communications, Inc.

American Fork, Utah

Copyright © 2020 by Tim Ballard

Printed in the United States of America

First Printing: April 2020

26 25 24 23 22 21 20   10 9 8 7 6 5 4 3 2

ISBN 978-1-52441-282-1

Contents

pilgrim/ˈpil-grəm/, noun: A person who journeys to a sacred place for religious reasons.[1]

Publisher's Note

A hypothesis is not a statement of fact, though it often reads like one. It is, rather, a jumping-off point, a tentative assumption made that provides a framework for examining and organizing facts. Most scientific or historical queries begin with a hypothesis, which is calculated based on the facts already known and then either supported or rejected by additional research.

The Pilgrim Hypothesis is a bold conjecture based on extensive historical research. The miraculous events of the discovery and colonization of America and the remarkable strength of character embodied in the explorers, pilgrims, and prophets are demonstrable facts. In this book, Timothy Ballard has shared many of those facts and drawn some fascinating conclusions from them. Not only that, but unlike a traditional historical work, *The Pilgrim Hypothesis* has a religious bias, specifically one based on The Church of Jesus Christ of Latter-day Saints, as described in the subtitle and throughout the book. Whether or not you come to the same conclusions—whether you support his "hypothesis" or not—we believe you will gain a new appreciation for the events that shaped America as a nation and for those historical figures who followed the inspiration they received to find and found this great American nation under God.

Author's Note

In researching for this book, I visited almost every city and location that I wrote about. I was astonished at the impact it had on me to actually walk on the same ground and enter the same buildings and spaces the historical personages in this book walked on and entered into. In an effort to share something of what I experienced on my journey, I have included QR codes throughout this book that will direct you to digitized videos. Using these QR codes, I will bring you, through video, to some of these historical spaces, introduce you to some of the experts who helped me on my way, and expound upon the lives and times of the men and women who built our American nation.

To access these videos, simply open the camera application on your phone and hold it over the QR code. When a prompt appears, press it, and you will be taken to your video. Depending on the model of your phone, you may need a QR code reader app to access this additional content.

Foreword by Glenn Beck

Christopher Columbus. William Bradford. John Winthrop. The *Mayflower* mothers. John and Abigail Adams. These are just some of the inspiring historical characters you will be introduced to in this book. One definition of *pilgrim* is "a person who journeys to a sacred place for religious reasons," which makes all of these people "pilgrims" in their own right.

For many years, as I thought upon these heroes of history, a recurring question dogged me. Where are our pilgrims today? Where is Bradford? Where is Abigail Adams? Where are Washington and Lincoln? God knows we need them now more than ever. For as *The Pilgrim Hypothesis* will show, they all knew the same secret to our national salvation. It is the secret that built the nation, that allowed us to conquer the world's superpower to gain our independence, and that allowed us to liberate slaves by the millions—that secret is a covenant with heaven. It's a two-way promise. *If* you are righteous, the Lord declared, *then* will I conquer evil and bless your land. It's the same covenant the ancient Israelites made, and it's the same covenant that, if lived, builds nations under God and blesses the world with the peace and light it so lacks today.

So again, I ask, Where are our American pilgrims today?

Shortly before Billy Graham passed away, I had the unique opportunity to sit with him one-on-one, and I asked him this very question.

"I don't know that we will see another Washington or Lincoln," Graham told me. Instead of seeking for a single national leader to command a revolution or liberate the captive, Graham explained that we should look to individuals—thousands of them—working independently of each other but toward that common cause. Working toward that national covenant with God.

I believe Graham. And I believe it is time to call these individuals together. This book by my good friend Tim Ballard *is* that call. Admittedly, *The Pilgrim Hypothesis* looks at history through the lens of the gospel as taught by The Church of Jesus Christ of Latter-day Saints. But the stories, the foundation of the book, are events all Americans share, and all who read this should feel free to plug their own faiths into these stories. For all faiths have grown and flourished because of what these pilgrims did. Let these stories, then, be our common foundation, our national standard, our rallying cry against the forces of darkness.

But I have to warn you: this book doesn't just ask you to recognize this national covenant with God; it shows you what is required to actually live it. And this may be the most difficult part of all. Darkness is real, and it is powerful. To fight it takes real grit, real commitment, and real dedication. Consider what the Pilgrims endured to keep their covenant in America. When they landed at Plymouth during the winter of 1620, they were starving, ill, and dying. In fact, during that first winter, of the 102 *Mayflower* passengers, roughly half (including about three-quarters of the women) perished.[2]

The remaining half—sickly widows, broken widowers, and shattered orphans—wallowed on the Plymouth shore. But they had an escape hatch, a portal that would have seemed almost magical to them, that could have carried them away from their hellacious existence and into the warmth and comfort of civilization. It was the *Mayflower*. It had not yet returned to Europe. The Pilgrims could easily reboard it and return to their homes in Leiden, Holland, where life had been good and where hundreds of the Pilgrims' family, community, and church members waited with opened arms.

Having recognized the short but seemingly failed American experience, Captain Christopher Jones invited the suffering Pilgrim remnant to return to England with him on his *Mayflower*. However, he was shocked when not a single one of the remaining survivors boarded the vessel. It is said that the Pilgrims fell to their knees and sobbed as they watched the sails of the *Mayflower* disappear over the eastern horizon. The date was April 5, 1621, and they all knew that that ship and those sails could be the last signs of civilization they would ever see again.

That is the commitment to God we are speaking of. That is what we need today, and it's what this book will inspire in you.

Not long ago, I was sitting in a chapel in Plymouth, Massachusetts, with Tim Ballard. The Sunday School teacher was talking about faith, using Hebrews 11 as the text for his lesson. Considering where we were, Tim couldn't contain himself and raised his hand high. Once called on, Tim turned to the congregation. "Do you know how lucky you all are to live in this promised land of the Pilgrims?" he asked. "Do you know what they did here? *That* is faith. The act of boarding that *Mayflower* and coming to this dangerous and untamed land because that is what God asked them to do—*that* is faith."

Still addressing the entire chapel-filled class, Tim then asked a question I still think about today. "What is your *Mayflower*?"

As you read this book, I would ask all of you to consider that question. By the end of your read, you may just have your answer.

And inspired by the characters in history you will have studied, you may just have the resolve to *live* that answer.

As a friend of Tim, I happen to know something about his impassioned plea to the class. I happen to know that in 2013, he was asked to board his own *Mayflower*. It almost killed him when he heard the Lord telling him to quit his very secure job as a special agent in the US government in order to start a private organization, Operation Underground Railroad, and head into the darkest corners of the earth to rescue slaves. Against the judgment of my legal team, I involved myself deeply in the risky endeavor and persuaded my audience to raise the start-up money for Tim. Later, I asked Tim to run a project I began in 2015, The Nazarene Fund, which rescues and restores persecuted and enslaved Christians and Yazidis in the Middle East from the evil grips of ISIS.

I have traveled with Tim and our teams to the four corners of the earth to combat the darkest forces on the planet. With the Lord's help, we have successfully rescued thousands of families and children. We have seen the hand of God over and over again. We have prayed for and seen miracles because we have dedicated our effort as part of the very covenant you will read about in this book. In fact, Tim has told me many times that it was his heroes in this book who gave him the example, the ideas, and the passion to launch his mission. Just as the history found in this book inspired Tim to board his *Mayflower*, so his telling of it to you in these pages will inspire and prepare you to find and board yours.

As I mentioned, one of these inspiring voices in *The Pilgrim Hypothesis* is that of Pilgrim governor William Bradford. One of the few first-person accounts we have of the Pilgrim voyage and settlement is Bradford's diary, which is titled *Of Plymouth Plantation*. Sometime after Bradford passed away, the diary manuscript disappeared. For some two hundred years, it was lost. Some believe it found its way into the tower of the Old South Church in Boston and that it was seized there by British forces when they occupied Boston during the American Revolution.

Then, in 1855, a researcher came across a London-published book in New England. In the book, he found a reference to what appeared to be a manuscript containing Bradford's first-person account of the Plymouth Plantation. Could it be a reference to the missing manuscript? Could it be *Of Plymouth Plantation*? According to the citation, the mysterious manuscript containing Bradford's writing was held in the Fulham Library in England.

Letters were exchanged across the Atlantic and to and from the Fulham Library. At last, it was confirmed. Bradford's lost manuscript had been found. A year later, in 1856, *Of Plymouth Plantation* was published in America.[3] And the timing was providential because America was falling apart and was only years away from its terrible Civil War. That war was largely an ideological one, a fight over what America really was and where America had actually begun. Was it the Jamestown colony in Virginia, built on gold and slavery? Or was it the Plymouth colony, built on God, faith, and covenant? Bradford's book reminded the Union of what they were fighting for. It reminded them of their covenant, which, in the end, was the thing Lincoln and the North utilized to save the country and bring forth a new birth of freedom for all.

Just as Bradford's book landed at a providential time, reminding Americans who they were and what they needed to become, I believe this book has as well. And not only because of its release date in 2020, the 400th anniversary of the Pilgrims' landing in America, but also, and more importantly, because this book's providential timing has to do with the fact that this country, with its hate, divisiveness, and ungodliness, in my opinion, is falling headlong into something as bad or perhaps even worse than the American Civil War. Let this book, then, be the *Of Plymouth Plantation* for our time. Let this book call you all to action. You may not be called to go undercover to rescue slaves, but you will be called to do something. Whether it's something that grabs the attention of thousands or something known only to your family or yourself, it matters little. Whatever it is, it will be equally important in furthering the purposes of God and building His kingdom on the earth.

So read this book. Find your calling. Live your covenant.

Introduction

Salem, Massachusetts, August 1836

Joseph Smith had arrived at the New England town of Salem—one of the very first towns established in America—along with his brother Hyrum, Oliver Cowdery, and Sidney Rigdon. The instruction from heaven was clear: "Tarry in this place, and in the regions round about . . . inquire diligently concerning the more ancient inhabitants and founders of this city; for there are more treasures than one for you in this city" (D&C 111: 7, 9–10).

The prophet could not have tarried long before learning of perhaps the most prominent ancient inhabitant and founder of Salem—Samuel Sewall. And Joseph might have been more than a little surprised to know that Sewall had something of a prophetic streak. Whereas most New Englanders understood America to be a "New Israel," Sewall went a step further and prophesied in the earliest days of the Puritan settlement that a new city, even the New Jerusalem, was to be built upon this American continent. But not to be built in New England, according to Sewall; rather, it would perhaps be somewhere closer to the middle of North America—south and west, to be exact, from where he stood in Salem.[4]

Years before his visit to Salem, Joseph prophesied almost these very same words and pointed to this same location—that is, the center of the continent—as the place of the New Jerusalem.[5] Was this a coincidence? Or perhaps there is more to America's settlers than first meets the eye. Perhaps there is deep meaning to the scriptural admonition to learn who these early settlers *really were*.

This story was one of many cues that compelled me to conduct an in-depth historical investigation into the discoverers, explorers, and settlers of America. Why was the Prophet of the Restoration commanded to take an interest here? Why did the Lord similarly command that we "obtain a knowledge of history, and of countries, and of kingdoms, of laws of God and man . . ." (D&C 93: 53)? Why did He ask us to study and teach "things which are at home, things which are abroad; the wars and the perplexities of the nations, and the judgments which are on the land" (D&C 88:79)?

All these questions sent me on a quest—a journey—that required me to travel to the most ancient parts of the Caribbean islands, to the most forgotten corners of Great Britain and Holland, then on to Cape Cod, Plymouth, Salem, and Boston. They sent me digging into libraries, exploring significant edifices, beachfronts, and islands, interviewing relevant locals, and turning over every rock I could. And I came to an astonishing conclusion: this historical narrative—from Columbus to the Pilgrims to the prophets of the Restoration—is the story of the prophesied and great latter-day gathering of Israel.

This fact alone, however, is not necessarily the astonishing part, as any student of scripture and history could make this same conclusion about these historical events without traveling the world for evidence. The real astonishing part of my findings is who these people of history really were and what they knew about their gospel-driven missions under God. Their lives, teachings, and sacrifices stand as a witness to the doctrines of the latter-day gathering, as taught and defined by the prophets of the Restoration. Astonishing indeed.

You may ask what I mean by *gathering*. After all, that can be a loaded term, with lots of definitions. For the purpose of this book, when I discuss *the gathering*, I am generally referring to the definition provided by the *Encyclopedia of Mormonism*: "The gathering of Israel involves bringing together the heirs of the covenant to designated places where they can enjoy the blessings of the temples. Latter-day Saints believe in 'the literal gathering of Israel' and hold that, along with a vital future role for the Old World Jerusalem, 'Zion (the New Jerusalem) will be built upon the American continent' (Articles of Faith, 10)."[6]

In other words, chosen people connected to God's covenant will, by prophecy, come to America—be gathered to America—to establish temples unto the Lord in the latter days. "It was the design of the councils of heaven before the world was," Joseph Smith taught, "that the principles and laws of the priesthood should be predicated upon the gathering of the people in every age of the world . . . . It is for the same purpose that God gathers together his people in the last days, to build unto the Lord a house to prepare them for the ordinances and endowments, washings and anointings, etc."[7] God has made clear that His "work" and His "glory" is to bring to pass the "eternal life of man" (Moses 1:39). Nothing prepares mankind for that blessing like the temple does. The covenants and promises made therein make the temple the ultimate portal to heaven, to exaltation, to eternal life for both the living and the dead. No wonder Joseph taught what he did about why God gathers His people.

But in the centuries and decades leading up to the latter-day discovery and settlement of America, there was no Zion, there was no place protected by liberty for a righteous band of disciples to gather and build God's temple. There was mostly only tyranny and general apostasy, as promised and commissioned by Satan himself, who reigned and ruled throughout the world.

But in His wisdom, the Lord had a plan for the great latter-day gathering of Israel. His plan was so important that it was documented and prophesied in the Old Testament, even as early as the days when Jacob (or Israel) walked the earth with his twelve sons.

Jacob Blessing Joseph

Before Jacob died, he took his sons and blessed them, prophesying over their posterities. To his son Judah, for example, Jacob promised that the Savior of mankind would be born through his line. And to his son Joseph, Jacob promised the covenant of America. "Joseph is a fruitful bough," Jacob said, "even a fruitful bough by a well: whose branches run over the wall" (Genesis 49:22). The authorities of The Church of Jesus Christ of Latter-day Saints have made it clear through official Church publications that this "wall" was the great ocean that separated the Old and New Worlds and that Joseph's "fruitful bough" that ran over the wall was, in fact, his posterity crossing the ocean and discovering and settling this New World—discovering and settling America.[8]

Jacob's grandfather Abraham made that most powerful covenant for all the house of Israel, which was to include all the blessings of the priesthood and temples. But as the LDS Bible Dictionary points out, this Abrahamic covenant was also to include "certain lands" to be given to Abraham's posterity as an "eternal inheritance." Said God to Abraham: "And I will make thee exceeding fruitful, and I will make nations of thee" (Genesis 17:6). Abraham bestowed his entire covenant, to include the covenant of "certain lands" and "nations" of "inheritance," down his line to his grandson Jacob, who conferred the blessing on the seed of his son Joseph. "The physical gathering of Israel," according to the LDS publication *Gospel Principles*, "means that the Israelites will be 'gathered home to the lands of their inheritance, and shall be established in all their lands of promise' (2 Nephi 9:2). The tribes Ephraim and Manasseh [Joseph's children] will be gathered to the land of America."⁹ The doctrine on this matter couldn't be any clearer.

Jacob's Old Testament blessing goes on to say that Joseph's people will prosper in this New World of America—that when the enemy strikes, Joseph's "bow [would abide] in strength, and the arms of his hands [would be] made strong by the hands of the mighty God of Jacob." Other American blessings would, according to Jacob, include "blessings of heaven above, blessings of the deep that lieth under, blessings of the breasts, and of the womb" (Genesis 49:24–25). Indeed, Joseph's people were to be fruitful and prosper as they gathered to America to build temples unto the Most High God.

We see this promise splendidly fulfilled in the Book of Mormon when Lehi and his family crossed that wall and were gathered to the New World to build those temples and carry out the mission of God. That Lehi and the Nephites were a branch of Joseph was not lost on them; they wanted their lineage known—and declared it often—because they knew they were fulfilling the grand prophecy of Jacob to Joseph.[10] "I am a descendant of Joseph," Lehi said. "And great were the covenants of the Lord which he made unto Joseph" (2 Nephi 3:4). Indeed, they were the people of Old Testament prophecy. They were descendants of Joseph. They were the people who had crossed over the wall, and they had every intention of fulfilling their prophetic mandate. It's no wonder Old Testament prophets foresaw this Book of Mormon, which would tell the rest of the story and fulfill those Old Testament promises made to Joseph. They even appropriately referred to this prophesied book as the "stick of Joseph" (Ezekiel 37:19).[11]

But what does this have to do with the *latter-day* gathering of Israel to America? What does it have to do with early discoverers like Columbus or early settlers like the Pilgrims and the Puritans? It has *everything* to do with them.

Remember, the ancient prophets knew there was to be an apostasy from religious truth that would stretch from the Old World to the New. All of Israel would eventually be scattered through their disobedience to God. They would be driven from their homelands, their covenants abandoned, the gospel and temples extinguished. Moses, Isaiah, Jeremiah, and Ezekiel wrote much concerning this worldwide tragedy.[12] Book of Mormon prophets knew of it and were equally concerned.[13]

But they also knew there would be a solution—a final latter-day gathering. A restoration of all that had been lost.[14] As I stated, this solution was provided in the beginning, when Jacob blessed Joseph with the American covenant. You see, the fulfillment of this national covenant was not limited to ancient America (Jaredites, Mulekites, and Nephites) only. Jacob (Israel) himself made this point just before blessing Joseph; while asking him and his brothers to gather for the blessing, he told them: "Gather yourselves together, that I may tell you that which shall befall you in the *last days*" (Genesis 49:1, emphasis added).

The ancient Book of Mormon heirs of the American covenant understood this connection to the last days. They knew that once the Apostasy and worldwide scattering of Israel occurred—and they knew it was going to occur upon their own land and people— their American blessings and promises would be restored to modern America, with specific emphasis on what would become the United States of America (more on this later). When the prophet Nephi was lamenting over one of the final waves of the scattering of Israel, even over the Great Apostasy following the Crucifixion of the Savior (2 Nephi 10:3–6), he immediately provided the solution: "And it shall come to pass," Nephi said, "that they shall be gathered in . . . to the lands of their inheritance . . . . And this land [America] shall be a land of liberty unto the Gentiles . . . for it is a choice land, saith God unto me, above all other lands" (2 Nephi 10: 8, 11, 19). With such a choice land in the latter days, God could start anew; He could bring a righteous branch of Gentiles to build a nation upon the principles of truth and liberty, thus laying a solid foundation for His temples to once again bless the world.

And who are these Gentiles Nephi saw? They are the discoverers, settlers, and founders of modern America (1 Nephi 13). Even at the end of the Book of Mormon narrative, as the prophet-historian Mormon is experiencing the final fall and end of his people, he, like Nephi before him, looked to a more glorious future for his covenant land: "The Lord," Mormon said, "hath reserved their [the Nephites'] blessings, which they might have received in the land, for the Gentiles who shall possess the land" (Mormon 5:19).

Often when we think of the gathering of Israel, our minds immediately take us to the Latter-day Saints of the early to mid-nineteenth century. And we are correct to include them. However, they were not the first ones brought over the wall. They were not the discoverers, explorers, settlers, revolutionaries, and nation builders Nephi saw in his 1 Nephi 13 vision. No, the Gentiles Nephi saw were, as we will see throughout this book, discoverers like Columbus, settlers like the Pilgrims and Puritans, and revolutionaries like George Washington, Thomas Jefferson, and John Adams. Not only did Nephi see them, but today, we also sing hymns dedicated to them, hymns like "America the Beautiful," "God of Our Fathers," and "My Country 'Tis of Thee." We must not forget to recognize the place of these early Americans in the great latter-day gathering, for in many ways, they started the very gathering that has since brought us our greatest gospel blessings.

This doctrine is so important in the story of latter-day America and its place in the house of Israel that Christ Himself spoke of it. While addressing the Nephite population, He explained how He would resolve the forthcoming Apostasy and general scattering of Israel. Just as the prophets He had sent did, He turned the people's attention to latter-day America: "For it is wisdom in the Father," the resurrected Christ said while standing upon the very land over which He was about to prophesy, "that they [latter-day Americans] should be established in this land, and be set up as a free people by the power of the Father . . . that the covenant of the Father may be fulfilled which he hath covenanted with his people, O house of Israel" (3 Nephi 21:4). Christ explained that it would be through this new nation that He would, in the end, "gather in, from their long dispersion, my people, O house of Israel, and shall establish again among them my Zion" (3 Nephi 21:1). "The whole of America," Joseph Smith said, "is Zion itself from north to south."[15]

Christ even made the point in the Bible. Speaking to the chief priests of old Jerusalem in the days leading up to His imminent death, which would mark the beginning of the Great Apostasy, He rebuked their wickedness, foretold their destruction, and, again, provided the ultimate solution: "Therefore say I unto you, The kingdom of God shall be taken from you, and given to a nation bringing forth the fruits thereof" (Matthew 21:43). The LDS King James Bible version of this very verse is cross-referenced with 1 Nephi 13, which tells the story of how the Gentiles would discover and settle the free world, even the *nation* of the United States of America, and ultimately usher in the Restoration of the gospel, which "shall make known the plain and precious things which have been taken away" so that all might know that "the Lamb of God is the Son of the Eternal Father, and the Savior of the world" (1 Nephi 13:40). Abraham Lincoln was perhaps more correct than he knew when he stated that America was "the last best hope on earth."[16]

With the benefit of all these scriptures, the light of the Restoration, and his own holy apostleship, Elder Erastus Snow took it a step further in explaining who Jacob might have seen when prophesying about America. He suggested that Jacob's promise to Joseph—the story of God's chosen ones crossing the "wall" and finding the American promised land (see Genesis 49)—was not solely fulfilled by the people of the Book of Mormon. Rather, he seemed to believe the prophecy also found fulfillment in the modern ocean crossing, which brought the early settlers of what would become the United States of America. These western Europeans, according to Elder Snow, were the ones we find "spreading over the waters a fruitful vine, as predicted by Jacob, whose branches should run over the wall."

Their blood has permeated European society and it coursed in the veins of the early colonists of America.

And when the books shall be opened and the lineage of all men known, it will be found that they have been first and foremost in everything noble among men in the various nations in breaking off the shackles of kingcraft and priestcraft and oppression of every kind, and the foremost among men in upholding and maintaining the principles of liberty and freedom upon this continent and establishing representative government, and thus preparing the way for the coming forth of the fullness of the Gospel.[17]

And this is where our investigation begins. This is where we ask, again, why the Lord commanded the prophet to "tarry in this place" and "inquire diligently concerning the more ancient inhabitants and founders of this city" (D&C 111: 7, 9). Who were these early American settlers and colonists? We know they were chosen, as the Book of Mormon states that "there shall none come into this land save they shall be brought by the hand of the Lord" (2 Nephi 1:6).

We also know that the land they inherited would be given only by covenant. Through the Nephites, we learn that "inasmuch as ye shall keep my commandments ye shall prosper in the land" (2 Nephi 1:20). To the ancient American nation of the Jaredites, it was similarly told: "And now, we can behold the decrees of God concerning this land, that it is a land of promise; and whatsoever nation shall possess it shall serve God, or they shall be swept off . . . for it is the everlasting decree of God" (Ether 2: 9–10).

The importance of the covenant on this land cannot be overstated. Too often this covenant is forgotten because we instead focus only on our more important priesthood covenants, such as those connected with baptism and temple worship. But God has been clear that the promised lands He gives are, in fact, given to a people—to a nation—*by covenant*. And those national blessings of liberty and peace are contingent upon national righteousness. "There is a law, irrevocably decreed in heaven before the foundations of this world, upon which all blessings are predicated—and when we obtain any blessing from God, it is by obedience to that law upon which it is predicated" (D&C 130:20–21).

This includes all the great promises and blessings streaming out of ancient Israel, as we've discussed above. To that ancient nation, the Lord declared: "For I will have respect unto you . . . and establish my covenant with you . . . . And I will walk among you, and will be your God, and ye shall be my people" (Leviticus 26:9, 12). "If my people . . . shall humble themselves, and pray, and seek my face," the Lord said, "and turn from their wicked ways; then will I hear from heaven, and will forgive their sin, and will heal their land" (2 Chronicles 7:14).

> "Joseph, son of Israel . . . was not forgotten when, as promised in the Abrahamic covenant, land was distributed to the tribes of Israel. Joseph's inheritance was to be a land choice above all others. (See Ether 13:2, 8). It was . . . choice because it was chosen. It was to be the repository of sacred writing on plates of gold from which the Book of Mormon would one day come, choice because it would eventually host world headquarters of the restored church of Jesus Christ in the latter days."
>
> —President Russell M. Nelson[18]

When this same covenant theology is applied to the ancient American Nephite and Jaredite nations, we should take note. Then, when we are told in that ancient book of American scripture that this covenant is *also* applicable to "whatsoever nation shall possess" the land, and that it is "the everlasting decree of God" upon the land (Ether 2:9–10), it is *then* that more than merely taking note, we should jump to attention. We should wake up and ask ourselves: *Does this mean the latter-day colonists of America were under this same covenant? And if so, did they know it?*

The purpose of this investigation is to answer these questions. It is to determine whether or not America's discoverers, explorers, and settlers—these pilgrims of the New World—fit the bill. Does history corroborate scripture? Did these early colonists really show an understanding of principles and doctrines connected to LDS revelations regarding the gathering of Israel and the restoration of the gospel—principles and doctrines that would only later be fully revealed through Joseph Smith and the restored Church? Did they know and live the covenant on this land, as defined in the Book of Mormon? Was there a deeper gospel reason for why they believed themselves to be the "New Israel"?[19] If so, the consequences for us today are immense.

First, it may prove to support our testimony of the prophets and scriptures of the Restoration, thus helping us increase our faith in The Church of Jesus Christ of Latter-day Saints and the gospel. And second, beyond our Church membership, it will help validate the notion that America was a covenant land—and *still is* a covenant land. If the covenant ideals prove true in America's founding, they should prove true today. In other words, if our investigation proves the reality of this covenant, the covenant obligations, actions, and consequences that affected these early colonists may still affect us today.

In the end, the findings of this investigation bridge a gap between them and us by placing us all under the same covenant understanding and gospel purpose. You see, their story did not end with them. They started a gathering that we are now in the middle of working through. And so this historical narrative should serve to inspire and energize us, who have taken the torch from these, our forbearers, to carry out their mission, even the mission of the Almighty: to gather in the righteous and bring them to the temple. As much as it is their story, it is our story. As much as it is their covenant, it is our covenant.

The Landing of the Pilgrims

Author Introduction to The Pilgrim Hypothesis

CHAPTER 1

The Pioneer

I sat at an outdoor bar in the Colonial Zone, wearing jeans and a T-shirt, sipping apple juice from a beer bottle. I had just returned from the bathroom, where, after ordering the Corona Extra, I had dumped its contents into the toilet, rinsed it out, then filled it with the juice from the Motts Apple Juice box I had purchased that morning. Though never a drinker, I had to play the role I had been playing for over a decade—my life depended on it in this moment. As I had before, first as a special agent with the US government and now as a deep-cover informant working for my private foundation, Operation Underground Railroad, I was playing the role of a criminal. That afternoon, while sitting and sweating in the thick humidity of Santo Domingo, Dominican Republic, I was a broker in the dark world of child trafficking.

"I got the girls," the waiter whispered with excitement in my ear as he filled my glass of water. "Just give me the address, and I'll make the delivery."

I glanced at my taxi driver, who sat patiently at a nearby table, ready to move upon my request. I took comfort in the small bulge slightly protruding out of the side of his Hawaiian-style shirt. Another bulge barely poked at the inside of his pant leg near his ankle. Though not readily apparent, and completely meaningless to a passerby, those tiny anomalies meant a lot to me. They were respectively his Glock 19 pistol and his Glock 26 ("baby Glock"), and he was wearing them for my protection. And, by the way, he wasn't *really* a taxi driver. He was an undercover detective for the Dominican Republic sex crimes unit. I actually worked for him.

Eventually, we would liberate those girls. In fact, altogether, we would eventually liberate over one hundred (and counting) on the island. Trafficking and slavery are everywhere. But we keep coming back to combat this evil upon this particular island. I somehow feel close to it—called to it. The whole of it is called Hispaniola, and it's divided in the middle and shared by the countries of Haiti and Dominican Republic.

And the very scene I was looking at while perched on my barstool, sipping apple juice from a beer bottle, summed up the deep meaning of the island to me. About a hundred yards from where I sat was one of the oldest remaining colonial structures in the Americas. The Alcazár de Colón, also known as Columbus's Fortress. Christopher Columbus's son Diego built it in 1510 and had, the previous year, been appointed governor of the Indies, a position his father had once held.

After the chat with the trafficker ended, I happily threw what remained of the false drink into the trash, then walked the short distance over to the fortress, which overlooked the rising shoreline of the Ozama River, near where its mouth emptied into the Caribbean Sea. As I walked, I felt the mixed emotions of the place. I realized that abuse and slavery had almost always existed on this island. When Christopher Columbus voyaged here, to the place he named Hispaniola, he brought with him crews who often acted untrustworthily at best and downright brutal at worst. After all, when soliciting help to make such a risky journey, it was not as though he'd had the luxury of picking saints. He took the sailors he could get. Though friendly with the Native populations at first, contentions arose, and viciousness and violence from both sides broke out. Slavery and abuse followed. And it never went away, as evidenced by the grotesque business deal I had just conducted. That abuse would haunt Columbus until the day he died. And it haunts his legacy still.

Columbus Fortress

I climbed to the top of the fortress wall, which boasted a beautiful view of both the river and the Caribbean Sea. I tried to picture Columbus's ships sailing into port. Beyond the river, I spotted a very unusual building. It looked like some giant, pyramid-like, modernized version of an Aztec temple. (Only later would I learn how significant that structure was.) As I walked along the wall, I thought of the immense challenges Columbus had faced on his journey and during his effort to settle and govern

Tour of the Alcazár de Colón

the colony. I thought of the smear campaign history has launched against him and his discovery because of these challenges, and after studying his entire history on the island, I knew he was not blameless.

But I also knew he had come to the New World in peace, and he had come to bring goodness and light. And he did. More than most people know, he truly did. But as the scriptures teach us: "For it must needs be, that there is an opposition in all things" (2 Nephi 2:11). This is especially true for one on God's errand. And Columbus was. As we will discuss in this chapter, he desired to use his discovery to redeem and save the world—a true gatherer of Israel, a true pioneer of the gospel of Jesus Christ.

For if it's true that a righteous group of Gentiles, a band who believed themselves to be the "New Israel,"[20] were waiting on the distant shores of the Old World, waiting to be brought "over the wall" and into the promised land, where God could do His work in the latter days, then someone needed to find this land and publicize its existence at the right time and to the right people. Indeed, someone needed to tell this New Israel what God had in store for them. With Satan's armies blocking the restoration of temple worship and, thus, eternal salvation throughout the world, the Lord needed this discoverer, this explorer, this pioneer.

As I continued to walk along the fortress wall, I thought of how this prophesied narrative, linked to the history of the world, was supposed to end. I thought of 1 Nephi 13, perhaps my favorite chapter in the Book of Mormon, which tells this history given to the ancient American prophet Nephi some 2,000 years before it all played out. And the whole of it reads like a strategy out of a great playbook that could be called *How to Gather Israel in the Last Days.*

1 Nephi 13 is bookended by two major historical events. It begins by describing how the world fell from God, attacking and

destroying His truths—a general state of religious apostasy (verses 1–9). By the end, we have been introduced to a new land, a land of promise, where God would begin the process of healing the world and gathering His people. This land is America.

The rest of the story is familiar to Latter-day Saints. First, the Bible was brought to America and blessed the people. Then, at the very end, God provided a powerful promise: "Other books, which came forth by the power of the Lamb [i.e., the Book of Mormon and other latter-day scripture] . . . these last records . . . shall establish the truth of the first . . . and shall make known to all kindreds, tongues, and people, that the Lamb of God is the Son of the Eternal Father, and the Savior of the world; and that all men must come unto him, or they cannot be saved" (verses 39–40). A restoration of God's gospel was to begin in America.

So what's in the middle of the chapter? What story builds the bridge between apostasy and restoration? The story of America. Nephi sees the Pilgrims coming to America "out of captivity, upon the many waters" (verse 13). He sees how they "prosper and obtain the land for their inheritance" (verse 15). He also sees the Bible in their hands, even that book that "contains the covenants of the Lord" (verse 23). He sees the Restoration beginning. He then sees the War for Independence: "Their mother Gentiles were gathered together upon the waters, and upon the land also, to battle against them" (verse 17). And the Americans were "delivered by the power of God" (verse 19). With freedom in the land, the foundation was set for "other books" to enter the scene and for the fulness of the gospel to at last be ushered in.

But there is one more thing. The first link Nephi reports in the chain of historical events that leads us from apostasy to redemption and restoration. Before pilgrims and revolutionaries, there is one verse—one verse that ignites the rest of the historical narrative: "And I looked and beheld a man among the Gentiles, who was separated from the seed of my brethren by the many waters; and I beheld the Spirit of God, that it came down and wrought upon the man; and he went forth upon the many waters, even unto the seed of my brethren, who were in the promised land" (1 Nephi 13:12).

Such a description is not consistent with the man of controversy so many historians have painted Columbus to be. And yet, according to LDS authorities, Columbus *is* the man Nephi saw.[21] Long frustrated by what I perceived as misrepresentations of the discoverer but also unable to fully reconcile his prophesied mission with the abuse of Native Americans that he is linked to, I've often wondered if somehow he was the reason I returned with my team so often to Hispaniola to help these island nations clean up the abuse and slavery. Somehow, perhaps, this helped me feel I was contributing in some small way to redeeming Columbus's memory. But as I later studied his life in depth, walking where he walked, I eventually realized that he himself left us all the evidence we need to prove who he was and what he accomplished for the kingdom of God on earth.

As can be said of so many of the Lord's anointed who seem to appear on the scene just in time from nowhere (or from nobody) significant, renowned Spanish diplomat and historian Salvador de Madariaga said this of Columbus: "Mystery surrounds him . . . . No one knows who he is, where he comes from, what he actually wishes to do."[22] The Lord—not man—qualifies His servants.

This much we do know about him: He was born near Genoa, Italy, to a lower-middle-class wool weaver, and Columbus seemed connected with God from an early age; he recognized heaven's direction in his life. And heaven directed him to the ocean. He wrote:

At a very early age I began to navigate upon the seas, which I have continued to this day. . . . I prayed to the most merciful Lord concerning my desire, and he gave me the spirit and the intelligence for it. He gave me abundant skill in the mariner's arts, an adequate understanding of the stars, and of geometry and arithmetic. He gave me the mental capacity and the manual skill to draft spherical maps, and to draw the cities, rivers, mountains, islands and ports, all in their proper places. [23]

From there, one event led to another, and he ended up moving to Spain, where his conviction and passion to take an ocean journey to discover unknown parts of the western world can only be described as overwhelming and obsessive. Only after his continued imploring to King Ferdinand and Queen Isabella of Spain did he finally convince the monarchs to fund his mission, which, of course, led to the discovery of America.

These simple facts alone are enough to secure Columbus's place as a prominent forerunner of the Restoration. And yet, the details of how this all happened represent the true power and validation of the story.

First, let's discuss what motivated Columbus to take his journey of discovery. What was in his heart? If I had to answer that in two words, I'd say *the Bible*. And Columbus would say, as we will discuss and source later, that without that book, there would have never been a New World discovery. According to two of the most important Columbus scholars who translated his personal writings, the discoverer "was a careful student of the Bible. He studied it systematically together with the opinions of learned scholars and commentators who were held in the highest regard in his day."[24] Such in-depth personal studies of religion were unusual in that day and show Columbus's commitment to God. But his commitment went

WHO *REALLY* DISCOVERED THE AMERICAS?

Some critics point out that other explorers actually found the New World before Columbus, and therefore, Columbus should not get the credit. It is true that others likely found it first. Certain Viking explorers, for example. But that does nothing to take away from Columbus, for those others did little to nothing with their knowledge. Columbus, on the other hand, was the first to find it, teach others about it, and help others get there. He was the one, in essence, to introduce the promised land to those whom God had preordained to eventually inherit it for His purposes.

beyond just studying. His son Ferdinand, who, like many others, referred to his father as the Admiral, explained: "In matters of religion he was so strict that for fasting and saying all the canonical offices he might have been taken for a member of a religious order. And he was so great an enemy to cursing and swearing, that I never heard him utter any other oath than, 'By San Fernando!'"[25]

Studying and living the gospel produced in Columbus the tools required to serve as a forerunner of the latter-day gospel gathering. Apart from his obvious understanding that Christ is the Lord, the Savior of the world, Columbus's understanding of the appendages to this greatest truth include (1) The reality of personal revelation given through the Holy Ghost, (2) A great missionary work to commence with the settling of the New World, and (3) (and perhaps most surprisingly) the importance of the temple and its restoration to the world in the last days. Each of these principles is consistent with those taught by and through the Restoration. Perhaps it is altogether fitting that this forerunner believed and acted upon each and every one of these doctrines in furtherance of his discovery. Indeed, as we will see, he could not have been clearer about the fact that these three doctrines were major motivating factors for his desire to take that trip.

Such a bold and surprising statement appears to contradict what some historians have long said about his motives. For example, we are taught that "the goal was not *land*, at least not in the Admiral's heart, but rather *gold* . . . .Time and time again . . . [Columbus] openly declared his single-minded interest in finding gold."[26] And another modern historian said, "His chief motive was one of the oldest and most powerful of all: money."[27] Though Columbus did seek monetary gain and though his aspirations for that gain and his sometimes overbearing desire for position and titles may have blinded him at times, it is important to balance the historical record with his spiritual motivation, which could not have been documented any clearer. Columbus wrote the following to the king and queen of Spain:

> With a hand that could be felt, the Lord opened my mind to the fact that it would be possible . . . He opened my will to desire to accomplish the project. This was the fire that burned within me when I came to visit Your Highnesses. All who found out about my project denounced it with laughter and ridiculed me . . . . Only Your Majesties had faith and perseverance. Who can doubt that this fire was not merely mine, but also of the Holy Spirit who encouraged me with a radiance of marvelous illumination.[28]

Columbus's belief in personal revelation through the Spirit was striking for the time in which he lived—a time when the clergy often sought to dominate theology and control the meaning of scripture. And yet, Columbus was so confident in the doctrine that he was bold enough to break further social norms, claiming that "the Holy Spirit" does not only work in him and other Christians but also "works in . . . Jews, Moors [Muslims], and in all others of every sect, and not just the learned, but also in the ignorant."[29] Certainly, this is a man who fits the Book of Mormon prophesy: "And I looked and beheld a man among the Gentiles . . . and I beheld the Spirit of God, that it came down and wrought upon the man" (1 Nephi 13:12).

Again, this is not to say Columbus wasn't also motivated by monetary gain. After all, he would not have been able to convince the Crown to send him on his journey without that justification. His desire for personal wealth and recognition even seemed to be a major weakness at times, particularly during his second and third voyages to the New World. But even that motivation was often tied to his spiritual mandate. For example, he wrote to the king and queen of Spain, asking them to use whatever gains his discovery brought to bring to pass the other two gospel principles that drove him, namely, missionary work and the temple. "I hope in Our Lord," Columbus wrote shortly after landing on the shores of the New World, "that Your Highnesses, with much diligence, will decide to send such [religious] persons in order to bring to the Church such great nations and to convert them."[30] Columbus was equally concerned about the temple in Jerusalem—how it had been overrun by foreigners, desecrated, destroyed, and made useless, as per the prophesies of the scattering of Israel. As one who seemed to seek a *gathering* of Israel, he sought to reverse this tragic state of affairs. "I urged Your Highnesses," he wrote again to the Spanish Crown shortly after his discovery, "to spend all the profits of this enterprise on the conquest of Jerusalem."[31]

Columbus clearly linked his discovery to the gospel themes of converting lost souls to Christ and rebuilding the temple. He referenced these points often. In terms of missionary work, Columbus stated, "I feel persuaded, by the many and wonderful manifestations of Divine Providence, that I am the chosen instrument of God in bringing to pass a great event—no less than the conversion of millions who are now existing in the darkness."[32] He would similarly inform the king and queen that with his discovery now completed, "the Gospel must now be proclaimed to so many lands in such a short time."[33] In a symbolic gesture of Columbus's divine missionary intentions and profound understanding about his voyages, he insisted on erecting a large cross upon every island he visited.[34] Considering what his discovery would eventually mean in a land that once knew the Christ but had since forgotten Him, his symbolic gesture was profound.

◆　◆　◆

Before continuing, we must pause here. For the critics (rightfully) will demand it. They will ask how I can possibly suggest that Columbus came as a Christian missionary to the Natives when his voyages, instead of leading to mass conversions, led to mass abuse. To make matters worse, the Native group hit the hardest was a generally peaceful people known as the Taínos, who even Columbus described as a people of "love and without greed .... They love their neighbors as themselves, and have the sweetest talk in the world, and gentle, and always with a smile."[35] In the beginning, Columbus enjoyed a peaceful relationship with these people.[36]

This part of the history becomes perplexing, and Columbus's role in it is perhaps the most perplexing. He led a total of four voyages to the New World, and the abuse began on his second voyage. On that second voyage, Columbus returned to the makeshift settlement at Hispaniola called La Navidad, where he had left thirty-nine of his men from the first voyage. Tragically, he found them all dead, many murdered by Taíno warriors. With over one thousand Europeans on this second voyage, opinions varied as to what to do, and the temptation must have been strong to avenge their brethren's deaths. But Columbus had come in peace, and he had come to bring Jesus. The royal mandate for this second voyage even laid out Columbus's original intent: the "principal concern" the mandate stated, was for "the service of God, Our Lord, and the enhancement of the Holy Catholic Faith." Columbus was "to win over the inhabitants of the said islands and mainland to our Holy Catholic Faith" and "if any person or persons should maltreat said Indians in any manner whatsoever," Columbus was ordered to "punish them severely." As further witness to this mission, Columbus brought twelve priests and teachers on the second voyage to preach the gospel of Christ.[37]

Though details about what had happened at La Navidad were hazy and no European was alive to testify and offer his side of the story, Columbus decided to give the Natives the benefit of the doubt and did not hold them accountable, declaring instead that "it happened through their [the Spaniards'] own fault"—through their thievery and plundering of Native villages and through their abuse of Native women.[38]

Columbus and his fleet then left La Navidad and sailed eastward around Hispaniola. When they came upon a deepwater port, Columbus decided to stop and commence construction of the first permanent European colony in the Americas. He called it La Isabela, after the queen of Spain. As he and his men built the colony, reports that Natives were planning an attack made everyone nervous. Perhaps he felt he had already played his one "mercy card" in dealing with the massacre at La Navidad. Whatever the case, he wasn't going to do it again. He was already feeling immense pressure from his more than one thousand complaining crew members, some of whom were already dying because of their dwindling food supplies. Furthermore, many of these men considered themselves above manual labor, so their laziness was halting the progression of all Columbus had set out to do.

Columbus then made a tragic decision. He sent his men into Native regions to look for gold and food and to execute a preventative strike (authorizing violence if necessary) on any Natives

Tour of the Ruins of Columbus's Colony, La Isabela

who were plotting against the colony. Knowing many of his men were ruthless, lazy, immoral, lustful, and greedy, Columbus should have known what would follow. Instead of managing the very delicate situation, he left them to their own devices and set off on his ship to explore the Caribbean. He didn't return to his new colony for five months.

In the end, every vow was broken; his men raped, killed, pillaged, and enslaved. The Natives responded with violence of their own. From that point on, Columbus could never bring the relationship back around. A constant state of violent contention ensued, and perhaps feeling that his own security demanded it and feeling that he needed to provide something profitable to the Crown, Columbus, at one point, tragically ordered the enslavement of hundreds of Native men and women, who he then sent back to the Spanish slave markets.[39] He also imposed forced labor on the Native populations in his quest to find gold and oversaw other violent preventative strikes against Native populations.[40]

While none of this can be justified, Columbus continued vouching for the Natives he did not see as a threat, still declaring that they "would be better delivered and converted to our Holy Faith by love than by force."[41] Furthermore, and to make matters even more confusing, in the midst of all the severe abuse, Columbus simultaneously conducted multiple slave rescue operations. Indeed, he and his men risked life and limb to extract and liberate innocent Taíno women and children who had been captured by the Caribe tribe. The Caribe were the enemy of the Taíno, and they were cannibals who feasted on some Taíno men, women, and children while sex trafficking others.[42]

In the end, critics will rightly point out that of the 250,000 or more Natives under Spanish rule, only 40,000 survived after fifteen years. Most of those deaths came about by European diseases accidently imported to the islands, though critics often unfairly blame the Europeans as though it were intentional. (Playing by those rules, a similar yet equally unfair argument could be made against Native populations for having introduced tobacco to Europeans, which has now led to millions of deaths by disease.) Notwithstanding, there is plenty of blame to lay at the feet of Columbus and his men.

Columbus did come as a missionary of Christ with good intentions, and he did convert many. But in the end, he could not endure it, and he could not maintain it, though other, more temperate, Christian leaders who followed Columbus had more missionary success. One of those, a contemporary of Columbus, a man who both admired and criticized Columbus, was the friar Bartolomé de las Casas. Las Casas lived among and loved the Natives—he was known as the "Apostle of the Indians"—and he abhorred how his countrymen, Columbus included, treated them. But even he, in his final analysis of Columbus, said that even "the Archangel Gabriel would have been hard put to govern people as greedy, selfish, and egotistical as the early settlers of Hispaniola."[43]

◆　◆　◆

Returning to our discussion of what drove Columbus to discover and explore the New World, we would be remiss to leave out further discussion of his love and desire for God's temple. As Hugh Nibley pointed out, "[Columbus] wished to discover the Indies to get enough money to rebuild the temple [at Jerusalem]" so God's people might "[go] back to the temple to the Holy of Holies."[44] In Stanford scholar Carol Delaney's 2006 article "Columbus's Goal: Jerusalem," she laments the fact that even today too many fail to see that "[Columbus's] ultimate goal,

the purpose behind the enterprise, was Jerusalem!" Delaney con-
cludes that Columbus firmly believed that "what he accomplished
was not so much a 'discovery' but a revelation—an important
step in uncovering God's plan."[45] Delaney's colleague Leonard
Sweet adds that Columbus's voyage was not a commercial ven-
ture as much as it was a "spiritual quest" and a "medium of
redemption."[46]

This begs the question: How much did Columbus really understand about these gospel themes as related to his discovery? In
hindsight, the picture becomes clear. Again, his discovery began
a chain of events that eventually brought prophets to the promised land. And these prophets, in turn, sent missionaries to all
the world, proclaiming the gospel everywhere; they also delivered temples to the earth. The temple-building project associated
with the Restoration will, according to the prophecies of Joseph
Smith and others, eventually lead to the rebuilding of a temple
in New Jerusalem (in America) and also in Old Jerusalem—just
as Columbus envisioned.[47] In short, whether or not he knew the
details of how this would all play out, Columbus's work did fulfill
and is fulfilling precisely what he believed it would. As President
Joseph Fielding Smith said in powerful simplicity: "The discovery
[of America] was one of the most important factors in bringing to
pass the purpose of the Almighty in the restoration of his Gospel
in its fulness for the salvation of men."[48]

But what do we know about Columbus's knowledge of these
things while he was working them out? The answer may surprise
you. Perhaps the most important artifact Columbus left behind
for us, which may answer this question, has often been ignored
or cast aside by historians who considered it "a late-life mental
aberration," "the religiosity of an embittered and ailing man,"
or an "unimportant excursion into fanaticism."[49] It was a book

Columbus himself wrote, *Libro de las profecías*, or the *Book of Prophecies*, after returning from his third voyage to the Americas. Perhaps the critics see the work as pointless because Columbus's understanding of the gospel as reflected in his book was too deep; perhaps they simply know too little of the gospel he loved. Either way, reading his words through the lens of the gospel, particularly through the lens of the Restoration, makes his words shockingly profound.

In introducing the book, Columbus wrote that his journey was fully inspired by "the forty-four books of the Old Testament, from the four Gospels, from the twenty-three Epistles of the blessed Apostles" and that his discovery of the New World later came to pass "just as our redeemer Jesus Christ had said, and as he had spoken earlier by the mouth of his holy prophets."[50] An astonishingly bold statement. Unless, of course, you believe the Book of Mormon, which does document the words of Christ's holy prophet predicting Columbus's discovery (see 1 Nephi 13:12).

Columbus did not have the Book of Mormon to cross-reference his life with, but he did have the Bible. And he believed his mission to the New World was a fulfillment of certain passages therein. In his book, Columbus listed these passages—these promises and prophesies he believed validated his bold claims. One familiar scripture he quoted in conjunction with his mission was John 10:16, which reads: "And other sheep I have, which are not of this fold: them also I must bring, and they shall hear my voice; and there shall be one fold, and one shepherd."[51] Jesus Christ Himself, in the Book of Mormon account, quoted this very scripture to the inhabitants of ancient America that they would know their worth in His eyes; that they would have His gospel (see 3 Nephi 15:21). Columbus understood that he was fulfilling this scriptural principle again—and again to America—in bringing Christ to a world that did not know Him. And it was more than just the Native population that would benefit. His discovery opened the way for the Restoration, which then brought (or will bring) Christ in His fulness to all lands.

Columbus might have understood this greater vision. In his letter introducing these scriptural passages, he recognized that his discovery was, in his words, part of the "evidence that our Lord is hastening these things . . . . The Gospel must now be proclaimed to so many lands in such a short time."[52] He knew he was living in the last days and that his work was associated with God's final attempt to gather His children in.[53]

Further evidence of his understanding of his role as a deliverer of Christ's message to a lost world comes from the fact that after his discovery, he changed his signature. He began using a Greco-Roman spelling of his name, "Xpo-Ferens." The fact that he changed his signature would naturally cause people to question why. It would cause them to think on his name, perhaps even take into account its meaning. And since the change happened at the time of his discovery, people would hopefully connect the meaning of his name to what his mission was all about. They would see Columbus as "Christopher," or "Xpo-Ferens," both of which mean "Christ Bearer."[54]

Columbus's understanding of his prophetic role only deepens as we dig further into his *Book of Prophecies*. In the introduction phase of the book, he wrote that his discovery was not aided by "mathematics or by maps. It was simply the fulfillment of what Isaiah had prophesied, and this is what I desire to write in this book . . . so that you may rejoice in the other things that I am going to tell you about our Jerusalem."[56]

Columbus then takes us to Isaiah's prophecies of Jerusalem to clarify what he is referring to. And this is where it gets shocking,

SAINT CHRISTOPHER: THE CHRIST BEARER

By some accounts, Columbus was born on the Christian holiday of St. Christopher's Day, which is why he was thus named. The holiday promotes a Christian legend about how a man named Offerus picked up the Christ child—not knowing who He was—and carried Him over dangerous waters. For his service, he was given the name of "Christ Bearer," or "Christopher." In that Christopher Columbus symbolically carried Christ (that is, His gospel message) over dangerous waters, his birth and name may have been stunningly prophetic from the beginning. Displayed upon the oldest known map that charts Columbus's voyages (the Juan de la Cosa map from 1509) is an image of St. Christopher bearing the Christ child over the waters—a homage to the great discoverer.[55]

particularly in light of restored truths. Like he did when quoting the "other sheep" passage (John 10:16), Columbus once again chose the same reference for his book that the prophet-historian Mormon chose for his own "book of prophecies." In this case, Columbus quoted Isaiah 2:2–3 (what we find in 2 Nephi 12:2–3). Under the heading "On the Present and the Future," Columbus quotes the verses in full:

> And in the last days the mountain of the house of the Lord shall be prepared on the top of the mountains, and it shall be exalted above the hill: and all nations shall flow unto it. And many people shall go and say: Come, and let us go up to the house of the God of Jacob: and he will teach us his ways, and we will walk in his paths. For the law shall come forth from Sion: and the word of the Lord from Jerusalem.[57]

The prophecy must have been important to Columbus because he also quoted Micah 4, which includes these same words. And the prophecy should be important to us because of what latter-day prophets have told us about it. According to the LDS-published *Old Testament Student Manual*, in this scripture, Isaiah sees the redemption of Jerusalem, the very thing Columbus sought in connection to his discovery. But Isaiah sees two cities— the New and the Old Jerusalem—"for out of Zion shall go forth the law" (which is the New Jerusalem in America) "and the word of the Lord from Jerusalem" (the old Jerusalem in Palestine). "These two cities," according to LDS doctrine, "one in the land of Zion [America] and one in Palestine, are to become capitals for the kingdom of God during the millennium."[58] In essence, though his mind and heart were always on the old Jerusalem, believing his journey would somehow lead to the redemption of the old city, Columbus found the lands of the *New* Jerusalem, thus paving the way for its prophesied creation. His prophetic interpretations were more tightly connected to his discovery than perhaps even he knew.

But he didn't see Isaiah's prophesied lands of promise as being in the New World, right? It seems as though when he made his discoveries and wrote his *Book of Prophecies*, he was focused only on the old Jerusalem in Palestine. Perhaps that is accurate. Perhaps he only partially understood Isaiah's words while still fulfilling them to the letter. Perhaps he didn't have it all figured out, but his promptings and revelations left him very close to the mark. Or perhaps he *did* know more. I suggest that idea only because of a strange revelation he appeared to have had after discovering the mainland on his third journey to the New World.

Columbus never made it to North America—to the land that would become the United States. But during that third voyage, he did hit the continent that connects to North America. (Before that, he had discovered only islands.) The areas of the continent he actually discovered as he sailed the coastline included parts of South and Central America. And when he did this, he seemed to feel something about the continent. He believed he had found the land wherein resided the Garden of Eden.[59] This is relevant to the Latter-day Saint student, especially in light of Columbus's Isaiah chapters that identify two holy cities in the end of days, because Latter-day Saints teach that the land of the Garden of Eden is the same location in Missouri as the New Jerusalem Isaiah saw.[60] Was Columbus on to something?

It seems he was. Leading Columbus scholar Delno West explains the significance of this purported revelation to the discoverer. Based on what Columbus studied and referenced, he would have believed, according to West, that "Eden was located in precise antipodal balance to Jerusalem. Eden was the exact center of one hemisphere while Jerusalem was at the exact center of the other." Columbus's understanding of the "two centers" theology familiar to Latter-day Saints becomes even more profound. "To Columbus, then," Professor West explains, "the finding of the geographic site of the Terrestrial Paradise meant human history was coming to an end. The two geographic areas had to be brought together, both had to be in the hands of Christians for Christ's return . . . . Instead of a crusade moving eastward across North Africa to recover the Holy Land, Columbus promoted a move westward that he believed was the prophesied path to the Holy City."[62]

> "I believed and I still believe . . . that there in that region is the Terrestrial Paradise."[61]
>
> —Christopher Columbus, in a 1502 letter to Pope Alexander VI

In a letter written to describe this new discovery of his third voyage, Columbus gave us more reason to believe he *knew* he was tapping into deep gospel truth. In the letter, he claimed that what he had discovered was "a New Heaven and a New World which had until now been hidden." He also added this bold and extraordinary claim: "Of the New Heaven and Earth which Our Lord has made, and as St. John writes in the Apocalypse, after he had told of it by the mouth of Isaiah, He made me the messenger for it and showed me where to find it."[63] Under the heading, "New Heaven and New Earth," the *Encyclopedia of Mormonism* relates this new heaven and new earth to "the Earth's destiny of renewal . . . . That renewal will include the restoration of its former components—for example, the return of the city of Enoch."[64] And that city, according to Elder Bruce R. McConkie, "shall return, as a New Jerusalem, to join with the city of the same name which has been built upon the American continent."[65] Indeed, upon the land and continent whose discovery Columbus made possible.

I still don't claim to know exactly what Columbus knew or what he fully meant when he referenced Jerusalem (new or old), the Garden of Eden, and the New Heaven and Earth, but in light of the fact that he connected all these things to his discovery of America—and the fact that LDS doctrine places all these things in connection with America—it's hard to write it off as a coincidence, especially when he saw himself as a "messenger," saying the Lord "showed me where to find it" and claiming he had found it in the New World. I say that because Nephi saw the same thing concerning Columbus, namely, that God showed him the way to the promised land (1 Nephi 13:12), and his discovery did and will, in fact (just as Columbus implied), lead to the fulfillment of the blessings related to the New Jerusalem, the Garden of Eden, and the New Heaven and Earth. Few if any faiths outside The Church of Jesus Christ of Latter-day Saints teach such connections to America, which makes us wonder how and why Columbus did. But what else could he have meant by all this?

Because this idea brings Columbus so close—maybe too close for some—to doctrine unique to Latter-day Saints, I recognize I am vulnerable to claims of interpretive bias. And so, like I did above with Professor West, I will bring in another outside, non-LDS scholar to expound on all this. Dr. Frank Graziano, distinguished professor of Hispanic Studies at Connecticut College, published the following: "As though [focusing only on old Jerusalem] was insufficient, however, Columbus then redoubled the millennial implications by equating the discovered lands with the New Jerusalem." Dr. Graziano then quotes Columbus's above-cited statement of how God showed him that the New Heaven and Earth were in the western hemisphere. Dr. Graziano then continues:

The allusions are to Revelation 21:1–4 and 21:22–27, where Jerusalem is transformed into a "new heaven and new earth" as the celestial city descends, and to Isaiah 65:17–25 [quoted in Columbus's *Book of Prophecies*], where the "new heaven and new earth" seem almost a fusion of Jerusalem and Eden . . . . Columbus will have his Jerusalem one way or another, by force of arms in a new Crusade at the old Jerusalem, by appeal to biblical New Jerusalem imagery superimposed in the Americas, or by the "discovery" of the Garden of Eden on his third voyage.[66]

In his *Book of Prophecies*, Columbus attached other chapters from Isaiah to his discovery, including Isaiah 11 and 49. From chapter 11, Columbus quoted, "The Lord shall set his hand the second time to possess the remnant of his people . . . And he shall set up a standard unto the nations; and assemble the fugitives of Israel."[67] LDS doctrine confirms that this prophecy refers to the last days, and the final gathering of Israel to the American Zion.[68]

Isaiah 49 prophesies of the same. One of several examples in that chapter is the following prophecy: "Behold, I will lift up mine hand to the Gentiles, and set up my standard to the people: and they shall bring thy sons in their arms, and thy daughters shall be carried upon their shoulders. And kings shall be thy nursing fathers, and their queens thy nursing mothers" (Isaiah 49:22–23). "Chapter 49 is one of the most important chapters in the whole book of Isaiah," according to the *Old Testament Student Manual*, "because it also clearly foretells the mission of the latter-day Saints and the destiny of the land of America in connection with the house of Israel."[69] Finally, Columbus quoted from Joel 2—yet another reference, per LDS doctrine, to the New Jerusalem in America.[70]

Another clue that Columbus might have believed he would discover a promised land is the fact that he brought a Hebrew man on his voyage. His original name was Yosef Ben Ha Levy Haivri (Joseph the Son of Levy the Hebrew), and Columbus stated that he was there to communicate with any remnants of the Lost Tribes they might find who were presumably sent to this same land before him.[71] Again, if that was Columbus's assumption, LDS doctrine— specifically the Book of Mormon—again seems to corroborate it. 1 Nephi 13:12 prophesied that Columbus would come to "the promised land" of the Americas, specifically to "the seed of [Nephi's] brethren," who were lost Israel.

It's astonishing to me to consider how right Columbus was. He believed these biblical scriptures were connected to his finding America—and they were!—but his assertions would not be confirmed until the Restoration, until latter-day prophets clarified what these Old Testament prophecies meant. It's also astonishing to consider that the *very* chapters Columbus cited from Isaiah (chapter 11) and from Joel (chapter 2) were also quoted by Moroni to Joseph Smith on the night he appeared to him in his room.[72] Furthermore, all these Isaiah chapters we discussed from Columbus's *Book of Prophecies,* from Isaiah 2 to Isaiah 11 to Isaiah 49 (not to mention others of the dozens of Isaiah chapters in his book), were also quoted by Nephi in the Book of Mormon, and both Columbus and Nephi were quoting these Isaiah verses to support the highly unique proposition that they were connected to the gospel purposes of latter-day America. Then, to close this amazing loop of history and prophecy, this same Isaiah-quoting Nephi actually saw in vision and documented in scripture this same Isaiah-quoting Columbus. Is this all one giant coincidence, or is there deeper meaning here?

To help us answer that, I think it's important to discuss more about Columbus's journeys to the New World. So far, we have gone into his mind and spirit, but what of his actions? Generally, miracles follow the Lord's forerunners, gatherers, and restorers. It's often evidence of their callings. Does Columbus's life follow this pattern? Though I won't attempt an entire biographical narrative here, I do want to introduce you to some of the miracles that seemed to follow this "man among the Gentiles" (1 Nephi 13).

◆　◆　◆

As best we can glean from the few historical clues that exist, Columbus was the oldest of five children living on the coast of Italy. As a child, he was naturally, even spiritually, drawn to the mariner arts. And so he began signing up as a common deckhand on merchant ships. As he grew older, his assignments became more extensive. At age twenty-five, he signed up for a longer trip on the ship *Bechalla*, which set off on May 31, 1476, carrying and trading goods from Italy to England and to other parts of Europe. While on this trip, French warships attacked the *Bechalla* (Europe was at war during this time, making any ship a potential target). Soon, sailors from both ships flooded onto each other's decks, where hand-to-hand combat ensued. Columbus was right in the middle of it. Crewmen started fires on both ships, and men had no choice but to abandon their posts and jump overboard. Many drowned. But Columbus managed to plunge into the Atlantic and swim eastward for six hours straight until landing, exhausted, on the shores of Portugal. By the grace of God, he was saved and brought to this new land.[73]

If God needed someone to find America at this time in history, there was no better place to put that person than in Portugal. No place on earth was busier in the field of ocean travel and exploration than Portugal's capital, Lisbon—it was a virtual university for would-be ship captains. Columbus arrived in this mariner mecca without a penny in his pocket. The ocean dreamer was thrilled. He set up a business charting and drawing maps, which he sold to sailors. He also learned to read and write in Spanish, which would eventually become his language of choice. He was then fortunate enough to meet Felipa Perestrello, the daughter of a former governor of the Madeira Islands, with whom he fell in love and married.

Columbus's father-in-law, who died before Columbus joined the family, had also been a great lover of the ocean. He had kept a large collection of notes and artifacts connected to the mysteries of the ocean, and Columbus's mother-in-law gave all these prized possessions to Columbus. He pored over the material as his life's mission became clearer and clearer. As his knowledge continued to grow, he eventually became the captain of his own merchant ship and moved with his wife to Portugal's Porto Santo Island, where their son Diego was born.[74] Part of the Madeira Islands, Porto Santo was in the western-most part of the known world. Surely it was here where Columbus stood looking westward, wondering what was out there.

Convinced that there was a western route to Asia and possibly other unknown lands to discover along the way, he stopped at nothing until he could go in search of it all. In 1483, he moved his family back to Lisbon so he could convince the king of Portugal to fund his mission. Then tragedy struck. First, his wife died, leaving him a widower and single parent. And second, the king of Portugal, unconvinced, refused to support his mission. Oftentimes, there is a descent before the ascent, and Columbus hit rock bottom. But he did not give up.

With Portugal's rejection, he moved with his son to Spain, sailing into the Spanish port town of Palos. But before traveling inland to track down and approach the monarchs, he apparently needed further instruction and preparation. He moved into a beautiful monastery called La Rábida, which overlooked the ocean. And it was here that he took his passion and scientific knowledge and learned to blend it with religious studies. He found a new purpose under God for his mission. And for the spiritually inclined Isabella, Queen of Spain, having God with him in abundance as he made his plea for support would be key.[75]

Though it took years of persistence and patience making his case at the Spanish court, his plan finally worked. The Spanish monarchs agreed to support his mission. Almost providentially, they ordered Columbus to leave their court and travel to, secure boats at, and launch his journey from Palos—the precious town of La Rábida, where he had learned to trust God. On August 2, 1492, he departed Palos with his three ships—the *Niña*, the *Pinta*, and the *Santa María*.

The journey was rough from the beginning. It was difficult for the discoverer to recruit sailors for a trip many believed to be a death trap. With few choices, he didn't have the luxury of finding those who shared a spiritual vision or who would be loyal to him and his mission. He would need to rely on the Lord and His miracles. One of those miracles occurred midocean when the wind stopped and the ships stood still. As his crew grew nervous, something inexplicable happened: the sea rose and moved the ships with no wind. The crew was astonished. But Columbus knew the secret; he knew God was with them, and he said, "The high sea was very necessary for me, [a sign] which had not appeared except in the time of the Jews when they left Egypt [and complained] against Moses, who took them out of captivity."[76]

A second possible miracle occurred on October 11, 1492. "I saw a light to the west," Columbus explained. "It looked like a little wax candle bobbing up and down . . . . [as if someone] alternatively raised and lowered it." Excited, he turned to a companion and asked if he was seeing the same thing. His companion confirmed it, but when they called others over, nobody else saw it.[77] Was it just a coincidence? Was it a sign? Was someone watching? Guiding them? Whatever it was, it convinced Columbus to continue with speed toward the light.

The next morning, October 12, 1492, the ships landed on the shore of a Caribbean island. With Natives watching in awe, Columbus disembarked triumphantly, then, with tears streaming down his face, gave thanks to the Almighty, in whose honor he named the land San Salvador ("Holy Savior").[78]

Columbus would make a total of four voyages to the islands and continent of the Americas, always facing new challenges, especially as he tried to colonize and failed to govern the island of Hispaniola, but he often (though perhaps not often enough) stood ready to receive God's miracles as well—tokens to remind him, and us, why he had done this.

One of these (possible) miracles is connected to an account published by the renowned American historian Washington Irving. In his work entitled *The Life and Voyages of Christopher Columbus*, Irving spent much time discussing the spiritual inspiration that accompanied Columbus's voyage. Irving then recounted a report he discovered while poring over documents in Spain that described an event that allegedly occurred during Columbus's exploration of the Caribbean. According to the report, one member of Columbus's crew, an archer, while hunting for wild game on the island of Cuba, encountered three strange-looking men interacting with a tribe of Natives. These men "were of as fair complexions as Europeans," wearing long "white tunics reaching to their knees," and were "so like a friar of the order of St. Mary of Mercy." Frightened at the scene, the archer ran back to the ship and told his commander what he had witnessed. Columbus then sent at least two separate expeditions to search for the three men but to no avail.[79]

Irving then apologized for including the account in his book, as no corroborating evidence existed that light-skinned people wearing such clothing existed in the New World. Though Irving concluded that the story was most likely born of error, he did feel so inclined to include it in his book.

Responding to Irving's account years later, Brigham Young University scholar E. D. Partridge wrote the following for the *Improvement Era*:

> No apology is needed . . . by the Latter-day Saints. The account given by the archer portrays conditions just as they would naturally be with the "Three [Nephite] Disciples." They lived among the people when the vision recorded in 1st Nephi was taught [Nephi's vision of Columbus]. They were, of course, looking forward to its fulfillment. They were to bring souls to Christ till he should come again, and had probably been busy gathering bands of followers all over the country . . . . Columbus and his sailors were looked upon by the natives as visitors from heaven, and their appearance was heralded all over the country. Their movements were watched closely from the shores, since whenever they landed they found themselves not unexpected. It does not take much imagination to see the "disciples" and one of their bands following the movements of the ships from the trees or mountains, awaiting a favorable opportunity to make themselves known. In fact, there is nothing in the report of the archer which is in the least at variance with what might be expected from our knowledge of the Book of Mormon.[80]

Another fascinating story with spiritual implications has to do with events surrounding Columbus's first journey back to Spain from the New World. Knowing that the news of the great discovery would begin a chain of events leading to a gospel restoration and gathering, the adversary seemed intent on doing all possible to deny Columbus's return. The ocean storms raged so violently that Columbus and his men believed they would perish—the gospel news they brought perishing with them. Things got so bad that Columbus, who was piloting the *Niña*, had lost sight completely of his companion ship, the *Pinta* (the *Santa María* had earlier wrecked off the coast of Hispaniola and couldn't make the return). The crew from the *Niña* believed the *Pinta* was lost forever and vice versa.[81]

Columbus was so concerned about news of the discovery being lost should he not make it that he wrote a letter with directions to the New World, wrapped it in a wax cloth, concealed it in a crate, and dropped it overboard.[82] If necessary, God could get the crate into the right hands. He then led his crew in prayers in hopes that his contingency plan would not be needed. "I have faith," Columbus wrote, "in Our Lord that He who brought me here will lead me back in His pity and mercy . . . . No one else was supportive of me except God, because He knew my heart."[83]

As days passed with no reprieve from the storm, the crew decided to make an offering to God. They covenanted with God and each other that if their lives were spared, they would make a series of pilgrimages to certain chapels back home and hold special worship services there. Lots were drawn on at least two occasions in the midst of the storms to determine who would lead the pilgrimages. And on both of those occasions, it fell on Columbus himself.[84] The crew believed it a sign from God, as the odds of this happening seemed impossible. [85]

When the ship finally arrived off the shores of Portugal, with hardly a single sail remaining intact, the people on the shore were shocked, for they had witnessed the storms and learned of so many ships that had perished off their coast in recent days. But the crew knew what had happened; they knew who had brought them safely to harbor.[86]

The Lord confirmed the miracle of it all shortly after their landing in Portugal. After taking about a week to rest and clean and refit the ship, Columbus and his crew departed Portugal for Palos, Spain, where they had initially embarked. They arrived at Palos on March 13, 1493. They were finally home in Spain. Though it had been nearly a month since Columbus had seen the *Pinta*, still believing it had been lost in the storm, as if directed by the hand of God Himself, the *Pinta* also somehow sailed into Palos on March 13—the very same day as Columbus.[87]

If all this weren't enough to convince men of God's hand in the affair, there is one more thing worth mentioning. Upon landing at Palos, Columbus knew there was still one last threat. One of his captains, Martín Pinzón, had led rebellions against Columbus during that first journey, and everyone assumed he would now attempt to discredit Columbus. They believed Pinzón would tell a different version of the facts to the Crown, which would elevate himself and attempt to hurt Columbus. But Pinzón got sick and died a few days after his return to Spain. The threat quickly sputtered to a full stop.[88]

One of the greatest miracles that accompanied Columbus was born, like so many other miracles, in a place of severe difficulty. During Columbus's third voyage, he had to confront a traitor, Francisco Roldán, who had usurped Columbus's power and staged a rebellion against him. To recruit Columbus's men to join the rebellion, Roldán had promised to share "all the wealth of the island" with them and, most disturbingly, give them the power to "use the Indians as they pleased, free from interference." Roldán used force to take Native women from their husbands and kidnapped daughters from their parents and forced them into labor and sexual slavery. With the allure of such wicked pleasures, Roldán eventually convinced most of Columbus's men to join the rebellion.[89]

Columbus fought back and eventually ended up hanging seven Spanish rebels and quashing the rebellion. But when word got back to the Crown that Columbus had lost control, the Sovereigns sent in an agent, Francisco de Bobadilla, to investigate. When Bobadilla got to Santo Domingo, Hispaniola (the colonial headquarters had since moved from La Isabela to the new colonial town of Santo Domingo, which has remained the capital until today), he reacted hastily and had Columbus arrested, placed in chains, and sent back to Spain to stand trial. The monarchs had unwisely told Bobadilla that if he found Columbus was guilty of crimes, then he himself would be the new commander and governor of the islands. With such a conflict of interest, Bobadilla's decision was likely made before his arrival. During the investigation, Bobadilla relied heavily on the biased testimonies of rebels who Columbus had punished (remnants of these biased testimonies are still unfairly used today to condemn Columbus). Incredibly, while Bobadilla imprisoned Columbus, he granted a full pardon to the wicked rebel Francisco Roldán.[90]

Columbus was humiliated. When he returned in shackles to Spain and to the king and queen and pleaded his case, they recognized their error in sending Bobadilla. They acquitted Columbus of all charges.[91]

Columbus then got support from the king and queen to make his last voyage back to his lands of discovery. And this was where the miracles began manifesting themselves once again.

When Columbus arrived at Hispaniola, Bobadilla and the others governing in Columbus's place made it clear he was not welcome. They did not permit the discoverer to leave his ship and step foot on the island colony he himself had founded.

Columbus did not fight back but instead appeared to become prophetic. He sent word to the island administrators that an enormous storm was about to hit the island. Columbus said he needed safe harbor for his ships. Columbus had learned that the administrators were about to send a large fleet of their own ships back to Spain soon. Columbus warned them to wait until the storm passed. Seeing no signs of any storm coming in, the governors of the island mocked Columbus as a false prophet, denied him safe harbor, and sent their fleet, consisting of twenty-eight ships, on their way back to Spain. Saddened, Columbus sailed his ships around the island and up a lonely river that emptied into the ocean. There he anchored his small fleet to wait out the storm.

And the storm came.

The fleet that left against Columbus's warning was decimated. Some five hundred sailors perished, and two thousand pounds of gold sank to the bottom of the ocean. Bobadilla, the man who had falsely imprisoned Columbus, was among those who perished in the storm. Francisco Roldán, leader of the rebellion that had led to Columbus's sham arrest, along with others who had rebelled and hurt Columbus, drowned alongside Bobadilla.[92]

Only one ship from the Spanish fleet made it through the storm and landed in Spain. The *Aguja*. And as if Bobadilla's and Roldán's deaths weren't enough to wrap this story up in poetic justice, you won't believe what cargo the *Aguja* carried. It was the gold the king and queen had ordered to pay Columbus for the work he had done. Columbus's son was at the Spanish port to receive it. The jealous nonbelievers who hated and despised

Columbus were dumbfounded. All they could say was that Columbus must have conjured up the "magic arts" to have "raised that storm" and thus taken his revenge. Columbus did not respond to their ridiculous comments. Again, he knew the truth; he knew whose mission he was on.[93]

He continued with his fourth voyage, exploring more lands and making more notes. He attempted to build a new settlement in Central America called Santa María de Belen but was run off by the Natives. He was later shipwrecked on Jamaica for a year before finally being rescued. He then sailed home to Spain, never to return to the New World again.

◆　◆　◆

Back in Hispaniola (Santo Domingo), I stood at the base of an elaborate outdoor staircase made of concrete. Remember that structure I first saw from the Columbus Fortress, the one that reminded me of an Aztec Temple? Well, several trips to the island later, I finally decided to check it out. And there I was, standing at the bottom of its staircase. The closer I got to it, the more certain I became that this truly was the strangest structure I had *ever* seen. The stairs led to an enormous building, a monument, a mausoleum stretching out several city blocks in length and shooting into the air at least ten stories. One unusual thing about it was that the entire thing was built in the shape of a cross, which you can only really see if you are flying over the top of the edifice. The other unusual thing about it is that the whole of it is a grave marker for the remains of Christopher Columbus. The structure is known as the Columbus Lighthouse.

Overwhelmed by it all, I began to walk up the stairs. *Are his bones really in here?* was the only question running through my mind. You see, nobody knows for sure. It's the strangest story. After Columbus died in Spain, he was buried in the city of Valladolid. His remains were then taken and interred at the monastery of Santa María de Las Cuevas near Seville, where he had lived while writing his *Book of Prophecies* between his third and fourth voyages. But he had requested to be buried in the Americas before his death, so years later, a family member sent his remains to be buried in a Santo Domingo cathedral. When the French took over Hispaniola, the Spanish didn't want Columbus's remains under French rule, so they moved what they thought were his bones to another Spanish-held island—Cuba. But when the Spanish-American war broke out over Cuba in 1898, Spain moved the remains back to Seville.

But before that, in 1877, workers digging around the Santo Domingo cathedral unearthed a leaden box of bones with an inscription—"Illustrious and distinguished male, don Christopher Columbus." Dominicans insist that the wrong remains (perhaps those of Columbus's son) were sent to Cuba in the first place and that they still had Columbus. And in defense, they built the Columbus Lighthouse to officially declare it.

After a DNA test on the bones in Seville seemed to suggest—without total confirmation—that Columbus is actually buried in Spain today, Juan Bautista Mieses, the director of the Columbus Lighthouse, dismissed the DNA results, stating that Hispaniola still has Columbus and that he wouldn't authorize a DNA test on the Lighthouse bones for religious reasons. Interestingly, the man who led the Seville DNA project, Marcial Castro, affirmed that the DNA results were probably accurate but that the remains in Santo Domingo might *also* be Columbus. He explained that the body was moved so many times it is possible that at some point the remains were divided so that Columbus is now buried in both the Old World and the New World.[94]

I liked that idea. By the time I was halfway up the concrete stairs—and already in a full sweat from the thick humidity that was inescapable on this island—I was *really* liking this idea a lot. *How appropriate*, I thought to myself. I thought of Columbus's love for both worlds—particularly his love for the Jerusalem in the Old World and the idea of the New Jerusalem (New Earth, Garden of Eden) in the New World. Buried in both!

I thought of the restoration of the gospel, built upon the lands Columbus discovered, and how that restoration has already led to the beginning of old Jerusalem's renewal. Indeed, it was that restoration that produced the Apostle Orson Hyde, who Joseph Smith asked to visit Jerusalem to dedicate it to the Lord, which he did in 1841. Elder Hyde climbed the Mount of Olives and dedicated the Holy Land for the return of the Jews and for the building of a future temple in Jerusalem.[95] Columbus would have been pleased. It was, after all, his discovery that started a chain reaction leading to this powerful event that touched his ultimate goal and mission.

How fitting that the same Orson Hyde, an Apostle of God, seemed to have had a vision of Columbus. While addressing the Saints in the Tabernacle in 1854, Elder Hyde proclaimed that the Angel Moroni "was with him [Columbus] on the stormy deep, calmed the troubled elements, and guided his frail vessel to the desired haven." The miraculous history of Columbus's travels certainly corroborate this idea. Elder Hyde continued: "This same angel [Moroni] was with Columbus, and gave him deep impressions, by dreams and by visions, respecting this New World."[96] Again, considering what he thought, felt, and wrote about in his *Book of Prophecies*, we have some corroboration.

The idea that the angel Moroni helped Columbus was, according to Elder Hyde, an indication of "an important reason why the discovery should be made: The history and record of a fallen people, containing light . . . and truth from heaven, were buried in the soil of the Western Continent; and although engraved on golden leaves in a strange and unknown tongue, still they must come forth."⁹⁹ After all, it was always Moroni's scriptural mandate to be sent to "reveal the Book of Mormon" in the last days (D&C 27:5).

But that was not all that was to be revealed. The crowning element of the gathering of Israel—the great Restoration of all things—was the temple. As I finally reached the top of the concrete staircase to the enormous Columbus Lighthouse, I could not help but think on the temple because I felt as though I was approaching one. Upon entering the open-air, doorless edifice, I was met by an enormously tall and long corridor that led directly to the elaborate tomb. I walked down to it. On both sides of me, I saw engraved in the walls Columbus's signature: *Xpo Ferens*. The Christ Bearer. That, along with the light-colored walls and the spiritual feeling within the building, almost brought me to tears. I thought of how Columbus must like this place—he was always fond of holy places. Temples.

Without even trying, my mind shot to Wilford Woodruff at the St. George Temple in August 1877. This was when, according to President Woodruff, some of the Founding Fathers of America visited him and asked that their temple work be done. Beginning on August 21, Wilford Woodruff was baptized for, or had baptisms done for, more than 160 eminent men and women, pursuant to the vision. Christopher Columbus was among them. Shortly thereafter, endowments were done for these deceased, and the men were ordained to the office of elder. Strangely, President Woodruff selected a few of these men to be ordained to the office of high priest, and Columbus was one of

DID AN ANGEL VISIT COLUMBUS?

While on his fourth voyage to the Americas, Columbus found himself alone on his ship, which was anchored near the mouth of the Belen river while his crew was on shore gathering supplies for their return to Spain. Columbus heard shots. His men had come under attack from a Native tribe, and Columbus could do nothing to help. He grew anxious and depressed. And this is when a miracle occurred. And it occurred, coincidently or not, on April 6, the date later given by revelation as the designated date that the Church of Jesus Christ was to be reestablished on the earth in the last days.[97]

Columbus himself tells the story in a letter to the Spanish monarchs:

> I was outside and all alone . . . . there was no hope of rescue . . . . I climbed in pain to the highest point of the ship and called in tears and trembling to your Highnesses' mighty warriors in all four corners of the earth for strength, but none of them answered me. At length, groaning with exhaustion, I fell asleep and I heard a most merciful voice saying: "O fool, so slow to believe and to serve your God, the God of all! What more did He do for Moses or for His servant David? He has had you in his care from your mother's womb. When he saw you a grown man, He caused your name to resound most greatly over the earth. He gave you the Indies, which are so great a section of the world, and you have divided them according to your desires. He gave you the keys to the gates of the Ocean which were held with such great chains. You were obeyed in many lands and you have won a mighty reputation for yourself among Christians. What more did He do for the people of Israel when He led them out of Egypt, or for David, that shepherd boy whom He made a king of the Jews? Turn yourself to Him and acknowledge your sins. His mercy is infinite. Even your old age will not prevent you from achieving great things for His domains are many and vast. Abraham was more than a hundred years old when he begat Isaac. And Sarah, was she a girl? You cry for help with doubt in your heart. Ask yourself who has afflicted you so grievously and so often—God or the world? The privileges and covenants which God has given you will not be taken back by Him. Nor does He say to them that have served

Him that He meant it otherwise, or that it should be taken in another sense; nor does He inflict torments to show His power. His way is to fulfill His promises with increase. Thus have I told you what your Creator has done for you and for all men. He has revealed to me some of those rewards which are waiting for you for the many toils and dangers which you have endured in the service of others.

Columbus continued. "I heard all this as if in a trance. The message was so positive that I could find no reply. All I could do was to weep over my sins. Whoever it was that had spoken, ended by saying: 'Fear not, but have faith. All these tribulations are written on tablets of marble and there is a reason for them.'"[98]

them. (George Washington, Benjamin Franklin, and John Wesley were also ordained high priests.)[100]

Columbus was not the only explorer on the St. George Temple list. His colleague Amerigo Vespucci was also there.[102] Inspired by Columbus, Vespucci began exploring the New World after Columbus discovered its existence. He became famous for determining that the Caribbean islands and the continental coastline were not Asia's eastern outskirts (as Columbus believed) but, instead, were the beginning of an entirely new and great landmass, a new continent altogether. How appropriate that this man, Amerigo, for whom America is named, would be on that very special temple roll along with Columbus.

> "The room was filled as with flaming fire."[101]
>
> —Wilford Woodruff, describing the St. George baptistry as he performed baptisms for the dead pursuant to his heavenly visitation from the Founding Fathers.

As my thoughts transported me to these amazing temple scenes, I found myself standing directly before the tomb itself. I stepped back from it and noticed that whereas I was hot and sweaty just moments earlier, I was no longer hot at all but actually had cooled off completely. This was strange since the tomb was in an outdoor chamber; the large corridors leading from the tomb to the parking lot had no roof or doors to close out the heat. A tour guide walked up to me in that moment and explained the phenomenon. "This open-air mausoleum," he whispered to me as we stood within a few feet of the tomb, "was built to capture the Caribbean breeze from all four entryways and bring it simultaneously to meet visitors here at the tomb." I thought of Isaiah's description of what the latter-day gathering of Israel to Zion would look and feel like. The same latter-day Zion Columbus seemed to have sought and believed (correctly) he had discovered in the New World. "And there shall be a tabernacle," Isaiah said, "for a shadow in the daytime from the heat, and for a place of refuge" (Isaiah 4:6; 2 Nephi 14:6).[103]

With Isaiah on my mind, I allowed my eyes to wander around the chamber. I smiled as I looked up and saw Isaiah's name engraved in large letters on one of the chamber walls. Of course! Columbus loved Isaiah. I read the words (engraved in Spanish): "For the execution of the journey . . . I was not aided by intelligence or mathematics. It was simply the fulfillment of what Isaiah had prophesied." Even Columbus's fiercest modern-day critics have to agree that he must have had something other than math and science to accomplish the impossible. Not likely to attribute his successes to God or miracles, critics instead have explained it like this: "All his maps and charts and painfully acquired formal education—so impressive, yet so misleading—were of little use to him. He relied on his instincts and experience . . . . His dead reckoning proved so accurate that he had already sailed from Spain to the New World without incident the very first time, and, incredibly, with no loss of life." In the end, all the critic can say is; "He had been spectacularly lucky."[104]

As I walked around looking at the other walls of the chamber, I noted other engraved words that proved again that Columbus would never have considered his discovery mere luck. "The Lord God opened my mind . . . and he opened my will to desire to accomplish the project." And finally, another set of engraved words memorialized the fact that Columbus had placed a cross on every island he'd discovered as a sign and symbol that this land was dedicated to "Jesus Christ and in honor of Christianity."

I exited through a different opening in the great edifice that led me to an exterior view I hadn't seen before. I tilted my head, looking up the outside wall, wishing I could get onto the roof to peer into another strange scene. *Lights*. Yes, there is a reason they call it the Columbus Lighthouse. Attached to the top, outlining the cross structure, are enormous searchlight-type lamps that shoot 157 light beams into the night sky. Symbolizing the light of Christianity that Columbus shared with the world, these light-house lights that make a cross shape in the sky have been seen as far north as Puerto Rico—a territory belonging to that scriptural nation of the Restoration, even the United States of America.[105]

Tour of the Columbus Lighthouse

As I visualized this symbol, my mind raced, trying to remember an ancient quote or prophecy connected to Columbus that always reminded me of the Prophet of the Restoration, even Joseph Smith. I pulled out my iPhone and started searching key words I could remember. Was it the spiritual manifestation Columbus had had as a child that told him his name "would be proclaimed throughout the world,"[106] just as the Angel Moroni had told Joseph Smith about his name the night he visited the boy Prophet (Joseph Smith—History 1:33)? *Nope.* That was a good one, but there was something else. This connection, however, made me think about the interesting fact that Moroni quoted a few scriptures to Joseph Smith that night, including Joel 2 and Isaiah 11 (Joseph Smith—History 40–41). Both of these scriptures were also included in Columbus's *Book of Prophecies*.

That's it, I thought. *Check the* Book of Prophecies.

Got it! I whispered to myself a few seconds later. Sure enough, there it was, directly from Columbus and written in his book. The reference was associated with a man, a very religious man, named the Abbot Joachim of Fiore. Born in 1135 AD, the Abbot was an Italian theologian who was very interested in prophecies of the last days. He had prophesied much himself, and Columbus saw him as a prophet of the medieval age. And there was his short yet profound prediction transcribed and applied to the great discoverer—this pilgrim to the Americas: "The restorer of the House of Mt. Zion," the prophecy states, "would come out of Spain."[107]

◆ ◆ ◆

And this brings us full circle, back to the main point of it all. For whatever his successes or failures were, Columbus had carried out his role in discovering and delivering the promised land to those pilgrims and prophets who would later come and usher in the Restoration of the gospel.

I realize that for some, that is still not enough in light of the death and destruction he ushered in to innocent Native Americans. In fact, some friends and colleagues of mine suggested I not even include a chapter about Columbus in this book for fear of stirring too much controversy. But let me leave you with one final thought regarding this controversy that has helped me come to terms with it. Oftentimes, especially with historical figures, we lock them inside a certain time and space of their own lives and then pelt them with criticism. And often, the time and space we lock them into are their low points. But let's review the larger narrative of Columbus's works, allow him to grow, sin, learn, repent, and evolve.

Remember, before he found success with Spain, he endured the tragic death of his wife and rejection of Portugal. He then humbled himself and made his life right with God. Only then could he begin his voyages.

Voyage 1 (1492)

He is a humble servant with three boats and a crew of less than a hundred. He prays often and seeks and receives many miracles. He beats the odds, finds the New World, then beats the odds again, escaping great storms and dodging enemies along the way, to get back home. It is a triumph, and he credits God, having made covenants with Him. If only he had been able to keep that spirit as he entered his next voyage.

Voyage 2 (1493)

Now a national hero, he is paraded through the streets of Spain with great fanfare and titles. This time, he has seventeen ships and well over 1,200 men under his command. He already knows the way and does not need to rely so heavily on God. Few if any miracles are recorded. In fact, in the few years following his abuse and enslavement of the Natives, there is a stunning lack of evidence that Columbus is guided at all by God as he had been before. Instead, only violence and abuse extend across the island. "But when we undertake to . . . exercise control or dominion or compulsion upon the souls of the children of men . . . the heavens withdraw themselves; the Spirit of the Lord is grieved" (D&C 121:37).

Voyage 3 (1498)

This trip is highlighted by the Roldán rebellion and further abuse to the Native populations. Columbus ends this voyage falsely arrested and in chains and is exiled from the land he discovered.

Voyage 4 (1502)

Columbus calls this his "Alto Viaje" (High Trip), and for good reason. After suffering bitterly at the end of his third voyage, he finds himself in a much-needed state of humility. He begins to repent. He claims that though he has sinned, "my errors have not been committed with intention to do ill" and that he had "fallen into error innocently and under compulsion." He explains that during those moments of poor decision, he was under constant pressure. "Not a day goes by," he said, "that I am not faced with the prospect of the certain death of us all." (The stress and illnesses he suffered caused him to lose partial or, at times, full use of his eyes.) But still, he laments that his discovery has brought so much destruction. "There are now many merchants," he reports to a friend of the queen, "who go seeking for girls; nine or ten are now for sale . . . if Their Highnesses would command a general inquiry to be made there, I declare to you that they will find it a great marvel that the island has not been swallowed up."[108]

Kneeling and sobbing before the queen, he further repents and takes responsibility for the dark works over the island. He pleads for forgiveness.[109]

Though he secures an acquittal from the Crown, he is not ultimately restored to his earlier status. He moves into the monastery of Santa María de Las Cuevas, where he would later be buried. Here he spends years in reflection, meditation, prayer, and repentance. He remembers his calling, that very first voyage, and he returns to his roots. It is at this time and in this monastery where he writes his *Book of Prophecies*, thus declaring the gospel truth to the world regarding what God has done through him, though until the days of Restoration, much of what he writes will make little sense.

The king and queen grant him his final voyage, his Alto Viaje, when he is fifty-one years old. Given his enlightened preparation, this journey begins very differently from the previous two. He even brings his thirteen-year-old son, Ferdinand, on this voyage. It is a redemption of sorts. He makes clear that he is not taking this voyage "to earn honors and riches" as he had before. He speaks kindly to and about the Natives and enforces his new and unbreakable covenant never to enslave one of them again. (Though he is attacked, and his men defend themselves.) Unlike before, Columbus has strict policies in place to check his men and ensure they don't hurt the Natives. He even makes his men stay aboard the ship and requires them to sign out if they want to go ashore.[110]

And the miracles return. It is on this trip that he warns and seems to prophesy about the storm that ends up taking out his worst enemies. It is also during this trip that the heavenly voice or angel appears to him, granting him forgiveness and redemption. He is told by the voice to continue repenting and relying on God's mercy, and he is reminded of the children of Israel and of King David, who, though severe sinners all, still maintain their heroic place in the gospel story.

Columbus: a Life of Struggle and Redemption

◆　◆　◆

After returning from his fourth and final voyage, Columbus lived for only two more years, mostly forgotten. Though he tried, he was never again able to reclaim his former status. "And so it was," Las Casas said in his eulogy of Columbus, "that a man who had, by his own efforts, discovered another world greater than the one we knew before and far more blessed, departed this life in a state of distress and bitterness and poverty . . . . He died dispossessed and stripped of the position and honors he had earned by his tireless and heroic efforts and by risking his life over and over again." Las Casas said, "His life was one long martyrdom, something which will lead others . . . to conclude that there is little to be gained and little rest to be enjoyed in the world for those who are not forever conferring with God."[111]

So what do we do now with Columbus's mixed legacy? Perhaps we learn from it, as Las Casas hoped. Perhaps we recognize that we all sin and fall short. Like Columbus, we can't go back in time and relive our lives, thus making it right this time. But we can, like Columbus did, reach out for the Atonement. "I am only a most unworthy sinner," Columbus said, "but ever since I have cried out for grace and mercy from the Lord, they have covered me completely."[112] His dying refrain was, "*In mansus tuas, Domine, commendo spiritum meum*" (Into thy hands, Lord, I commend my spirit).[113]

Before writing this chapter, I was warned by friends and colleagues that I would never be able to write anything that would redeem the sinful Admiral, especially in the current national environment of virtue signaling, which has specifically included Columbus bashing. I agree that I cannot. But I know the Lord can. What I can do, however, is provide proof and evidence that notwithstanding his mistakes, he was still a forerunner of the Restoration. The Lord still allowed him to participate and still commended him in the Book of Mormon. What hope this gives to the rest of us sinners! That in spite of Columbus's errors, an Apostle of God, President George Q. Cannon, could still stand and say: "Columbus was inspired to penetrate the ocean and discover this Western continent, for the set time of its discovery had come . . . . This Church and kingdom could not have been established on the earth if [Columbus's] work had not been performed."[114]

CHAPTER 2

The Pilgrims

John Howland was a Pilgrim, one of the originals who came over on the *Mayflower*. For reasons I'll explain later, he is my favorite. I like him, in part, due to his age and circumstance as he boarded the *Mayflower*. He was single, in his twenties, and still figuring things out as he went to an unknown and dangerous land where there were few prospects for marriage, family, or social progression, things men his age tend to desire and seek. With no guarantee that he would ever return, *what was he thinking?* For that matter, *what were any of them thinking?*

Whatever they were thinking, I know they were special. There were only 102 who came over on that ship, so they were few in number—a special group. A chosen group. Too often, we picture the Pilgrims as exiles running from tyranny and oppression—outcasts with nowhere else to go. Not true. Yes, they had been a group of religious separatists who had sought religious independence from the oppressive English monarchy, but they had actually already found that freedom. At the time they took their overseas voyage to America, they had fled the religious oppression of England and were enjoying full religious freedom and solid employment in the commercially growing town of Leiden, Holland.

Admittedly, some of them weren't always thrilled in Holland, as they felt their children were not living their English culture properly. Others didn't like Leiden's city philosophy of putting kids to work rather than encouraging school. Some were also concerned about what they perceived as moral decay in the Dutch city. For example, having so many commercial endeavors in the city influenced its businesses to ignore the Sabbath and keep working. This was unacceptable to the Pilgrims, and they didn't want their children to be led in the wrong direction. These are some of the reasons Pilgrims William Bradford and Edward Winslow gave as to why they were looking at places to migrate outside of Holland.[115]

Scholars have given other reasons for why the Pilgrims might have left to America. As a city friendly to the outcast and refugee, Leiden's population was on the rise. This population boom might have contributed to fewer available or lower-paying jobs and more disease. As it was, workdays were long and often difficult. Furthermore, the Dutch treaty with Spain was going to sunset in 1621, allowing for the possibility of hostilities between the two nations and, thus, the possibility of throwing the Pilgrims into an unwanted war.[116]

Notwithstanding these problems (some of which were still hypothetical), the Pilgrims also recognized the blessing it was to worship freely and participate in the growing economy of Leiden. William Bradford, who was able to start his own successful textile business in Leiden and eventually purchase his own home there, stated: "[Leiden is a] fair, & bewtifull citie, and of a Sweete situation."[117]

These English separatists should not be thought of as exiles or second-class citizens in Holland. To the contrary, their congregation had grown to around 300, and their members were counted among the most respected citizens in town, known for their hard work and industry. Like any group, some members were wealthy, while others struggled, but they pulled together and took care of each other. Edward Winslow described his Pilgrim community in Leiden, saying, "Never people upon earth lived more lovingly together."[118]

Pastor John Robinson, the Pilgrim leader in Leiden, was looked upon by his peers, including the eminent Dutch intellectuals, as one of the great thinkers in all of Holland, and he was regularly sought out to lecture and participate in great academic debates and events. Members of his congregation, including William Brewster and Edward Winslow, ran a press (known today as the Pilgrim Press), from which cutting-edge content was published and distributed with the help of Leiden University and prominent figures such as Jan Jansz Orlers, a known historian and one of Leiden's mayors. Even when the British monarchs pressured the Dutch to shut down the Pilgrim Press (as the Pilgrims published material critical of their former nation's corruption and authoritarianism), the Dutch, as best they could, stood by their promise to protect the Pilgrims.[119]

But notwithstanding, if the Pilgrims really wanted out of Leiden, there were other places in the Dutch regions where they could have migrated to establish themselves. In fact, they considered offers to relocate to other parts of Holland where they could improve their situation.[120]

And yet, because of Columbus's work, they knew of this other option—this distant land called America. And that was where they went—to this wild, dangerous, untamed, and unknown land, where Natives were known to kill European settlers. *Why?* Certainly, whatever hardships they faced in Holland would pale in comparison to the hardships of starting over in America. It seemed an unnecessary and ridiculously risky move.

I have tried hard to understand the academic reasons for the Pilgrims' coming to America, but the answers I get, while honest and valid, never fully add up. I understand wanting to shield children from moral decay—but at the cost of these children's very lives in a dangerous land? I understand wanting to avoid the possibility of an economic downturn—but in exchange for what? A *certain* economic downturn in America? Incurring a huge debt in order to afford shipping off to the New World to live in the mud? Exchange a *possible* economic recession for a *certain* economic depression? Exchange *possible* disease in Leiden, for almost *certain* disease in America? Or avoid a *possible* war with Spain in order to confront an almost *certain* war with Native Americans? Furthermore, the Pilgrims would have known that any Spanish war could easily result in aggression against vulnerable, infant American colonies, such as the one the Pilgrims sought to build. Indeed, the Spanish maritime giant was watching every movement.[121]

Further, if things were so dire, why did only a fraction of the Separatist congregation get on a boat and go through with it? It could accurately be argued that more of the congregation would have gone had there been more resources or more space on the boat. But how hard did the others really push to get over to America? And what about the thousands upon thousands of other Dutch citizens, all confronted with many of these same hypotheticals? We didn't see them jumping on ships and heading to the New World.

In the end, historical hindsight allows us to be witnesses to what happened next. Once the Pilgrims got to America, there was nothing hypothetical anymore. Almost immediately, they were attacked by Natives, they were starved out, and then, one by one, they began to die. Within months, they lost roughly half of their total number to disease and starvation.

Now how do the academic arguments for leaving Leiden compare? We have hypotheticals in Leiden against certain and lived hell in America. And yet, still, they stayed. Even as the *Mayflower* was preparing to pull out of Plymouth harbor and travel back to Europe on April 5, 1621, the small band of remaining survivors, still sick, still dying, and now widowed and orphaned could have returned. But they stayed.[122] And it wasn't because things were "just better" in America than in Leiden. This is why I've never been satisfied with the answers given for why the Pilgrims did what they did. There *had* to be something more.

As is often the case, it is through the lens of the gospel that history is rounded out. Just as only the gospel could explain why Lehi and his family left a good situation in the Old World to come to the New, only the gospel can expound on why the Pilgrims did the same in their time. Nothing was certain, of course, in the eyes of mortal understanding. Not Holland. And less so America. But God knew what was certain. He knew the outcome if only He could convince them to board the *Mayflower* and stay in America. Nothing makes satisfactory sense unless and until we consider the gathering of Israel. Unless and until we consider the need for God to bring a pure-hearted, religious, and covenant-minded people to begin the miraculous process of establishing a covenant land to host the restoration of God's gospel and temples on the earth. This was key.

It couldn't have been just any group. It had to be a special group, a chosen group, because the first settlers would set the precedent for all to follow; the first settlers needed to be believers in God and His covenant upon the promised land of America. If not, the covenant wouldn't take effect. The miracles born of the covenant, which miracles built the nation and brought us the liberties found in the Constitution, wouldn't take effect. And the gathering of Israel and the restoration of the gospel, which require that liberty born of miracles, would be severely jeopardized. That's how important the Pilgrims were.

The Book of Mormon teaches us that "there shall none come into this land [America] save they shall be brought by the hand of the Lord" (2 Nephi 1:6). History seems to corroborate this scriptural promise. Like I said, this wasn't a reactive move; it was totally proactive. It wasn't something necessary for survival. Their existence or livelihood wasn't being threatened in Holland as it had been in England. On the contrary, in many ways (as discussed above), they were doing just fine. Scripturally, the Pilgrims—if they were who we think they were—were called of God to come to this land.

John Howland worked at the time as the servant of John Carver, who would become the first governor of the Pilgrims once they landed on the shore of America. Howland likely worked, studied, and prayed alongside his kind benefactor in England and later in Holland. He would have participated in or, at least, would have known about members of his congregation who participated in the great solemn assembly over the America question. According to one member of the group who attended the special assembly, "The Lord was solemnly sought in the congregation by fasting and prayer to direct us."[123]

By the time the service was over, it was decided. The Lord had spoken. They would go to America. Pastor John Robinson drafted a letter stating the reason for the voyage. The principal reason he gave was that "we verily believe and trust the Lord is with us . . . and that He will graciously prosper our endeavors . . . [and] we are knit together in a body in a most strict and sacred bond and covenant of the Lord."[124] Bradford added that their move to America was also inspired by their desire to spread the gospel of Jesus Christ to parts of the world that did not have it.[125]

In summation, while the Pilgrims were looking for ways to improve their situation, as they always did, the option of moving to America (irrational as it may have seemed to many) fell before them. They took it to the Lord, who they felt consecrated the idea. Knowing God was with them and knowing they were to take the gospel to all the world, they trusted in the protection of a covenant they made with each other and the Lord. Indeed, they were called. That was why they went. And that was why they stayed.

The Pilgrims in Leiden

But what else did they know? If these Pilgrims truly were the advent guard of the Lord to establish the land and nation that would facilitate the gathering of Israel and restoration of temples to the earth, they should have followed a certain pattern, the same pattern every group called of God to migrate as pilgrims to a promised land has always followed. First, they receive the land under covenant, for that is how the Lord can provide the blessings of liberty to support and protect their religious endeavors. Then, as they act on the Lord's will, miracles follow and the way is opened for them. Only then, once that protective foundation is set, do we see the building of temples in those special lands. Only then are God's purposes fulfilled.

Think about Moses and the children of Israel when they migrated to their promised land. Before they could build their temple, they were given a law from Sinai and a covenant, and they wandered for years being tested by the law and covenant until the temple finally came. And the liberty and power to sustain that temple continued to be contingent on their national covenant: "If my people . . . shall humble themselves, and pray, and seek my face, and turn from their wicked ways; then will I hear from heaven, and will forgive their sin, and will heal their land" (2 Chronicles 7:14).

Lehi laid the same national-covenant foundation. Once he found the land of promise, before he or his people built temples, they too needed to build that protective foundation, that covenant on the land. "We have obtained a land of promise . . ." Lehi said, "a land which the Lord God hath covenanted with me . . . And if it so be that they shall serve him according to the commandments which he hath given, it shall be a land of liberty unto them" (2 Nephi 1: 5, 7).

Did the Pilgrims follow the pattern? Just before they left, Pastor Robinson, who decided to stay in Holland to oversee those who could not make the voyage, led them in fasting and prayer. He then sent them off to America with profound instructions: "We are daily to renew our repentance with our God," he stated, "especially for our sins known . . . [For] sin being taken away by earnest repentance, and the pardon thereof from the Lord . . . great shall be [your] security and peace."[126] The national covenant was invoked.

William Bradford, who would succeed Howland's boss, John Carver, as second governor of the Pilgrims' American colony, also recognized this covenant relationship. After landing in America, Bradford pondered on the dangerous journey that had led them there. According to Bradford, just when the Pilgrims thought they would perish in the wilderness from starvation, sickness, and other threats, "they cried unto the Lord, and He heard their

voice."[127] Bradford continued to describe how his people's inten-
sified relationship with God took on a covenant nature: "So," he
said, "they committed themselves to the will of God, and resolved
to proceed."[128]

Though the national covenant was clearly invoked, it appears
the Book of Mormon requires more historical corroboration.
Indeed, the Book of Mormon seems to expect the Pilgrims to
connect their national covenant with the covenants of ancient
Israel. "And it came to pass," Nephi said, "that I beheld the Spirit
of God, that it wrought upon other Gentiles; and they went forth
out of captivity, upon the many waters . . . . And it came to pass
that I, Nephi, beheld that they did prosper in the land; and I
beheld a book, and it was carried forth among them . . . [and it]
contain[ed] the covenants of the Lord, which he hath made unto
the house of Israel; wherefore, they are of great worth unto the
Gentiles" (1 Nephi 13:13, 20, 23).

Prophesying over these American Gentiles, Christ repeated
the suggestion, stating that they shall be "established in this land,
and be set up as a free people by the power of the Father . . . that
the covenant of the Father may be fulfilled which he hath covenanted with his people, O house of Israel" (3 Nephi 21:4).

But did the Pilgrims themselves say or do anything to
corroborate this? Did they feel this connection to the ancient
covenant and to the restoration of Israel? Before boarding the
ship bound for America, they would have heard Pastor Robinson
explain to them:

> Now as the people of God in old time, were called
> out of Babylon civil, the place of their bodily bondage;
> and were to come to Jerusalem, and there to build anew
> the Lord's temple . . . so are the people of God now to
> go out of Babylon spiritual, to Jerusalem [America] . . .

THE MAYFLOWER COVENANT

Even in the Pilgrims' first written charter, the national covenant is made clear. Before disembarking from the *Mayflower*, they joined together and signed it. Consider the following introductory words of this document, known as the Mayflower Compact of 1620:

> In the name of God, Amen . . . Having undertaken for the glory of God, and advancement of the Christian faith . . . a voyage to plant the first colony . . . do by these presents solemnly and mutually in the presence of God, and of one another, covenant and combine ourselves into a civil body politic, for our better ordering and preservation, and the furtherance of the ends aforesaid.[129]

and to build up themselves as lively stones into a spiritual house, or temple for the Lord to dwell in.[130]

The Pilgrims indeed fit the bill. As Pilgrim historian Rebecca Frazier explained, "The [pilgrim] church believed they had a covenant like the Jewish people of old. Their comparison was the working of God's will to save the chosen people in the Old Testament. They constantly looked to the Bible for guiding examples."[131]

They understood that the covenants of the Bible, particularly those of the Old Testament, connected God to His nation—to Israel. Just as Moses led Israel through the Red Sea and out of captivity, so the Pilgrims "went forth out of captivity, upon the many waters" (1 Nephi 13:13). Those many waters included, first, the North Sea, which brought them from oppressive England, where they truly were captives, to Holland, where they weren't feeling completely certain, satisfied, or permanently settled, and, second, the Atlantic, which carried them to their ultimate promised land in America.

Indeed, the Old Testament provides the formula for how a people can truly build a covenant nation under God. As discussed in the introduction, when Abraham made his great covenant with God, which would bless all the children of God, it was made clear that certain lands, bound by the covenant, would be part of the equation. When Abraham's children went to these promised lands and invoked the covenant, miracles occurred and the people achieved great success. This is the power of a national covenant.

The Pilgrims needed that same covenant to build this new nation under God because America always was one of the designated promised lands that fell under the Abrahamic covenant. They needed it, and because of that, they wanted the Lord to know what kind of nation they intended to be. When they got to the shore of America, they went so far as to imply that they themselves were the New Israel.[132] They, and those who followed them into America, even named their villages and towns after biblical locales—Bethel, Bethlehem, and New Canaan, to name a few. More than a thousand New England towns were eventually named this way. They also regularly gave their children ancient Hebrew names from the first five books of the Old Testament.

After the *Mayflower* anchored near Plymouth Rock, and as the Pilgrims were disembarking, William Bradford exclaimed, "Come, let us declare the word of God in [Zion.]"[133] This mission to America, according to Bradford, was as important as that of "Moses and the Israelites when they went out of Egypt."[134] Indeed, these certainly seem to be the people of Nephi's vision.

The ancient covenant even played into the first Thanksgiving. It is widely believed that the feast was based on the Hebrew holiday of the Feast of Tabernacles. Biblically, it was a multiday holiday, a time of praying, feasting, and giving thanks. That ancient feast, known as *Sukkot* in Hebrew, was, according to historian

Pilgrim Thanksgiving

Barney Kasdan, "to be a time of bringing in the latter harvest. It is, in other words, the Jewish 'Thanksgiving.'" The concept of giving thanks or *Thanksgiving* is mentioned dozens of times in the Bible. William Bradford, a great student of the Bible, presided over the first American Thanksgiving and followed this biblical pattern. Like with Sukkot, Bradford made Thanksgiving a multiday holiday to celebrate the fall harvest and to pray, feast, and give thanks to God. The Hebrew tradition, as per the book of Deuteronomy, directs that "thou shalt rejoice in thy feast, thou,

It was not by coincidence that Bradford, in his written history *Of Plymouth Plantation*, paid homage to Israel. In the very first pages of his book, we see him attempting to write several phrases in the ancient Hebrew language. Above the handwritten, ancient characters, he wrote: "Though I am grown aged, yet I have had a longing desire, to see with my own eyes, something of that most ancient language, and holy tongue, in which the law, and oracles, of God were writ, and in which God, and angels, spake to the holy patriarchs of old time."[137] This precedent set by pilgrims like Bradford spread through the New England colonies. Eventually, the early colonists sought to make Hebrew, not English, the official language of the American colony. They also moved to make the Mosaic code the basis for the Massachusetts legal system.[138] We see why Bradford's people referred to him as their Moses.[139]

and thy son, and thy daughter . . . and the stranger." Dutifully, the Pilgrims invited "the stranger," even the local native tribes, to join in the festival of thanksgiving. And they came.[135] No wonder Kasdan suggests that these early American settlers, "who were great students of the Hebrew Scriptures, based the first American Thanksgiving on Sukkot."[136]

Comparing Bradford to Moses made perfect sense. As a descendant of Abraham, Moses understood the Abrahamic covenant and the lands associated with it. When he led the great exodus from Egypt to the promised land, he knew he had to invoke the law of the covenant and encourage the Israelite nation to live the law of the covenant. Only then would the national covenant be activated. Only then could they reap the blessings. Bradford followed suit as he led his group of new Israelites.

Speaking of the Pilgrims and those who followed them to the New World, historian Dr. Gabriel Sivan concluded: "They themselves were the children of Israel; America was their Promised Land; the Atlantic Ocean their Red Sea; the Kings of England were the Egyptian pharaohs; the American Indians their Canaanites . . . the pact of the Plymouth Rock was God's holy Covenant . . . . [They] saw themselves as instruments of Divine Providence, a people chosen to build their new commonwealth on the Covenant entered into at Mount Sinai."[143]

Clearly the Pilgrims sought the power of the ancient covenant, so they lived after the biblical model so God might honor their request and bless them. But why? Was it just so they could be protected from danger in this new and strange land? Or was there a deeper meaning that drove them? Perhaps a deeper meaning connected to God's plan for them and America? Again, we return to Pastor Robinson and his farewell address to the Pilgrims:

MOSES IN AMERICA

The precedent the pilgrims set of connecting America to the national covenant through Moses is still seen today. For example, engraved in bronze upon the floor of the entrance to the US National Archives, which houses the original Constitution and the Declaration of Independence, are the words of the ancient national covenant, even the Ten Commandments.[140] Also, in no less than four locations in and around the US Supreme Court building are depictions of Moses and the Ten Commandments (this imagery is at the center of the sculpture over the east portico of the building, on the bronze doors of the building, inside the courtroom itself, and engraved over the chair of the Chief Justice).[141] Similarly, perched upon the wall of Congress, overlooking the interior of the House chamber, is a large image of the Prophet Moses. Other an-

cient lawmakers are depicted around the chamber as well, but all have their heads turned to Moses, who is the only full-figured image and the only one who hangs directly in the middle of the room.[142]

Here also [God] put us in mind of our church covenant, at least that part of it whereby we promise and covenant with God and one with another, to receive whatsoever light or truth shall be made known to us from his
written Word . . . . For, saith he, it is not possible the
Christian world should come so lately out of such thick
anti-Christian darkness, and that perfection of knowledge
break forth at once . . . . For I am verily persuaded the
Lord hath more truth and light yet to break forth from
His holy word. [144]

Pastor John Robinson in Leiden

The connection here is astonishing. In 1 Nephi 13, which
outlines how the Lord will use latter-day America as the gathering place of Israel and the host nation of the Restoration, we
are told that the Pilgrims will play their part as forerunners of
this Restoration and will do so in connection with the covenants
of Israel. Then, once again, history corroborates scripture when
the Pilgrims' pastor sends them off, saying, in essence: *You are
the New Israel. Now go and use that ancient covenant to seek more
light and knowledge of the gospel in America.* Forerunners of the
Restoration, indeed.

Bradford also seemed to connect the Pilgrims' New World
mission to the Restoration. He recognized long before what
Satan had done to the Old World. "What wars and oppositions

ever since [the true gospel was on the earth], Satan hath raised, maintained and continued against the saints," Bradford said. He went on to explain that Satan did this to prevent the "truth [from] prevail[ing], and the Church of God [from] revert[ing] to their ancient purity, and recover[ing] their primitive order, liberty, and beauty."[145]

Again, we see parallels to Nephi's America vision, which also recognized (in the beginning of the vision) that Satan's church "slayeth the saints of God . . . and bringeth them down into captivity"(1Nephi 13:5). And just as Nephi understood that all this was to change, at least in part, with the coming of the Pilgrims to America (per the rest of the 1 Nephi 13 vision), so did Bradford, Robinson, and the Pilgrims themselves understand. They knew who they were and why they had been called. "In coming to God's New Israel," according to historian Jim Baker, "[the Pilgrims] viewed themselves as recreating God's original kingdom that had been occluded by the manmade church."[146] For as Frazier points out, it was always their goal to come "as close as possible to the primitive church of the Apostles."[147]

But there is one more thing that seals the deal. Miracles. Miracles follow the covenant. That's how you know the covenant is in force. Moses parted the Red Sea. Nephi learned how to build a boat to cross the ocean. Would the Pilgrims have a miracle as they crossed *their* great waters?

I wonder if young John Howland had similar thoughts as he boarded the *Mayflower* and began his journey. He would have had so much to ponder. So much to take in. Certainly, it was overwhelming for him and every other passenger on the boat. Perhaps all of this made the young man anxious as he sat below deck while the tempestuous sea rolled the *Mayflower* to and fro en route to the promised land.

At one point during the voyage, when the storms were particularly rough and the passengers were compelled to confine themselves below deck for safety, it appears Howland had had enough. Against his better judgment, he stood, climbed to the deck, and took a little stroll. Perhaps he was seasick. Or perhaps his own young, curious, somewhat fearless, maybe a bit naïve character tempted him to peer into the powerful, white-foamed waves plowing into the side of the boat.

Bam!

Before John Howland knew it, the water knocked him off his feet and threw him into the ocean.

The *Mayflower* wasn't a speedboat. There was no turning that thing around and hoping to trace over the same waters where the man overboard had last been seen, especially in stormy weather. Statistically, Howland was a dead man.

As he plunged into the water, several "fathoms under," as Bradford described it, Howland must have been thinking that his life was finished.[148] Or perhaps he was thinking about the covenant he had just made with his fellow Pilgrims. Perhaps he considered the miracles of biblical Israel, who had made the same covenant. Perhaps he had an inkling of the importance of every person, including himself, on that boat. They were starting a nation. A nation prophesied of God to play an indispensable role in His latter-day work. Today, there are more than 35 million living Americans who are direct descendants of these *Mayflower* Pilgrims. If Howland had died, millions would have been affected.[149]

As he plummeted to what would have appeared to be his imminent death, Howland reached out his hand in a last-ditch effort to save himself. And there it was. Somehow, someway, he was all of a sudden gripping firmly to the topsail halyard, the rope sailors used to raise the upper sail. There was no reason that the rope should have been dangling off the decks and dragging in the waters below. According to one historian, "Only a very shoddy boatswain would let a halyard dangle into the water, instead of making it fast to a cleat."[150] Yet it was there, precisely, even within inches of, where Howland needed it at that moment. The young man climbed back onboard.[151]

Howland Overboard

◆ ◆ ◆

I need to pause this narrative for a moment. When I first learned of the Howland miracle, I knew what I needed to do. I began looking for cheap airline tickets to Boston. I wanted to learn the rest of the story at the place where it had culminated. I wanted to "meet" the *Mayflower* at its destination point: Cape Cod, Plymouth Rock, New England. There had to be other miracles that proved the chosen status of these people. Stories that proved the covenant. But something told me I was starting in the wrong place. I found my fingers typing "London" instead of "Boston" on the travel websites.

Why? Because there seemed to be something deeper to who these English women and men were. The evidence was adding up too rapidly to ignore the connections to ancient Israel, the applications of the ancient covenant, allusions to a restored gospel of Jesus Christ, and the evidence of a new gathering in America. And now I knew they did experience mind-boggling miracles. I needed to go to England to seek further knowledge, not only because that was where the Pilgrims had come from but because there was something else I needed to discover as well.

Remember in the introduction when I quoted Elder Erastus Snow? He made an interesting application of the Genesis 49 prophecy, which foretold of Joseph's posterity crossing "over the wall" and into America. He suggested that America's settlers, Howland and the Pilgrims for example, were that prophesied group. But wouldn't that mean they were from the seed of Joseph, like Lehi before them who made a similar ocean journey? After all, the Genesis 49 prophecy definitely seemed limited to Joseph and his people. I recognize we are entering deep doctrinal waters here, and I'm not certain any conclusion can be proven indefinitely, but I like the hypothesis.

And so did Elder Snow, apparently. I didn't reveal his whole quote in the introduction. The rest of it goes like this:

> Now the same spirit of revelation that sought out the Prophet Joseph [Smith] from the loins of Joseph who was sold into Egypt, and that raised him up in this last dispensation to receive the keys of the Priesthood and to lay the foundation of this great work in the earth, has also called the children of Abraham from among the kingdoms and countries of the earth to first hear and then embrace the everlasting Gospel; and the remnants

of the seed of Ephraim [children of Joseph] who were scattered from Palestine and who colonized the shores of the Caspian Sea and thence made their way into the north of Europe . . . penetrating Scotland and England . . . and mingling their seed with the Anglo-Saxon race, and spreading over the waters a fruitful vine, as predicted by Jacob, whose branches should run over the wall. Their blood has permeated European society, and it coursed in the veins of the early colonists of America.[152]

He then goes on to not only identify these American colonists and revolutionaries as being from this British line born of Joseph through his son Ephraim, but he also explains their role as Ephraimites in fighting tyrants, bringing and upholding liberty upon the American continent, and "thus preparing the way for the coming forth of the fullness of the everlasting Gospel."[153]

Elder Erastus Snow

For me, the most compelling part of Elder Snow's statement is his reference to Joseph Smith being from the loins of Joseph of old. For that is scriptural. The Lord told Joseph of Egypt: "A choice seer will I raise up out of the fruit of thy loins" (2 Nephi 3:7). "And his name shall be called after me," Joseph of old said, "and it shall be after the name of his father" (2 Nephi 3:15). Brigham Young added his testimony: "[Joseph Smith's] descent from Joseph that was sold into Egypt was direct, and the blood was pure in him . . . . Joseph Smith was a pure Ephraimite."[154]

And where did Joseph Smith, this pure Ephraimite, hail from? Where does his lineage begin? *The British Isles.*[155] The pieces were adding up.

Does this corroborate what Elder Snow said? Was it just Joseph Smith and his line, or was there a larger ancient migration of the tribe of Joseph through his son Ephraim, as Elder Snow suggested? Did they settle in Britain? Did God pluck the early American Pilgrims from that covenant group? A *literal* regathering of these lost tribes in the promised land of America? Is that why Christ told the Nephites the new nation of America would be "set up as a free people by the power of the Father . . . that the covenant of the Father may be fulfilled which he hath covenanted with his people, O house of Israel" (3 Nephi 21:4)? Is this why so many thousands, maybe millions of patriarchal blessings of those with British ancestry in America and elsewhere have identified their recipients as being from Joseph via Ephraim? According to a Church publication, "The lineages declared in patriarchal blessings are almost always statements of actual blood lines; they are not simply tribal identifications by assignment."[156] Does it not seem likely that early Americans, from William Bradford and John Howland to George and Martha Washington and John and Abigail Adams, would be proclaimed as Ephraimites in a patriarchal blessing?

This is why I had to go to Britain. I wanted to search out answers to these questions. They mattered to me as I studied the Pilgrims because if it were true, it would provide tremendous insight into who they were in both scripture and history. It would shed light on why they believed themselves to be the New Israel. Why they acted like they were. And whereas they did not have the opportunity to be baptized into the house of Israel due to the time in which they lived (baptism brings any person, no matter their blood or background, into the house of Israel with *all* its blessings), a heritage back to Joseph and his great-grandfather Abraham would help validate their sacrifice and mission as forerunners of the Restoration.

As I began researching the places I wanted to visit in England, one name continued to surface. A contemporary British man and Christian author named Stephen Spykerman. Spykerman intrigued me for several reasons. Born in Holland during the Nazi occupation of that land, he and his family were part of the secret Dutch resistance. Both of his parents were Jews, but because they attended Catholic mass and because his mother was British, they were able to conceal their Jewish heritage. They hid many Jews in their home during this dark era and eventually weathered that storm.

As Stephen grew into adulthood, he sought God and moved to Israel to find his religious roots. He lived on and off in the biblical promised land of old and dedicated himself to the study of his people. Though Stephen became a great believer in the ancient biblical texts of his people, God had revealed to him that there was no salvation without Jesus of Nazareth. So instead of following Judaism, he became fully converted to Christianity. But he became a Christian who refused to ignore the story of his Israelite ancestry because he recognized that this story was also the story of Christianity. Indeed, he learned that the prophesied future of the Old Testament people was, in fact, the gathering of Israel under Christ the Lord.

Stephen eventually settled in Britain with his wife and children and founded Mount Ephraim Publishing with the support of Viscount Michael Allenby of Megiddo, a member of the British House of Lords and direct descendant of General Allen Allenby, who defeated the Ottoman Empire and liberated Jerusalem in 1917.

Stephen's biography alone made him worthy of a visit, in my eyes. But it was his published research that intrigued me the most because his findings so closely paralleled the teachings of The Church of Jesus Christ of Latter-day Saints in regards to the movements of the lost tribes and the gathering of Israel in Britain and America. I sought to corroborate these LDS teachings. I thought it would be a wonderful idea to seek some validation from a teacher who, while not of my faith, came to similar conclusions using only scripture, history, and personal revelation as his guide.

One email was all it took, and within hours, Stephen wrote back and instructed me to meet him in London. I dutifully bought a plane ticket.

I boarded the plane with a bag full of books and scriptures, which I had been studying feverishly during the weeks leading up to this trip. I wanted to be as prepared as I could for my meeting in London. My goal was simple: I wanted to review everything I could about Joseph of Egypt and his heir of the covenant, Ephraim. I wanted to confirm the notion that the tribe of Ephraim, as possibly suggested in Genesis 49 and as taught (or suggested) by LDS leaders, had migrated to Britain, then inherited the promised land of America in the form of the Pilgrims.

As the plane took off, I dug into my bookbag. Right off, I remembered that the last time we really heard from Joseph and his tribe of Ephraim in the Bible was when they led a rebellion against Judah and separated themselves. Ephraim and his companions thereafter became known as the Northern Kingdom, or Israel. The Southern Kingdom became known as Judah. Ephraim and his ally tribes lived independently until their wickedness and disobedience allowed the Assyrians to conquer them and carry them off to a land north of Nineveh around 721 BC.[157] But what land? Then what? Until Joseph Smith and the scriptures of the Restoration began speaking of Ephraim and his role in the last days, the record was pretty quiet.

The only other ancient references made about Joseph/Ephraim reveal something about the prophecies and promises of their ultimate destiny. For example, whereas the Lord could have completely destroyed them for their wickedness, He instead chose to hide them away and preserve them for a later mission in a later day. As the prophet Hosea said, though "Ephraim is smitten," the Lord would only "cast them away" to be "wanderers among the nations" (Hosea 9:16–17). Furthermore, and in spite of their wandering state, they were to strongly present themselves again. Said the Lord: "I will save the house of Joseph, and I will bring them again to place them . . . and they shall be as though I had not cast them off . . . . And they of Ephraim shall be like a mighty man, and their heart shall rejoice . . . . And I will sow them among the people: and they shall remember me in far countries" (Zechariah 10:6–9). "Is Ephraim my dear son?" the Lord asked. "I will surely have mercy upon him" (Jeremiah 31:20).

In light of these and related prophecies, one might surmise that Ephraim was carried to "far countries" in order to support and build up such lands unto God. After all, it was given anciently to Ephraim, through his lineage from Abraham and Joseph, to "make" and "bless" nations (Genesis 17:6; 22:18). There certainly was a reason God promised to "sift the house of Israel among all nations" (Amos 9:9). There is a reason His prophet Isaiah prophesied (as he did on multiple occasions) that "Israel shall blossom and bud, and fill the face of the world with fruit" (Isaiah 27:6).

So after migrating to the north, where did Joseph/Ephraim go to build the covenant nations? "For, lo, I will command, and I will sift the house of Israel among all nations, like as corn is sifted in a sieve, yet shall not the least grain fall upon the earth" (Amos 9:9). That they were heading north is clear, not only from the fact that Assyria is in that direction but also from the words of the prophets. When the Lord called on Israel to return from its lost state, it was clear where the messengers would find them: "Go and proclaim these words toward the north, and say, Return, thou backsliding Israel" (Jeremiah 3:12). Some may argue that the Lord is speaking to Israel in the Northern Kingdom within Palestine (they were always north of Judah, after all). However, Jeremiah, who recorded these words, lived well after Joseph/ Ephraim had abandoned Palestine altogether. They had already migrated north of the ancient promised land. In later chapters, Jeremiah again referred to the land of the lost tribes as the "land of the north" (Jeremiah 3:18; 16:15).

But it was not just a northern migration. According to Hosea 12:1, "Ephraim . . . followeth after the east wind." In their book *A Guide to Scriptural Symbols*, Joseph Fielding McConkie and Donald Parry confirm that an east wind "originates in the east, the symbolic direction of Deity's presence."[158] Just as an east wind travels west, we might consider that Ephraim, in addition to being carried to the north, also predominately traveled to the west. Some scholars believe Isaiah also provided clues as to Joseph/ Ephraim's coordinates when he said they would be called "from the north and from the west" (Isaiah 49:12). According to some scholars, ancient Hebrew has no distinct word for the coordinate *northwest*. Accordingly, the thought is that Isaiah was doing his best in these verses to convey that lost Israel had migrated to a northwestern location—that Isaiah's use of "the north and the west," was simply his designation for what we would call "northwest." Hosea perhaps indicated the same when speaking specifically about Ephraim. Said Hosea: "The children [referring to Ephraim] shall tremble from the west" (Hosea 11:8, 10).

If Joseph/Ephraim and the lost tribes had followed this general northwesterly direction, they would have landed squarely in Western Europe. From there, the Lord might have called them "over the wall" to America. After all, Jacob-Israel, when describing the blessed land of "everlasting hills" (America) that Joseph/

Ephraim were to inherit, prophesied that Joseph was a "fruitful bough by a *well*." This perhaps indicates that Joseph/Ephraim would migrate to the coast (i.e., a place by a "well") in preparation for the discovery, settlement, and establishment of America and her covenant.

Jeremiah, who, as recently noted, indicated a northern migration of Israel, added more to the geographic location: "Behold, I will bring them from the north country, and gather them *from the coasts* of the earth" (Jeremiah 31:8, emphasis added). Again, it appears Ephraim would be brought to the water's edge of the north country in order to cross "over the wall," to be a colonizing people God would plant abroad. Isaiah also spoke *after* Israel had already been scattered, calling Israel to "gather" in order "to restore the preserved of Israel" (Isaiah 49:5–6). He referred to them alternatively as "Israel" *and* as the "isles." "Listen, O isles, unto me," he stated (verses 1–3). Later, Isaiah again addressed Israel, stating, "Keep silence before me, O islands; and let the people renew their strength" (Isaiah 41:1). Is it possible that Isaiah is calling Israel to America—to a place where they can be "gathered" and "restored"—and that he is calling them *from* the British isles, where they await in "silence" and where they "renew their strength"?

If the clues above indicate that Joseph/Ephraim would travel from Palestine in a *northwest* direction until they landed on an island *coastline*, their destination becomes very clear. While I was flying somewhere over the Atlantic Ocean, moving toward Britain, I was thrilled to think of Ephraim moving toward the same land many, many years prior. I began playing with the map on the television screen in front of me, the one that shows the plane's location. Using my fingers on the touch screen, I moved the map over so I could see Palestine and Britain in the same frame. Following the scriptural instructions, I placed my pointer finger on Palestine/Israel and moved it precisely in a northwest direction. My finger landed squarely on the British Isles!

Map of Europe and Middle East

Another fascinating clue may shed some light on this question. Elder George Reynolds of the Quorum of the Seventy, in his book *We Are of Israel*, explains how ancient writings indicate that a large portion of the lost tribes of Israel, particularly the tribe of Ephraim, settled in what is now Europe. Elder Reynolds quoted the apocryphal writer Ezra (also known as Esdras), who described the lost tribes' trek northward, showing that by geographic necessity, they swung near or through modern-day Europe.[159] Elder Reynolds then explained:

Is it altogether improbable that in that long journey of one and a half years, as Esdras states it, that from Media the land of their captivity to the frozen north, some of the backsliding Israel rebelled, turned aside from the main body, forgot their God, [and] by and by mingled with the Gentiles? The account given in the Book of Mormon of a single house, its waywardness, its stiffneckedness before God, its internal quarrels and family feuds are, we fear, an example on a small scale of what probably happened in the vast bodies of the Israelites who for so many months wended their tedious way northward. Laman and Lemuel had, no doubt, many counterparts in the journeying Ten

Tribes. And who so likely to rebel as stubborn, impetuous, proud and warlike Ephraim? Rebellion and backsliding have been so characteristically the story of Ephraim's career that we can scarcely conceive that it could be otherwise . . . Can it be any wonder then that so much of the blood of Ephraim has been found hidden and unknown in the midst of the nations of northern Europe . . . until the spirit of prophesy revealed its existence?[160]

According to Ezra, these lost and fleeing tribes (presumably en route to Europe) "entered into Euphrates by the narrow passages of the river," then traveled to a region called Arsareth (4 Ezra 13:43–45). Professor Terry Blodgett, writing for the Church's *Ensign* magazine, proposed that this narrow passage is the modern-day Dariel Pass (also known as the Caucasian Pass), which begins near the headwaters of the Euphrates River and moves north, thus fitting Ezra's description of where the tribes traveled, presumably on their way to Europe. (Arsareth has been identified by scholars as a region north and west of the Euphrates, stretching even to the northern shores of the Black Sea. Indeed, right into Europe.)

Dariel Pass

Professor Blodgett points out that Russian archeologist Daniel Chwolson explored Dariel Pass and found an ancient inscription on the mountain ridge running through the pass. The inscription reads: *Wrate Israilia,* or "the gates of Israel." Chwolson's team discovered more than 700 such Hebraic inscriptions in the regions where Ezra purportedly put the lost tribe's northern migration, namely in the regions north of the Black Sea. One of these inscriptions calls the Black Sea the "Sea of Israel." [161]

It is quite possible that the apocryphal writings of Ezra from which these conclusions were made are accurate, for the Lord said to Joseph Smith that "there are many things contained therein [referring to the Apocrypha] that are true" (D&C 91:1). However, the book of Ezra also teaches things apart from the movement of the lost tribes that contradict gospel teachings and the standard works, causing us to question the credibility of this particular book.[163] Either way, it is worthy of consideration.

Again, the Old Testament prophets who revealed the geographic location and spiritual destiny of Ephraim—Ezekiel, Hosea, Zechariah, Isaiah, Jeremiah, and Ezra—all lived during or after the northern migration of Joseph/Ephraim and the lost tribes. This is important, as it reveals that their prophecies related to Joseph/Ephraim have to do with some future time—a time the Bible account does not fully cover. Indeed, they leave us with great prospects for Joseph/Ephraim, but then the Bible account of this family ends.

"There are but two tribes in Asia and Europe subject to the Romans, while the Ten Tribes are beyond the Euphrates till now, and are an immense multitude, and not to be estimated by numbers."[162]

—Flavius Josephus, ancient Romano-Jewish historian who lived during the first decades after Christ's death.

And so, it is incumbent upon us, in the latter days, to seek these biblical fulfillments in our known histories.

The suggestion thus far is that Joseph/Ephraim landed in Western Europe, occupied the British Isles, then migrated to the promised land of America. The prophet Jeremiah leaves us with one of the strongest witnesses in favor of this theory.

Indeed, in his famous Old Testament prophecies regarding the gathering of Israel, it is possible that, like Nephi, Jeremiah foresaw the early American settlers. Jeremiah spoke of the "Children of Israel" being brought by the Lord from the "land of the north, and from all the lands whither he had driven them" into "their land that I gave unto their fathers" (Jeremiah 16:15). He taught that they would be gathered from "the coasts of the earth" (Jeremiah 31:8). He further detailed this migration, stating that "Ephraim shall cry, Arise ye, and let us go up to Zion." Recall what William Bradford said as he stepped off the *Mayflower* and onto American soil: "Come, let us declare the word of God in [Zion]."[164]

Jeremiah foresaw them traveling from the "north country" (Europe?), being gathered from "the coasts" (the British Isles?), and being delivered into this new land of its inheritance (America?), saying they will come "with weeping, and with supplication" (the historical record, as we will see below, is clear on the difficulties the Pilgrims faced, particularly in their first year).

But as Jeremiah points out, the Lord would also bless them with the very blessings of the national covenant. God would indeed "lead them" and protect them "from the hand of him that was stronger than [them]." The Lord further promised to provide for them that they might "come and sing in the height of Zion" and receive "the goodness of the Lord," even "wheat," "wine," "oil," "the young of the flock and of the herd," and thus sayeth the Lord, "My people shall be satisfied with my goodness" (Jeremiah 31:6–14).

In Jeremiah 31, he defined the relationship between God and Ephraim as the "new covenant" (verse 31). He also pointed out that on an earlier occasion, God made this covenant with Israel when He "took them by the hand to bring them out of the land of Egypt" but that they had broken that covenant (verse 32). And finally, Jeremiah stated that in the last days, the Lord would bring this covenant back and "put my law in their inward parts, and write it in their hearts; and [I] will be their God, and they shall be my people" (verse 33).

In comparing this new covenant with what was clearly an ancient *national* covenant—even that covenant made with the children of Israel on their exodus from Egypt—we find that this new covenant is but another iteration of a *national* covenant. The fact that this new covenant must be "writ[ten] in their hearts" perhaps implies that these national covenant-makers would need to *feel* their responsibility under the covenant more than they would actually deduce the details in an academic sense. When the time came for Ephraim to enter America, they were already a "lost tribe." Their identity was lost—but their covenant was not. Their covenant was *written in their hearts* because of who they really were. This might explain why the Pilgrims almost inherently turned to ancient Israel, seizing upon their customs, languages, and holidays.

Some may ask how it can be suggested that the Pilgrims and America's other founders could possibly be directly from Ephraim when the Book of Mormon constantly refers to them as "Gentiles." The answer to that is found in the LDS Bible Dictionary, under the term *Gentile*: "As used throughout the scriptures [the term *Gentile*] has a dual meaning, sometimes to designate nations that are without the gospel, even though there may be some Israelite blood therein. This latter usage is especially characteristic of the word as used in the Book of Mormon."[165]

◆　◆　◆

The flight went quickly for me, with my mind so focused on scripture and history. I should have been asleep (it was somewhere in the middle of the night back in the US), but the day was just beginning in London. As we touched down, I turned on my phone to check my emails. When I saw Stephen Spykerman's name with the subject, "I'm here waiting," a shot of adrenaline went through me, and I was wide awake. He told me he was taking tea in the basement of an old London house (hundreds of years old), now converted into a hotel, and that I should meet him there as soon as possible. I wrote down the address and headed there from the airport.

When I walked into the basement café, I saw him. I couldn't miss him. There he was, white beard, fedora hat, poring over documents, maps, and books. The table before him looked like the desk of some busy university professor who had been parked there for decades.

He looked up. "Timothy!" he said with a smile, and he stood to greet me.

Nobody calls me Timothy (just "Tim"), but I wasn't going to correct him.

After we sat, I wanted to catch him up on my understanding of the theory of the tribe of Joseph and his ancient movements. He listened patiently as I recounted what I had reviewed on the plane—the movements from Palestine to Britain to America. He nodded and said I was correct in my understanding. He also warned me that many people would use this information and twist it into justifying racism. He said those twisted ideas are both false and appalling and that the only reason we study the movements of Israel is to understand how the Lord has chosen to deliver His gospel to the world.

"If we want to help God," he said with a wink and a smile, and in his classic British accent, "we better understand something about His plan."

Excited, I began to recite more scripture and prophecy.

He put his hand up and politely cut me off. "You can study that stuff at home. I want to show you something else. I want to show you why you traveled all the way out here."

I was all ears.

"Heraldry!" he exclaimed, throwing his arms in the air as if he were scattering flowers or confetti over my head. "Historians and politicians," he explained, "they can write and rewrite history all they want according to their agendas. And they do. But they can't change the lessons taught to us through heraldry, or in other words, symbolism. The ancient signs and symbols delivered by our forefathers are permanent. Untouchable. God speaks to us through them."

He whipped out a poster-size image that he himself had created. It was the Great Seal of the United States. "Do you think this could possibly just be a coincidence?" he asked as he pointed to the Seal. He first pointed to the thirteen stars that sit above the eagle's head. "The stars form a perfect Star of David."

I couldn't deny what was right before my eyes.

"And surrounding the star, look!" He pointed to what appeared to be a circle of light or fire around the star; according to the image, it was the Pillar of Fire defined in Exodus, which protected migrating Israel (Exodus 14:24; Exodus 33:9).

"And in case you don't believe me," he said, "what's around the fire?"

"Clouds," I said. Again, I could not deny what was there.

"Yes," he replied, "the clouds that hovered over the Tabernacle of the Camp of Israel. Do you know what Thomas Jefferson and Benjamin Franklin proposed for the original Seal of the United States?"

Ben Franklin's Proposed US Seal   *The Great Seal of the United States*

"I do," I replied, my eyes still fixed on the symbols of ancient Israel. I looked up at a smiling Stephen. I pulled out and referenced one of my history books. "They wanted to show depictions of Moses freeing Israel from its Egyptian oppressors through the power of God, represented by 'Rays from the Pillar of Fire in the Clouds.' They wanted to show the children of Israel being led in the wilderness 'by a cloud by day and a pillar of fire by night.'"[166]

"That's right!" Stephen confirmed. "So if those Americans were the tribe of Joseph and they came from these British Isles, let's go out and find corroboration!" He stood up and began gathering his documents and books and placing them in his book bag.

"Are we leaving?" I asked.

"Timothy, I didn't have you travel three thousand miles to sit in a London basement and talk about the United States Seal. Especially," he continued with a grin, "since you apparently have no interest whatsoever in the tea that's being served here."

I smiled.

He stood up, his bag packed. "If America is Joseph," he said, looking me straight in the eye, "then Britain has to be . . . . And we have heraldry too!" As he rolled up the poster, I narrowed my focus on the eagle—the central figure of the United States Seal. There was something about the eagle that I had learned years earlier, something connected to the Puritan era of American history. Something that only now fully made sense after hearing what Stephen had just taught me about the Seal. I knew I didn't have time to bring it up with him in that moment, just like we didn't have time to talk about the volumes written (many by Stephen himself) concerning these ancient Israelite movements and their connections to

Westminster Abbery

Britain and America.[167] So much additional evidence that falls outside the scope of this book. (But don't worry, I will tell you about the eagle in the next chapter.)

Before long, Stephen and I were in and out of taxis and darting across streets and alleyways, dodging the rapidly moving traffic of downtown London. Stephen's movements were stunning for a man his age. I smiled in amusement as I struggled to keep up with him. There were a few stretches where he was literally in full sprint—one hand grasping his closed umbrella as if it were a joust, the other holding his fedora on his head—in order to beat oncoming cars heading directly toward us.

"Here we are!" he stated abruptly and matter-of-factly.

I looked up, and there it was. Westminster Abbey.

"This religious building dates as far back as the seventh century," Stephen explained, "and its walls don't lie about who we Brits really are."

I recognized the building immediately as the place I'd seen dozens of times on television and in photos. The place where the Royal family gets married and where the coronation ceremonies take place.

Stephen pointed out many important things inside the Abbey, but the thing that stuck out the most was the enormous and elaborate stained-glass window depicting full-body images of Abraham, Isaac, and Jacob, along with full-body images of Jacob's twelve sons.

"British history reflects the reunion of Israel," Stephen explained. "This window is not a coincidence. Nor is it a coincidence that the sovereigns who are coroneted here are adorned with a crown—a crown with exactly twelve jewels embedded around it. Nor is it coincidence that the symbols on the Arms of Westminster are adorned with the breastplate of the high priest of Israel."[168]

I had seen that familiar breastplate symbol throughout London, with its grid-like shape creating exactly twelve spaces, presumably to hold twelve jewels, one for each tribe. The breastplate symbol also included a looped chain on each side, presumably showing how easy this breastplate could be fitted onto a high priest. It was familiar to me from LDS gospel art depictions of

Priests of Israel Wearing Breastplate and the Arms of Westminster

the high priests of ancient Israel, who used the breastplate, according to scripture, as a Urim and Thummim (Exodus 28:30).

"The breastplate," Stephen explained, "is the principal symbol of Britain's Houses of Parliament."

As we exited the Abbey, Stephen began unloading several books and documents and giving them to me. "Go over this material," he instructed me. "I need to leave you for a while to go make preparations for our next stop. It's my favorite place. I'll call you when I'm ready for you."

I began looking around for a library or somewhere I could sit and study.

"Remember, Timothy," he said as we parted. "You must understand the unfaltering, the unchanged, and the unalterable parts of history. Heraldry . . . and *language*."

I found an empty table on the second floor of a pub down the street from the Abbey. As I read, I understood more about what Stephen meant. I reviewed the findings of linguist Dr. Courtney James. In his book *Hebrew and English: Some Likenesses Psychic and Linguistic*, he concluded, "The similarities between the English language, which has come in great part from the Celtic and Germanic languages, and Hebrew, are more than structural."

The similarities represent harmony in both "etymology and in the thought processes involved in verbalizing ideas."[169] Another scholar and linguist, Dr. Edward Odlum, agreed. In his book *God's Covenant Man: British Israel*, Dr. Odlum stated the following:

> Much has been said and written in relation to the foundation of the English language . . . . I wish to say that as a result of long years of careful work and comparison, I am safe in saying that the construction of the Hebrew, the old British and the English of the King James Translation of the Bible are more similar than any other known language is to either the present or old British construction. The order of words to express a simple statement, the very spirit and genius of the thoughts, nature and sentiment, the strength and directness, conciseness and lofty ideality, and the predominating religious feelings permeating the whole manifest aims and temper of the people, are common to the Hebrew, ancient British, Welsh and English languages, and mark them in a class apart from all other systems of human speech.[170]

When we discussed the ancient apocryphal writer Ezra and the proposal that his writings indicated an Israelite migration into Europe, I quoted the work of Professor Terry Blodgett. As you recall, Blodgett provided archeological evidence that corroborated this idea. But the thing that originally brought Blodgett into this field of research wasn't archeology but *language*. He is a professor of languages and linguistics at Southern Utah University and has done extensive research into the connection between Hebrew and English (and the other Germanic languages). After running analytical comparisons between the Hebrew and the English/ Germanic languages in the areas of pronunciation, grammar, and vocabulary, he found that in each area there were profound similarities. He documented his findings in an *Ensign* article called "Tracing the Dispersion: New Linguistic Studies Help Tell Us about the Scattering of Israel."

According to Professor Blodgett, "Although ancient Israelites were eventually scattered throughout the entire world (Amos 9:9), at least one general geographical area contains significant linguistic evidence to suggest that Israelite migrations did in fact occur there. That area is Europe." More specifically, Professor Blodgett points out that in the centuries following 700 BC (about the time Ephraim and the ten tribes were purportedly beginning their migrations out of their homeland, following their Assyrian captivity), European languages, especially the Celtic and Germanic languages, whose concentration was in Britain, experienced profound changes. These changes (e.g., alterations in pronunciation, added vocabulary, etc.) were, according to Blodgett, "marked by tremendous outside influences."

This European linguistic phenomenon was profound enough for scholars to give it a name: the Germanic Sound Shift. (They call it that since the changes were most profound in Germanic languages, such as English, Dutch, and German.) Blodgett described a *sound shift* as "the gradual evolving of the sounds that make up words in a language, particularly when two languages merge." He explained how scholars "have long pondered what caused this sound shift and the increase in vocabulary." Though several theories exist, Blodgett concluded the following: "The research shows that the changes in language resulted from an influx of Hebrew-speaking people into Europe, particularly into the Germanic- and Celtic-speaking areas."[171]

Other scholars have noted the interesting construct of words like *England* and *Anglo-Saxon*. The word *England* might be derived from the word *Angle-land*—the Angles being a Germanic tribe that migrated to the British Isles during the fifth and sixth centuries BC. *Angle* is a Hebrew word meaning "Bull" or "Ox." These animals are the biblical symbol for Joseph, as in, "Let the blessing come upon the head of Joseph . . . His glory is like the firstlings of his bullock" (Deuteronomy 33:16–17). Other examples of the same are also very present in the biblical account.[172]

Saxon also has a fascinating proposed origin. Some scholars propose that it has its origins in the name Isaac. Dropping the *I* from Isaac (vowels are not used in Hebrew spelling) leaves us with *Saac*. God told Abraham: "In Isaac shall thy seed be called" (Genesis 21:12; see also Romans 9:7; Hebrews 11:18). The Israelites are called "the house of Isaac" (Amos 7:16). If the theory is correct, the Anglo-Saxons were derived from this same biblical house—they are "Isaac's sons." Or in Hebrew, they are "Saac's sons"—hence the name Saxons.[173]

As I studied, I paused to check other online sources regarding these theories. I found some sources that corroborated what I was reading, while others took a different angle to explain the linguistic development of the English language. While I found the arguments for a Hebrew-English connection to be both compelling and fascinating, I also found them to be inconclusive.[174]

Many of the sources I was consulting had very interesting points about the word *British*. Bible scholars and linguists explain how the Hebrew word for "covenant" is *Berith*. "In the original Hebrew language vowels were never given in the spelling. So, omitting the vowel *e* from berith, but retaining the *i* in its anglicized form to preserve the *y* sound, we have the anglicized Hebrew word for covenant: *brith* . . . . The Hebrews, however, never pronounced their *h*'s . . . . Incidentally, this ancient Hebrew trait is also a modern British trait . . . . The Hebrew word for 'covenant' [therefore] would be pronounced, in its anglicized form, as *brit*." Finally, the Hebrew word for "man" is *ish*, which means "of or belonging to." Put them together and the translation is quite incredible. *British* in its Hebrew form literally means "Covenant Man" or "Covenant People." It should also be noted that the Hebrew *ain* means "land"; *Britain*, therefore, is translated *Land of the Covenant*.[175]

My cell phone rang.

"Timothy!" It was Stephen. "Come to the Palace of Westminster. I'll be waiting at the visitors' entrance."

I was excited. The Palace of Westminster is the famous structure that sits along the River Thames and is home to the British Parliament. I met Stephen, and we walked in and were met by a tour guide who began walking us through the building. Again, the guide showed so much to me, but to stay within the scope of this study, I will limit my comments here to describing just a couple images present throughout the building—on walls, windows, and paintings. I recognized the images, having seen them many places throughout London. They are found within the Royal Coat of Arms of Britain, which is Britain's version of the US Seal. The symbol in the Coat of Arms is supported by the predominant figures of a rearing Lion and a rearing Unicorn facing each other.

"The Bible is clear, Timothy," Stephen whispered to me as the tour guide spoke monotonously about different points of interest. "The lion is the symbol of Judah, and the Unicorn the symbol of Joseph," he continued.

"Judah is a lion's whelp . . . he crouched as a lion, and as an old lion, who shall rouse him up?" (Genesis 49:9); "[Joseph's] glory is like the firstling of his bullock, and his horns are like the horns of unicorns: with them he shall push the people together to the ends of the earth: and they are the ten thousands of Ephraim, and they are the thousands of Manasseh." (Deuteronomy 33:17)

Royal Coat of Arms

Stephen looked at me.

"Timothy," he said, "what do you see wrapped around the unicorn?"

"Chains," I said. And I noticed the lion had no such restraints.

"Yes," Stephen replied. "Joseph is in captivity. That is the message. And only God can unlock the chains, liberate him, then bring him into the lands of his inheritance."

My mind flashed to the Pilgrims and the Book of Mormon. "And it came to pass that I beheld the Spirit of God, that it wrought upon other Gentiles; and they went forth out of captivity, upon the many waters" (1 Nephi 13:13). Joseph waited upon the covenant isles until being freed, being called to the promised land of America—called to commence the great latter-day gathering.

As if he could read my mind, Stephen picked up where my thoughts left off. "You see how they face each other, Timothy. The lion and the unicorn. They were to reconcile. Isaiah predicted, 'Ephraim shall not envy Judah, and Judah shall not vex Ephraim' (Isaiah 11:13). This unification process has its roots in Great Britain. That's what we learn from the Coat of Arms."

As the tour guide rambled on, I sensed a bit of frustration in Stephen's body language. Nothing the guide said came close to the significance of Stephen's whisperings to me.

"Excuse me, sir." Stephen spoke politely but firmly. "Please take us to the Moses room."

"Sir?" the guide responded.

"The Moses room, please," Stephen repeated without skipping a beat.

"There is no such thing here in the palace, sir," the guide said.

"Sir!" Stephen's voice grew louder. "We are here at the invitation of a standing member of the House of Lords. There *is* a Moses room, and we will see it now, thank you kindly."

I found the showdown quite entertaining. There's nothing like a back-and-forth in British English. The confusing blend of intensity and politeness. My American ears didn't know if a fight was breaking out or if they were about to take tea. I was lost in a Jane Austen novel.

"Excuse me, sir," the guide spoke quietly. "I will return shortly." The guide walked away, and Stephen stood firmly with the slightest hint of a smile on his face.

I didn't dare say a word.

Moments later, an older woman approached us with a key in her hand. With a smile on her face, she said kindly, "Follow me, gentlemen."

She walked us through a corridor until we came to an unassuming door, where she inserted the key and it opened wide.

"Take as much time as you need," she said as we entered the room.

I was instantly overcome. Speechless. Spirit-filled. There before me was a long table, chairs neatly placed around it. Each chair contained the breastplate symbol of the high priests of Israel on its backrest, the same symbol Stephen had introduced me to earlier in the day. But the thing that dominated the room was the enormous oil painting that filled the entire back wall. It was a painting of Moses carrying the tablets containing the law and the covenant down from Sinai.

Britain, I thought to myself. *The land of the covenant.*

I sat in one of the chairs and pondered Britain's truly miraculous history. Due to its small size and easy accessibility for foreign aggressors (it is surrounded by water), Britain has been an easy target for thousands of years. Yet, all who have tried could not conquer it. Roman invasions lasted years, the Spanish Armada took a stab, the French under Napoleon gave it a go, and Germany attempted to subdue it two distinct times during the two World Wars. Yet Britain would not fall. She had a mission under God to preserve and support its inhabitants for a wise purpose.

Dr. H. A. Wilson, the Bishop of Chelmsford, England, said: "If ever a great nation was on the point of supreme and final disaster, and yet saved and reinstated, it was ourselves . . . . It does not require an exceptional religious mind to detect in

Said Sir Winston Churchill: "I have a feeling sometimes that some Guiding Hand has interfered. I have a feeling that we have a Guardian because we have a great Cause, and we shall have that Guardian so long as we serve that Cause. And what a Cause it is."
—From *The End of the Beginning*

all this the hand of God. It has been a miracle . . . . We have been saved for a purpose."[176]

These are the signs of a covenant land. As I exited the Moses room, I was as convinced as ever.

Symbols of Israel: An Interview with Stephen Spykerman

◆　◆　◆

As I boarded the plane to return to the United States, my mind took me to all those people in history who had embarked on the same voyage from Britain to the promised land, only under much worse conditions than I was about to enjoy. And I'm not just talking about the Pilgrims. Arguably, the early Latter-day Saints from Britain saved the kingdom of God on earth by coming to America and building Zion. Within ten short years of LDS missionaries landing in Britain, nearly 18,000 British converts had joined the Church, many of them flowing into Nauvoo and later into Salt Lake City. In subsequent years, nearly 85,000 British were converted and then immigrated to America in support of the Restoration. Around 75 percent of the immigrants who came to the Salt Lake Valley in the late 1800s were from Britain.[177] Was it a coincidence that the Lord gathered so many from this land? A land that had so many connections to ancient Israel? Were these people not the children of Joseph? Were they not of Ephraim?

When President Heber C. Kimball was a missionary in England, he experienced inexplicable spiritual manifestations as he walked the old streets. He said he would just feel things within his mind and soul, things "I never before felt in my life . . ." he explained. "And I did not know what to think of it." When he returned, he reported the experiences to Joseph Smith. "Did you not understand it?" Joseph replied. "That is a place where some of the old Prophets travelled and dedicated that land, and their blessing fell upon you."[178] On another occasion, the Prophet Joseph revealed that John the Revelator had been ministering to the lost tribes in the place where they had been led away "to prepare them for their return, from their long dispersion."[179]

> "For behold, the Lord God has led away from time to time from the house of Israel, according to his will and pleasure. And now behold, the Lord remembereth all them who have been broken off."
>
> —2 Nephi 10:22

"The Lost Tribes are not lost unto the Lord," Elder Bruce R. McConkie said. "In their northward journeyings they were led by prophets and inspired leaders. They had their Moses and their Lehi . . . [and] the resurrected Lord visited and ministered among them following his ministry on this continent among the Nephites (3 Nephi 16:1–4; 17:4)."[180]

Admittedly, so much of what I learned in Britain was based in hypothesis and interpretation. But put together with LDS scripture and teachings on the subject, these pieces of circumstantial evidence became enlightening to me on my journey.

Not long after the plane took off from London, it was already descending. I had a brief layover in Holland. I thought of the Pilgrims, who had also had a layover of sorts in this very region of the world on their journey from the covenant land of Britain

THE SAVIOR IN ENGLAND?

To this day, some Brits maintain a long-held tradition that the Lord Jesus visited their nation in ancient times. These traditions are prevalent in southwest England. One historian listed over twenty locations in the region where these traditions are still celebrated.[181] Even today, William Blake's *Jerusalem* is a celebrated British anthem. The lyrics are impressive:

> *And did those feet in ancient time,*
> *Walk upon England's mountains green?*
> *And was the holy lamb of God,*
> *On England's pleasant pastures seen?*

to the promised land of America. The layover refocused me and reminded me again why I had come to London. I had come to build a case for the Pilgrims—to understand what great powers and influences might have driven them.

Mission accomplished.

At last, I was prepared to visit the Pilgrims' Plymouth Plantation (or what was left of it) in New England. I was prepared to meet John Howland and his companions from the *Mayflower* at their final destination in America.

I could only imagine what treasures would be awaiting me there.

CHAPTER 3

The Plantation

The *Mayflower* left England on September 6, 1620. The port book documented that there were a total of sixty-five fishing boats traveling in a convoy home from Newfoundland and heading for the same port from which the *Mayflower* was about to depart. One of the boats in the convoy led the rest, and that one landed at port alone on the very day the *Mayflower* launched out. The two ships must have passed each other, the passengers in each perhaps looking upon each other. If the Pilgrims caught a glimpse of the name of the inbound vessel, they might have thought it a happy omen. But if they remembered this fishing boat after a year in America, they might have instead reflected upon it and thought it a prophecy fulfilled. The boat was called *Covenant*.[182]

If the Pilgrims believed the Lord taught through symbols and patterns, perhaps they considered a deeper meaning in the name of their own vessel. As a ship, the *Mayflower* was not the optimal choice. It was old and in bad shape (sold for scrap just four years after the Pilgrim voyage), and it was not an ocean-going vessel (it was reserved as a short-distance cargo transport, mostly between Britain and France).[183] There is no record to show that its captain and owner, Christopher Jones, had ever even made the journey across the Atlantic before.[184] But the ship was available for hire, and it was all the Pilgrims could afford. Notwithstanding its inferior nature, its name was *Mayflower*. "Mayflower" was another name for the hawthorn plant. According to legend, the hawthorn (or hawthorne mayflower) "sprang from a drop of Christ's blood on the crown of thorns at the Crucifixion."[185] The power of the Pilgrim covenant was, especially in their own minds and hearts, fueled directly by the atoning sacrifice of Jesus Christ. That a vessel called *Mayflower* carried them safely to their covenant land was wholly fitting.

On November 11, 1620, the *Mayflower* at last landed on the shores of America. William Bradford said they "fell upon their knees and blessed the God of heaven, who had brought them over the vast and furious ocean."[186] It is no coincidence that the earlier Jaredite arrival to ancient America was described in the Book of Mormon in almost identical fashion: "And when they had set their feet upon the shores of the promised land they bowed themselves down upon the face of the land, and did humble themselves before the Lord, and did shed tears of joy before the Lord, because of the multitude of his tender mercies over them" (Ether 6:12). The Pilgrims and the Jaredites (and also the Nephites) were, after all, brought to the promised land for the same purposes under God.

As happy as they were to see land after over two months at sea, it didn't take long for the Pilgrims to realize they had missed their mark—by over 250 miles. They were supposed to have landed south of where they were. They were supposed to have landed at the mouth of the Hudson River, near to where New York City is today. Instead, due to unexpected wind, weather, and ocean currents, they accidently arrived at Cape Cod, near the place known as Plymouth. So they turned the *Mayflower* southward in order to arrive at their desired location. But as they moved south, they ran into shallow and treacherous waters caused by a series of shoals, or submerged sandbars. The wind dropped, and the waves picked up. For a moment, the *Mayflower* was close to running aground, which might have ended the entire Pilgrim story. Suddenly, the wind picked up and changed directions, offering a small window of opportunity for the *Mayflower* to turn around and head back north. They took it.

Once they were out of harm's way, they stopped the *Mayflower*, and the Pilgrims huddled up to decide what to do. They felt they should return to where they had originally seen land, and they made a huge historic decision: they would begin their settlement in present-day Massachusetts, at a place they would soon discover called Plymouth.[187]

Knowing what I did about the Pilgrim mission and its connection to God and the gathering of His latter-day Israel, I couldn't believe that this decision was a mistake. There had to be a reason the Lord had kept them from settling where they had intended to settle. There had to be something special about Plymouth. And I was going there to find out what it was.

As I was preparing my trip, I began researching the area. I needed to find the right people to show me what I needed to see. I was shocked at the lack of anything that advertised a Plymouth tour based in the Pilgrims' faith. It seemed everything about the Pilgrims was being taught in Plymouth except for their faith and religion, even though their faith and religion had meant *everything* to them. I grew frustrated.

But I believed in the American spirit. I believed enough people still sought truth. So I went to TripAdvisor, a travel website that lets the people speak and leave reviews. And there I found it: The Jenney House, one of the oldest homes in Plymouth and the site of the Jenney Museum, run by an older couple, Leo and Nancy Martin. And from what I could tell by the reviews, the focus of their tour was the Pilgrims' faith. I had to meet them. I was pleased to see that the Jenney Museum tour was the highest-ranked tour on TripAdvisor. Indeed, I still believe in the American spirit.

I exchanged emails, and they gave me the coordinates of where I should meet Leo in Plymouth for my "walking tour."

As I drove to the mysterious location, I became confused. The GPS told me I was within 100 feet of the destination, but all I could see was a quiet residential neighborhood around me. Nothing commercial and nothing that seemed obviously historic.

But then I saw it. And when I did, my heart skipped a beat. *How could such an amazing thing exist and I never knew about it?* I thought to myself. *And here, of all places, in an obscure neighborhood in Plymouth.*

Its existence seemed so out of place and surreal that I quickly parked and exited my car to get a better look. It was an eighty-one-foot-tall granite sculpture dedicated in 1889, and it was entitled *The National Monument to the Forefathers*. It stands as a

National Monument to the Forefathers, Plymouth, MA

tribute to, and a reminder of, the very national covenant I had learned about in scripture and history.

The morning was beautiful, and I was the only one at the site. It was peaceful and quiet. I walked up to the monument, which was configured in an octagonal shape, and began my examination. I noted that the monument contained several pedestals, upon which stood several figures and depictions. Upon its tallest, most centralized, and principal pedestal stood the heroic figure of "Faith," with her right hand pointing toward heaven and her left hand clutching the Bible. Upon the other pedestals were seated figures emblematical of the principles upon which the Pilgrims founded their land. The figures were named Freedom, Morality, Law, and Education.

The monument included four large panels with powerful verbiage. The front panel was inscribed as follows: "National Monument to the Forefathers. Erected by a grateful people in remembrance of their labors, sacrifices and sufferings for the cause of civil and religious liberty." The right and left panels contained the names of those who came over on the *Mayflower*. The rear panel contained a quote from William Bradford:

> Thus out of small beginnings greater things have been produced by His hand that made all things of nothing and gives being to all things that are; and as one small candle may light a thousand, so the light here kindled hath shone unto many, yea in some sort to our whole nation; let the glorious name of Jehovah have all praise.

As I read these words, I thought about the fact that these "small beginnings," or this "one small candle," had in some ways been even smaller than I'd recognized before. Of the 102 *Mayflower* passengers, only about half were from the Leiden congregation.[188] The others weren't necessarily traveling for religious reasons and, therefore, were not necessarily American covenant-makers. (The Leiden group invited these others so as to share the large cost of the voyage.) The Leiden passengers still evolved into the dominant group, commanding the leadership roles by the consent of all the settlers. This made it possible for the covenant to be invoked powerfully upon American soil, thus paving the way for greater blessings to follow. But it truly was only a remnant that ignited it all.

As I pondered all this, lost in emotion and spirit, and with my eyes still locked on the monument, I was suddenly jolted back to my surroundings by a voice coming to me in a heavy New England accent.

"Hello, you must be Tim!"

I thought I was looking at a ghost. There before me stood a man with a white beard. He instantly reminded me of the character John Hammond from Jurassic Park. Only this guy was dressed head to foot in Pilgrim clothes—hat and knickerbockers included.

"Leo Martin?" I asked.

"At your service!"

I liked Leo immediately. I asked him how he got into giving Pilgrim tours, and his answer made me all the more anxious to hear what he had to say about these early settlers. He told me he had spent an entire career as a carpenter, living and working in a town many miles from Plymouth, and then one day, years earlier, he and his wife had a revelation to abandon their lives and leave everything they knew. They were to move to Plymouth to tell the true story of what happened there because few others really were.

"Did you know a lot about the Pilgrims when you worked as a carpenter?" I asked, expecting to hear that Pilgrim history had been his hobby for years.

"Not a thing," he admitted.

The scripture came to my mind: "And he saith unto them, Follow me, and I will make you fishers of men. And they straightway left their nets, and followed him" (Matthew 4:19–20).

"Leo," I said, "I have three questions I want answered today."

"I'll do my best." He smiled.

"First, why did the Pilgrims do it? It was irrational. Crazy. So why? Second, why didn't the Lord let them go south to the Hudson? In other words, why Plymouth when it wasn't their plan? And third, what can you tell me about John Howland? Because that guy totally fascinates me."

"John Howland?" he asked rhetorically with a huge grin. "Well, you must know what happened to him on the way over, right?"

"Yeah," I said. "He should have been fish food."

"That's right," he replied with a chuckle. "I'll tell you what ended up happening to him at the end of the tour. You won't believe it! But first, let me answer your other two questions."

He then walked me around the monument, describing each scene and symbol. Though he presented himself as a simple carpenter, he was a walking encyclopedia. I learned later that he had an extensive historical library and had even authored his own book.

I was overwhelmed with what he was teaching me.

"And so," he said after a forty-minute lecture that enthralled me, "you see why they did it. I can sum it up in two words: faith and covenant."

Leo Martin Presents the National Monument to the Forefathers

Leo had spoken truth. Gospel truth. His words reminded me of all that I had recently learned about the Pilgrims' invocation of, and at times obsession with, the ancient covenants of Israel. As we were walking away, I turned and gave the monument one more look, focusing on the central figure—Faith. I narrowed my focus on the woman's Bible. I recalled the Pilgrims' intense love of and dedication to the Bible—"And it came to pass that I, Nephi, beheld that they did prosper in the land; and I beheld a book, and it was carried forth among them . . . which [book] contains the covenants of the Lord, which he hath made unto the house of Israel" (1 Nephi 13:20, 23).

"Now, I need to take you to the water's edge," Leo said, "so I can properly answer your second question regarding why they landed here. You will see it was a result of this faith and covenant because the whole thing was a miracle from God. They *had* to settle here. Anywhere else and they all would have died!"

He had my attention.

Before traveling the short distance to the beach, we stopped over at the Jenney House Museum. I met his lovely wife, Nancy, who held down the fort and ran the small gift shop. I also took a short tour of the historical house, which provided further insight into the lives and faith of these settlers.

I noticed the old house was in bad shape. The roof, for example, was so old it looked like it was about to collapse. I was worried because I knew this place *had* to hold up. To me, Leo and Nancy seemed to be the last bastions of hope in this town, which seemed to be getting more and more secular and less and less religious in its approach to its own history—actually, in its approach to *all* of our history. After all, this was the birthplace of America.

Leo and I eventually made it down to the water, where the famous Plymouth Rock is on display, along with a replica of the *Mayflower* docked in the harbor.

THE MISSING MANUSCRIPT

Perhaps the most important piece of literature recording the Pilgrims' history is *Of Plymouth Plantation*, written by one who witnessed it all, Governor William Bradford. Before copies could ever be made, the original manuscript mysteriously disappeared from America. It is believed by some that during the Revolutionary War, the British stole it from the tower of the Old South Church in Boston, where it had reportedly been kept, and sent it back to London. Sadly, key portions of the Pilgrim history, particularly the spiritual elements so important to Bradford and the Pilgrims, were lost to Americans. Many years later, in 1855, an American researcher came across a London-published history book that seemed to reference a passage directly out of Bradford's elusive volume. In the footnotes of the book, it was learned that the Bradford reference came from a manuscript held in the Fulham Library in England. *Could it be the missing manuscript?*

After weeks of correspondence and cooperation with interested parties on both sides of the Atlantic, it was ultimately confirmed. It *was* Bradford's book. The administrators of the Fulham Library provided a copy of the manuscript as soon as possible, and in 1856, *Of Plymouth Plantation* was published in Boston by Little, Brown, and Company and made widely available for the first time.[189]

And the timing seemed providential, for at that time, the nation was deeply divided and heading into Civil War. The national climate fueled the longstanding debate about America's true roots. Was its foundation the Jamestown, Virginia, settlement, made famous by gold seekers and the introduction of slavery into the land? Or was it Plymouth, with its Godly and covenant-based foundation? The newly published *Of Plymouth Plantation* reminded Northerners that they were on the right side of history and that theirs was a legacy worth fighting to preserve.

In early 1861, as the Civil War was just getting underway, Abraham Lincoln made a ten-dollar donation to the building of the National Monument to the Forefathers.[190]

As we stood near the shoreline, Leo explained the miracle that was Plymouth Plantation. "You need to remember," he began, "the Pilgrims were delayed in England. When they got here, it was already winter. They were starving. They were dying. As it was, half of them died the first year. They should have all died, given the circumstances. The Lord let them die, perhaps, so that we could appreciate the miracle required to save the other half."

I remembered Jeremiah's prophecy about the gathering of Israel: they will come "with weeping, and with supplications" (Jeremiah 31:9).

Leo referred me to the book *Mayflower* by the award-winning historian Nathaniel Philbrick. Whether by disease, lack of food, or dangerous Natives who had slaughtered other Europeans who dared to enter their lands, things could have been much worse. "By all rights," Philbrick stated, "none of the Pilgrims should have emerged from the first winter alive."[192]

"They lived though," Leo said, "because they came *here*." As he said this, he pointed to the water, to the shoreline, and to the steep hill that overlooked the bay.

He then began his second full lecture. I took notes so I could later corroborate what he was telling me with the published historical record—something I was able to do in full.

I learned that when the Pilgrims landed at Plymouth, their diseased bodies made it almost impossible for them to start hacking and clearing the densely wooded New England land in an effort to prepare crops of any kind. But they didn't have to. Someone else had already done it. Indeed, acres of cleared and fertile land were awaiting them. Three years earlier, up to 3,000 Native Americans (the Patuxet Indians) were farming and thriving happily along this shoreline, precisely where the Pilgrims built their settlement. But a plague had hit the Patuxet paradise,

MAYFLOWER MOTHERS

During their first winter in America, half of the recently landed Pilgrims died. But the *Mayflower* mothers were hit the hardest. They were the first to go without food. The first to go without shelter. They, more than any of the others, took what little they had and gave it to their children. They sacrificed for the survival of the next generations. They died for us. During that first winter, about three-quarters of the women died.[191]

Not far from the Plymouth shoreline today, there stands the Monument to the Pilgrim Mothers. It reads, "They brought up their families in sturdy virtue and a living faith in God without which nations perish."

causing them to either die or abandon the area. The land seemed cursed, and nobody dared return. This tragic event ended up saving the Pilgrims.[193]

Leo pointed out the steep slopes that overlooked the bay. He explained how the setup was perfect. The Pilgrims could build a fort atop the hill and use the advantageous position to survey the landscape and waters for signs of danger. The sloping hillside was also home to a brook, called Town Brook, which was supplied by naturally sand-filtered spring water and, thus, provided all the fresh water the Pilgrims could drink. The steep, downward flow of water was also ideal for building grist mills. And finally, between the harbor and the brooks, the Pilgrims had an endless supply of fish and eel. But these miraculous features were just the beginning.[194]

Though the Pilgrims recognized these benefits, they still needed more help. They were in an unfamiliar land and did not know the finer points of farming in this foreign environment. They had to trust in the Lord that somehow He would provide. And He did, in the most unusual way.

The day had started like any other. The settlers were working to build their new home, and it was proving difficult. Suddenly, the alarms sounded and the women and children were rushed to the safe zone within the camp. The men grabbed their guns and stood their ground. The reason? A large, scantily-clad Native American man was walking right toward the camp, with no indication of halting. Tensions rose as he came nose-to-nose with the armed settlers. He stopped. Smiled. Then, in a simple act that would shock all present, the man opened his mouth and spoke in clear English.

"Welcome, English!" he exclaimed.

His name was Samoset, and he had come as a friend. He had come to help. Shortly thereafter, another Native American walked into the camp who also spoke English. His name was Squanto, and he would become a close friend and ally. Not only did Squanto also speak English, but he stayed with the Pilgrims during their first year in the wilderness and taught them how to plant corn, hunt, and fish. He showed them, for example, the Native art of how to use dead fish for fertilizer, then add bean sprouts to the already sprouted corn. The creepers from the beans would attach to the cornstalk, creating a blanket of shade to protect against the heat of the sun. The traditional planting techniques of the Pilgrims failed to produce. Without Squanto, they would have starved. Bradford called Squanto a "special instrument sent of God."[195]

And then there was the Indian Chief of the whole region. His name was Massasoit, and with one order, he could have destroyed the Pilgrim settlement, and at first, he had intended to do it.[197] But something stopped him and instead convinced him to make friends with the English. What it was, nobody knows for sure. Historian Rod Gragg asked, "Why did Massasoit not order a massacre of the Pilgrims and wipe out the weak, struggling colony in its infancy? Why was Plymouth spared the repeated attacks and bloodshed that marked the early history of Virginia's Jamestown Colony? . . . Again, to William Bradford, it was all an act of divine grace, in which 'the powerful hand of the Lord did protect them.'"[198] According to another historian, "Massasoit was a remarkable example of God's providential care for the Pilgrims. He was probably the only chief on the northeast coast of America who would have welcomed the Europeans as friends."[199]

Instead of war, the Pilgrims (using Squanto as an interpreter) entered into the most successful treaty ever negotiated between European colonists and Native Americans. Both sides respected and enforced the treaty, and they kept the peace under its law for

THE "SPECIAL INSTRUMENT FROM GOD"

In 1614, only six years before the Pilgrims arrived, Squanto was kidnapped by a Captain Hunt, taken to Spain, and sold into the Spanish slave market. He escaped slavery and got himself over to London, where he learned English. He eventually found a sea captain to take him back home to his village in America. When he finally returned in 1619, he found that his people had been wiped out by a plague and that his village was completely abandoned. Squanto was a Patuxet Indian, and it was his land in Plymouth that the Pilgrims had ended up settling on within a year after his return. And so it was with some satisfaction and consolation that he was able to use his language skills and his knowledge of his homeland to help the Pilgrims develop the very land and soil upon which he himself had been raised.[196]

over fifty years. Though later generations on both sides would allow the treaty to be violated, these first-generation Pilgrims made it work. In fact, the peace they built with Massasoit blossomed into deep friendship. When Massasoit was threatened by outsider tribes, the Pilgrims, as per their promise, risked life and limb to come to his rescue. And Massasoit did the same in return.[200]

One of the most tender stories ever told of this time was when panic-stricken Natives sent word to Plymouth Plantation that Chief Massasoit was sick and dying, apparently from typhus. His people had seen this before and had determined he was past the point of no return. Pilgrim Edward Winslow decided to see what could be done. He packed fruit preserves that were easy to digest, then hiked most of the day to Massasoit's village. There he found him blind, unable to eat, and half dead. Over the next couple days, Winslow stayed by his side, fed him the preserves, and scraped away the poisonous,

Edward Winslow, a *Mayflower* Pilgrim who served as the third colonial governor of Plymouth, said:

I desire they may really know what we do . . . assuring myself that none will ever be losers by following us so far as we follow Christ . . . that the Lord our God may still delight to dwell amongst his plantations and churches there by his gracious presence, and may go on blessing to bless them with heavenly blessings in these earthly places, that so by his blessing they may not only grow up to a nation, but become exemplary for good unto others.[201]

furry bacteria that had grown on the inside of his mouth and tongue. Through Winslow's love and care, Massasoit made a full recovery. "Now I see the English are my friends and love me," the recently healed Massasoit said, "and whilst I live, I will never forget this kindness they have showed me."[202]

The Relationship Between Pilgrims and Native Americans

"And now, as ye are desirous to come into the fold of God, and to be called his people, and are willing to bear one another's burdens . . . . Yea, and are willing to mourn with those that mourn; yea, and comfort those that stand in need of comfort" (Mosiah 18:8–9). This is the covenant. And adherence to it continued to bring blessings to the Pilgrims.

Indeed, there was a reason the Pilgrims had been brought to Plymouth, with its providential land features, its English-speaking Natives, and its friendly Native American chief. There was a reason that, though the suffering Pilgrims had landed in New England during an unusual cold streak that had lasted for years—what climatologists have called the "little ice age" in America—miraculously, the first Pilgrim winter saw an unexpected reprieve. A warming. An early spring. And it likely saved many sick Pilgrims from dying.[206] Yes, there was a reason that when, a couple years later, a drought hit the land and was about to destroy all the Pilgrims' crops (threatening the end of their

KING PHILIP'S WAR

Unfortunately, the peace at Plymouth did not last. Greedy deals, bad-faith agreements, and unnecessary aggression from both sides caused later generations of European settlers and Native tribes to reject the more peaceful traditions of their fathers. It ended in terror and bloodshed. King Philip's War (named after Massasoit's son, Phillip), lasted from 1675–1678 and claimed the lives of thousands of Natives and colonists.

Sadly, too many ignorant commentators (often peddling some modern agenda), conflate these later conflicts with the *Mayflower* Pilgrims in an effort to smear the Pilgrim name. As Pilgrim historian Rebecca Fraser points out, historians today "emphasize the symbiotic nature of Indian and English life, and talk more of a middle ground than a battleground. Indians are no longer seen as doomed passive victims. They were as cunning as their English neighbors."[203]

Though these Pilgrims did experience armed conflict with certain tribes and though they did have to defend themselves and defend Massasoit and his people, nothing is clearer than that the *Mayflower* Pilgrims honored and re-spected their Native friends. They did not believe themselves superior. Edward Winslow wrote glowingly about the Natives, declaring them "worthy of the name Covenant."[204]

What is equally clear is how saddened these Pilgrims were when those who followed them to America failed to see the Natives as brothers and sisters un-der God. "At some point a serpent was bound to enter paradise," Fraser wrote. "The arrival of many more English from 1630 was the death knell of easy relations between them and the Indians."[205] If only all those newcomers, and if only all Americans *today*, could have better remembered the true covenant, with all its principles, established by those first American Pilgrims.

plantation), the Pilgrims called for a special day of fasting and prayer. And there was a reason that on that very day of fasting and prayer, which had begun hot and cloudless, consistent with the drought, by the afternoon, the clouds had rolled in and spilled their rain into the land—a rain that continued for fourteen days and saved the plantation.[207]

The reason was the covenant and the Pilgrims' efforts to live it in the land.

By the time Leo and I were done, we had walked the shoreline, explored Plymouth Rock, toured the *Mayflower 2* (replica of the original), and discussed everything each of us could think of regarding the miraculous settlement. We were exhausted physically, mentally, and even spiritually.

But I could not shake one nagging question: How did the Pilgrims turn this little village into the United States of America, even the host nation of the Restoration? None of these miracles would have meant much at all if they could not have produced such a nation. More pilgrims needed to come. More settlements needed to be built. But how could they make that happen?

I said goodbye to Leo, hopped in my rental car, and headed north for the answer. I was on my way to Salem, Cambridge, Boston, and other nearby cities that represented the next major wave of settlements to follow Plymouth. This was the home of the Puritans, who came to America from Britain and founded the Massachusetts Bay Colony in 1630, some ten years after the *Mayflower* landed. Like the Pilgrims, the Puritans were a religious group that sought to improve and purify the church of Christ. I knew the Puritan colony had grown rapidly and had eventually taken in Plymouth and all it had originally created. But what exactly had brought the Puritans here? Did they follow the same covenant traditions of the Pilgrims? Were they a product of that legacy?

The answers to these questions begin with yet another Pilgrim miracle. It began one day about a year after the Pilgrims had landed at Plymouth. The day had begun like any other. The settlers were going about their business, building their colony, when a warning shot rang out from the Pilgrim fortress on the hill above the camp. A ship was heading into harbor, and the Pilgrims had to assume the worst. Perhaps it was a French vessel or one from another potentially hostile land coming to make trouble. Fortunately, it was an English ship called the *Fortune*, sent by the Pilgrims' sponsors back home to bring more settlers and to pick up any valuable imports the Pilgrims had acquired as a return on their investment. The Pilgrims loaded the ship with New England timber, loads of sassafras, and dozens of beaver pelts.

They also sent a secret weapon, a manuscript recounting the eventful, adventurous, and miraculous first year at Plymouth, written by Edward Winslow and William Bradford, entitled *A Relation or Journal of the Beginning and Proceedings of the English Plantation Settled at Plimouth in New England*. (Later, for reasons not entirely known, the title was reduced to *Mourt's Relation*.)

Upon the *Fortune's* return to England, French privateers attacked it and stole everything the Pilgrims had worked so hard to acquire and send back to Britain in order to pay down their debt to their investors. But the French pirates missed the most valuable thing. One of the passengers had hid Bradford and Winslow's manuscript, and it was later given to an English publisher. The book was a huge success and a tool the Lord then used to inspire and recruit more of His chosen ones to migrate and settle in the American promised land.[208]

The Puritan governor John Winthrop, who brought the Puritans in 1630, led many of the first recruits. They called themselves the Massachusetts Bay Colony and founded Salem,

Boston, and the surrounding areas. It didn't take long for me to conclude that Winthrop and his people most certainly followed in the example of their friendly Pilgrim neighbors to the south. Before landing in America, Winthrop gathered the Puritans and offered what some scholars today deem the "Ur-text of American literature."[209]

Winthrop stated: "Thus stands the cause between God and us. We are entered into Covenant with Him for this work . . . . Now if the Lord shall please to hear us, and bring us in peace to the place we desire, then hath He ratified this Covenant and sealed our Commission."[210]

Winthrop then famously prophesied:

> [God] shall make us a praise and glory . . . that men shall say of succeeding plantations: the Lord make it like that of New England. For we must consider that we shall be as a City upon a Hill, the eyes of all people are upon us; so that if we shall deal falsely with our God in this work we have undertaken, and so cause Him to withdraw His present help from us, we shall be made a story and a by-word through the world.[211]

Upon internalizing Winthrop's words, we can almost hear echoed exhortations from an earlier American Covenant–maker, even the Prophet Lehi, who said: "Serve him according to the commandments [and] it shall be a land of liberty . . . . Inasmuch as ye shall keep [God's] commandments ye shall prosper in the land; but inasmuch as ye will not . . . ye shall be cut off" (2 Nephi 1:7, 20).

Winthrop continued utilizing concepts we might recognize in the Book of Mormon, when, in this speech, he detailed the covenant obligations. Winthrop explained that his people must, under their covenant, "delight in each other, mourn together, labor and suffer together, always having before our eyes our Commission and Community in the work"[212] (compare to Mosiah 18:9). As one Puritan wrote of his early America countrymen, "They joyned together in a holy Covenant with the Lord, and one with another, promising by the Lords Assistance to walke together . . . and to cleave to the Lord."[213]

Winthrop went on to list the promised blessings for living this covenant, which included God's "wisdom, power, goodness, and truth," along with the promise that the "God of Israel is among us, when ten of us shall be able to resist a thousand of our enemies." And finally, Winthrop reminded his people that by "obeying [God's] voice and cleaving to him," they secure "our life, and our prosperity."[214]

As the Book of Mormon prophesies and as the Pilgrims at Plymouth might have presaged, Winthrop and his Puritans also adhered closely to the ancient covenants of Israel. In fact, in his speech, Winthrop reminded his early American migrants and covenant-makers what happened to ancient Israel when they failed to live their end of their national covenant: "It lost [them] the Kingdom." And that his people might not fall into the same tragic state, he implored them to live the covenant correctly lest the Lord "make us know the price of the breach of such a Covenant."[215]

John Winthrop

Winthrop's colleague in the cause, Pastor John Cotton, also weighed in on the power and importance of this national covenant. Using 2 Samuel as the basis for his sermon, he applied Old Testament principles to his Puritan congregation. Quoting the Bible, Pastor Cotton said, "Moreover I will appoint a place for my people Israel, and I will plant them, that they may dwell in a place of their own, and move no more; neither shall the children of wickedness afflict them any more, as before time." Cotton went on to explain that such would be their covenant blessing if they "with a public spirit" lived in righteousness, "that they do not degenerate as the Israelites did." Only then would the covenant take force, and only then, as Cotton concluded, would the Puritans "prosper and flourish . . . . [For] when He promiseth peace and safety, what enemies shall be able to make the promise of God of none effect?"[216]

And yet, further evidence that the Puritans knew their national covenant was somehow an extension of the ancient covenants with Israel is found in the fact that they oft referred to their founder Winthrop as *Nehemias Americanus*, thus comparing him to the ancient Israelite leader Nehemiah. The Bible records that Nehemiah led his people out of Babylon back into the promised land, rebuilt the walls of Jerusalem, and inspired his people to return to their national covenant.[217]

Furthermore, and as aforementioned, the Puritans named one of their first towns Salem, which name is a root of the word *Jerusalem* and translates from the Hebrew meaning of "peace." They also called their colony the "New Jerusalem" and believed they were somehow fulfilling prophecies regarding the last days.[218]

And like the Pilgrims before them, they tapped into the ancient power of this ancient covenant for a wise purpose—for the enlargement and restoration of the gospel. Winthrop taught that the Puritans had come to America in order "to carry the Gospel into those parts of the world . . . [away from] all other Churches of Europe [that] are brought to desolation . . . and who knows, but that God hath provided this place [America] to be a refuge for many whom he means to save out of the general calamity."[219]

Another early American Puritan of New England who shared this vision was the minister Jonathan Edwards. A major participant in developing a God-centered nation during early eighteenth-century America, Edwards said, "God presently goes about doing some great thing in order to make way for the introduction of the church's latter-day glory—which is to have its first seat in, and is to rise from, [this] new world."[220]

Historian Perry William summed it up succinctly:

> Winthrop and his colleagues believed . . . that their errand was not a mere scouting expedition: it was an essential maneuver in the drama of Christendom. The Bay Company was not a battered remnant of suffering Separatists thrown upon a rocky shore; it was an organized task force of Christians, executing a flank attack on the corruptions of Christendom. These Puritans did not flee to America; they went in order to work out that complete reformation which was not yet accomplished in England and Europe.[221]

And so my question about how the Plymouth legacy led to the building of a nation had been answered. Indeed, the Puritans had not only followed the Pilgrim's trek across the ocean, but they had also followed the Plymouth model, invoking the ancient covenants for the purposes of establishing the kingdom of God on earth. Upon their arrival, the Puritan pastors even sought advice from Plymouth about how to covenant with God in America. As Fraser explained, both Salem and Plymouth realized that they "shared the desire to recreate a purified church on the lines of Christ's ancient church—and that drew them together."[222] Thus, a nation was born. And with its growth, this nation would soon

SHARED ANNIVERSARIES AND SHARED GODLY PURPOSES

1620—Mayflower Pilgrims arrive on the promised land.

1820—Joseph Smith has his First Vision.

1630—Massachusetts Bay Colony (Puritans) arrive on the promised land.

1830—The Church of Jesus Christ of Latter-day Saints is established.

be prepared to enter into the next phase of Nephi's chapter 13 vision—that is, to lead a revolution for independence (see 1 Nephi 13:17–19). This revolution made a nation-state, which, as Nephi's vision indicated, would then usher in the Restoration (1Nephi 13:34–40), even that "purified church on the lines of Christ's ancient church," which was the motive of America's earliest settlers from the beginning.

◆ ◆ ◆

One Puritan who took the idea of a restored gospel in America even further was Roger Williams. Many believed Williams's beliefs on religion and government went too far, and he subsequently fled the Massachusetts Bay Colony under threat of arrest. During his exile, he found safety and refuge with Massasoit, whom Williams loved and greatly respected. He later purchased land from Massasoit and eventually founded his own colony called Providence in what is now Rhode Island.[223] Once secure in his new colony, he helped organize a new church. However, he eventually left that church as well. His reason for doing so was that there was "no regularly-constituted Church on earth, nor any person authorized to administer any Church ordinance; nor could there be, until new apostles were sent by the great Head of the Church, for whose coming he was seeking."[224]

Another gospel visionary of that day was the prominent Puritan and judicial officer, Samuel Sewall. Sewall is known in history for his participation in the reprehensible Salem Witch Trials. In the centuries leading up to the new settlements in America, European courts had executed up to 50,000 people for witchcraft. Fortunately, in America (Salem), only twenty people were executed before enough people saw the sin in what was happening to end the revolting tradition.[226] There is no question that

Roger Williams

the adversary knows the promised land and will stop at nothing to influence it with evil. This is one reason the Lord needed to bring the inspired US Constitution to the land in order to protect against such wickedness.

In the meantime, Samuel Sewall was one of the few who stood and publicly apologized for his role in letting the trials proceed. He was penitent and remorseful for the rest of his days. Interestingly, his humility in the matter might have been the thing that prepared his spirit to receive some of the most incomprehensible revelations pertaining to the gospel and America.

For example, as if he were reading Article of Faith 1:10, Sewall predicted that the New Jerusalem was to be built upon the American continent. Others used the name "New Israel" or "New Jerusalem" to describe their early American settlements. Sewall, however, like Joseph Smith, was calling for the *actual* Millennial city.

"Why [may not America] be the place of the New Jerusalem?" he would ask. He believed the Lord answered this question for

AN APOSTLE DESCENDANT OF WILLIAMS SPEAKS OUT

"In the tumultuous years of the first settlements in this nation, Roger Williams, my volatile and determined 10th great-grandfather, fled—not entirely of his own volition—from the Massachusetts Bay Colony and settled in what is now the state of Rhode Island. He called his headquarters Providence, the very name itself revealing his lifelong quest for divine interventions and heavenly manifestations. But he never found what he felt was the true New Testament church of earlier times. Of this disappointed seeker the legendary Cotton Mather said, 'Mr. Williams [finally] told [his followers] 'that being himself misled, he had [misled them,' and]

Roger Williams.

he was now satisfied that there was none upon earth that could administer baptism [or any of the ordinances of the gospel], . . . [so] he advised them therefore to *forego* all . . . and wait for the coming of *new* apostles.' Roger Williams did not live to see those longed-for new Apostles raised up, but in a future time I hope to be able to tell him personally that his posterity did live to see such."[225]

—*Elder Jeffrey R. Holland in his October 2004 general conference address "Prophets, Seers, and Revelators."*

him one evening while he was pondering over a sermon he had heard regarding stars being a "sign in the heaven."[227] He was astonished to then see a shooting star fly over his house. Using a ship's globe and consulting a sea captain, Sewall determined that the star had been heading in a southwesterly direction, in a trajectory toward Mexico. He believed God was pointing him in the direction of the future site of the New Jerusalem.[228] Depending on what Sewall understood about the vast territories of "Mexico" at the time, such a trajectory would likely have included, in Sewall's mind, territory over the middle of North America, perhaps directly over what would become the state of Missouri. Again, it was as though Sewall had access to the same inspiration Joseph Smith received, who also pointed to the middle of the North American continent—specifically to Missouri— as the sacred site of the New Jerusalem.[229] It's easy to believe that this Puritan and that Prophet were inspired by the same divine, all-knowing source above.

Sewall argued that New England was but "a preface" to the New Jerusalem. America "stands fair," he claimed, "for being made the seat of the divine metropolis." He continued, "I hold that [God] set His right foot in the New World and His left, in the Old."[230] LDS authorities have interpreted Isaiah 2:2 as saying the same thing. According to President Harold B. Lee, when Isaiah prophesied that "out of Zion shall go forth the law, and the word of the Lord from Jerusalem," Isaiah was seeing two Millennial capitals: one in America and the other in the Old World.[231]

But then Sewall tapped even deeper into the teachings of the restored gospel. The title page and introduction to the Book of Mormon teach that "the Lamanites" who are "ancestors of the American Indians" are "a remnant of the house of Israel." We are further taught that the gospel of Jesus Christ must be delivered to the Lamanites, that they "might come to the knowledge of their fathers, and that they might know the promises of the Lord, and that they may believe the gospel" (D&C 3:19–20).

Astonishingly, Sewall believed the same thing. He believed, as many of his fellow colonists believed, that Native Americans were remnants of the lost tribes of Israel. He quoted John 10:16: "And other sheep I have, which are not of this fold: them also I must bring." These other sheep were, for Sewall, the American Indians. "The English nation," he taught, "in shewing Kindness to the Aboriginal Natives of America, may possibly, shew Kindness to Israelites unawares . . . . Instead of being branded for Slaves with hot irons in the Face, and arms; and driven by scores in mortal Chains: they shall wear the Name of God in their foreheads, and they shall be delivered into the glorious Liberty of the Children of God."[233]

And as the Book of Mormon and D&C direct, so Sewall complied: he not only called for equal rights for the Natives but also personally took it upon himself to see that they were taught the gospel of Christ. He personally funded these efforts. (Not coincidentally, Joseph Smith also followed the commands of God and sent missionaries to the North American Indians, who were identified as the Lamanites, as D&C 32 explains.) "Desire then," Sewall pled, "pray that the Gospel may be preached in all the world; in this Indian end of it. For till then, Christ himself tells you, He will not, He cannot come. The door is, as it were, shut against Him . . . For love, or shame, get up! And open the door!"[235]

Another thing Sewall perhaps shared with LDS teachings on this matter was a belief in true brotherhood. Consistent with LDS teachings, Sewall believed the American settlers from Britain

THE SELLING OF JOSEPH

In the year 1700, Samuel Sewall published the first antislavery tract in English North America and titled it "The Selling of Joseph." Using legal, moral, practical, and biblical arguments, Sewall warned against the evil act of slavery invading America.[232]

WILLIAM PENN ON NATIVE AMERICANS

The famed Quaker William Penn, founder of Pennsylvania, spent much time visiting with and studying Native Americans. He recognized something familiar in their "countenance," in their "rites," holidays ("they have a kind of feast of tabernacles," he said), and in their "customs." His conclusion: "I am ready to believe them of the Jewish race, I mean of the stock of the ten tribes . . . [when with them] a man would think himself in Duke's Place or Berry Street [Jewish quarters] in London."[234]

were, like the Native Americans, also a remnant of Israel. "You have this for your encouragement," he wrote, "that the people [here] are a part of the Israel of God, and you may expect to have . . . the prudence and patience of Moses . . . it is evident that our almighty Savior counseled the first planters to remove hither, and settle here."[236] This means the early settlers of America and the Natives they met here were, at least in Sewall's mind, both from Jacob's family and were literally brother tribes of Israel.

◆ ◆ ◆

I want to pause here. Remember when I mentioned that as I studied with Stephen Spykerman in a London basement, I focused silent attention on the American eagle? Remember I said that as Stephen pointed out the signs of Israel on the US Seal, something about the eagle came to me? Something I would share with you? Well, it's time I present to you my eagle hypothesis. It has its base in this early American idea that there be a desired brotherhood between American settlers and American Indians.

The Book of Mormon identifies the family of Lehi as being from Joseph, specifically as being from the tribe of Manasseh (see Alma 10:3). It would appear then (and patriarchal blessings given to Native Americans tend to confirm this) that the Lamanite remnants the American colonists possibly made contact with were largely from Manasseh. If the British-Israelite theory holds true, the Pilgrim and Puritan settlers were Ephraim. So is this latter-day connection between settlers and Natives really a powerful reunion of two brother tribes who have been long lost from each other? Is this what we see in the treaty between the Pilgrims and the local tribe? In the service Squanto rendered to the dying settlers? In the love between Winslow and Massasoit? In the missionary work between Sewall and the Natives around New England?

If so, there is perhaps something remarkable about the Great Seal of the United States. We know the Lord loves to teach us the gospel through symbols. Perhaps He has done so again here. And it begins with the eagle.

We discussed in the last chapter how the eagle in the US Seal is surrounded by emblems of Israel, including a Star of David, a pillar of fire, and the clouds of the Tabernacle. The eagle is also clutching arrows in one talon and an olive branch in the other. Some speculative historians have identified the symbols of a bundle of arrows and an olive branch as being connected to the tribe of Joseph (Ephraim and Manasseh). They base this theory on the Genesis 49 scripture that calls Joseph a "fruitful bough" and equips him to fight his enemies with a "bow [and presumably arrows]"—and "his bow abode in strength," so the prophecy states (Genesis 49:22, 24).[237] It should be noted that the reference to "a fruitful bough" is cross-referenced in the LDS scriptures with the Topical Guide subject of "Vineyard of the Lord"; the Topical Guide reference to Vineyard of the Lord then points us to Jacob 5:3 and to Isaiah 5:7, which teach us that the Vineyard of the Lord is associated with the "olive tree" and "the house of Israel."

The implications here are quite amazing. Think about it. Jacob/Israel blessed Joseph, per Genesis 49, with the land America and did so using the symbol of a bough/vineyard/olive tree or branch and the symbol of arrows. Then, when the prophecies were fulfilled, when Joseph (Ephraim) entered the land America and created the United States, even the host nation of the Restoration, that nation chose as its emblem an eagle. And with that act, the symbolic and scriptural loop was closed; the talons of the eagle emblem hold traces of the Old Testament promise of America. All this seems to further corroborate the importance of America as a promised land and is enough to make us think twice about our American eagle symbol. But it gets *way* more interesting than just that.

The shockingly profound part of the eagle connection comes to light when we begin to consider where the Founders might have gotten the idea for the eagle in the first place. There is reason to believe that these Founders, presumably Ephraim, picked up the symbol from their neighbors, the ancient Native tribes, presumably Manasseh, who we know through the Book of Mormon inherited the same land anciently.

In order for me to explain how the eagle symbol might have been transferred from Native Americans (Manasseh) to American settlers (Ephraim), I need to first set up the argument appropriately. First, the eagle emblem as used on the US Seal has been deemed by historians to be an "open mystery."[238] Some propose that the eagle design may have come from an earlier proposed design that included a phoenix. But where it ultimately stemmed from is unknown. In fact, it was so unknown that Benjamin Franklin questioned its relevance and use as a national symbol. He preferred the turkey.[239]

Any attempt, then, to figure it out requires us to look into the only man who may know—the seal's designer, Charles Thomson. Thomson worked as secretary to the Continental Congress during the Revolution. Congress commissioned him on that spiritual and historic day of July 4, 1776, to design the seal. He was a spiritual man, a biblical scholar who had translated the Greek Bible into Latin. He was also a moral man, known as the Soul of Congress, with John Adams referring to him as "the Sam Adams of Philadelphia, the life of the cause of liberty."[240] Significant to our study here, he also had a profound affection and appreciation for Native Americans. He had even been adopted into a Native American tribe and given the name Wegh-Wu-Law-Mo-End, or The Man Who Tells the Truth.[241] His connection to the Natives has left many wondering if he borrowed from them ideas for the seal and whether the eagle may have had its origins there.[242]

One group of Natives with whom Thomson associated was the Iroquois League, or the Iroquois Confederacy, which was a confederation of six North American Indian nations (originally, it was five nations). Iroquois archeology suggests that these Indian nations, which generally resided in and around modern-day New York state and southern Ontario Province, began sharing territory, which eventually led to the Confederacy as early as 500 AD.[243] (For context, this would have been some eighty years after Moroni finished the Book of Moroni, part of the Book of Mormon, and buried the plates at Cumorah.)[244]

Though nobody knows for sure when the six nations *officially* confederated, this Iroquois Confederacy broke the mold of Native Americanism by establishing peace through law set forth on principles of equality, justice, and division of power. Their politics obviously intrigued the Founding Fathers, who were working to similarly confederate the Thirteen Colonies. It appeared that Thomson and the other Founders borrowed directly from them in writing portions of American policy. In fact, in 1988, the US Congress passed a Concurrent Resolution that acknowledged the contribution of the Iroquois Confederacy in the development of the "democratic principles which were incorporated into the Constitution itself."[245] Perhaps we should think more expansively when reading Doctrine and Covenants 101:80: "And for this purpose have I established the Constitution of this land, by the hands of wise men whom I raised up."

And here's the pivotal point: the *eagle* is the prominent symbol of the Iroquois; it's the prominent symbol of *their* "Great Seal." If the Iroquois government influenced American government, perhaps it follows that Iroquois symbolism influenced

United States Congress: Iroquois Confederacy—Recognizing Contributions to the United States, Concurrent Resolution, October 21, 1988

"Whereas the original framers of the Constitution, including, most notably, George Washington and Benjamin Franklin, are known to have greatly admired the concepts of the Six Nations of the Iroquois Confederacy;

Whereas the confederation of the original Thirteen Colonies into one republic was influenced by the political system developed by the Iroquois Confederacy as were many of the democratic principles which were incorporated into the Constitution itself . . . .

Now therefore, be it resolved by the House of Representatives (the Senate concurring), that the Congress, on the occasion of the two hundredth anniversary of the signing of the United States Constitution, acknowledges the contribution made by the Iroquois Confederacy and other Indian Nations to the formation and development of the United States."

AGREED TO OCTOBER 21, 1988.[246]

American symbolism. In other words, perhaps Charles Thomson borrowed the eagle for the Great Seal of the United States.

If the American eagle did come from the Iroquois, it becomes more significant as a symbol of America's national covenant because the Iroquois eagle reflects the principles found in that book of scripture that, more than any other, promotes this American covenant—even that book of scripture written quite possibly by close contemporaries of the Iroquois's ancestors, if not the ancestors themselves. Indeed, within the context of the great symbol of the Iroquois, the eagle finds itself in the middle of Book of Mormon ideals.

Front and center in the Iroquois League's national symbol is a tree, known as the Tree of the Great Peace—the ultimate Iroquois ideal.[247] We might compare this tree to the Book of Mormon's tree of life, which represents the peace and salvation provided by the pure love of God (see 1 Nephi 11:25). Beneath the Iroquois tree is the symbolic placement of a weapon of war. The Iroquois's constitution, also known as the Great Law of Peace, states, "Into

Iroquois Nation Symbol: Tree of Peace

the depths of the earth, down into the deep . . . we cast all weapons of strife. We bury them from sight forever and plant again the tree."[248] We might compare this obvious Book of Mormon theme to the recorded actions of the people of Anti-Nephi-Lehi, who buried their weapons of war as a sign to God that they intended to keep peace at all costs (see Alma 24:16–18).

And then the sign of the national covenant: Hovering above the Iroquois tree is an eagle. The Iroquois constitution explains, "We place at the top of the Tree . . . an Eagle who is able to see afar. If he sees in the distance any evil approaching or any danger threatening he will at once warn the people of the Confederacy."[249] We might compare the eagle to the power of the national covenant promised to the peoples of the Book of Mormon—that their gospel and religion (even that most prized possession represented by the tree of life) would be ever-protected and ever-preserved.

If Thomson did, in fact, borrow the eagle from his Native American friends, perhaps he was on the receiving end of a divine transfer of powerful symbolism of the American covenant, from the ancient version of that covenant (Lehi/Manasseh) to the modern one (American settlers/ Ephraim). It would serve as a symbol of the brotherhood of the lost tribes, who at last had come together. Indeed, if Thomson borrowed the symbol, the eagle on the seal today represents in every way that national covenant as defined in the Book of Mormon—a defender and protector of the rights and principles that directly sustain the gospel of Jesus Christ, even a defender and protector of the tree of life.

I stress again, this is only a theory, difficult to prove. But will you ever look at the American eagle the same way again?

◆　◆　◆

THOUGHTS ON THE GREAT LAW OF PEACE

The articles of the Iroquois constitution, or the Great Law of Peace, were established by their prophet, the Great Peacemaker, Dekanawideh, who scholars estimate lived in pre-Columbian America.[250] The Iroquois tradition holds that Dekanawideh was the lawgiver who provided the symbols and imagery of their national standard, namely the Tree of the Great Peace, the buried weapons of war, and the Eagle. He also offered arrows as a symbol of their ideals. "Five arrows shall be bound together very strongly," states the Great Law of Peace, "and each arrow shall represent one nation."[251]

The Tribe of Manasseh, or whom we might call the Lehites, who arrived in the Americas in 589 BC, possessed the brass plates (Old Testament) and, therefore, might have known that the arrow was a symbol of their tribe from the promises Jacob/Israel gave Joseph of old, as discussed earlier in the chapter. These Lehites/Nephites also knew about good government from the books of the Old Testament contained in those brass plates. For example, ancient Israel set up a government that included principles employed by the Iroquois and the American founders, namely elections, laws by consent of the people, and divisions of power.[252]

The Book of Mormon also demonstrates principles of good government, including government by the consent of the people instead of a king, along with the divine system of checks and balances, "higher judges" checked by "lower judges," and "lower judges" balanced by "higher judges," so that "if these people commit sins and iniquities they shall be answered upon their own heads" (Mosiah 29:26, 29–30).

Seeing that the Iroquois practiced so many of these political principles that are manifested in the brass plates, as well as in the Book of Mormon, and considering that they also possessed symbols unique to both Book of Mormon and Old Testament accounts (i.e. Tree of Peace, buried weapons, bundle of arrows), one naturally wonders what connection, if any, there was. How, for example, did the pre-Columbian Iroquois chief Dekanawideh come upon this valuable information?

What we do know is that by 421 AD, the prophet Moroni, son of Mormon, finished the Book of Moroni, which completed the Book of Mormon account as we have it today. [253] We might assume that at this point Moroni had a pretty good understanding of all these scriptural principles discussed above, many of which he possessed in written form (i.e. the gold plates), others of which he likely knew about through the teachings passed down from the brass plates. We also know that regardless of where he or his people originated or resided before, Moroni ended up in what is now New York State sometime after 421 AD and deposited the plates into the Hill Cumorah. We don't know how many years after that he lived, nor do we know what he did or who he associated with. Based on archeology, scholars put the date of the first gatherings and territorial occupation of the Iroquois tribes only about 80 years after Moroni likely deposited the plates in Cumorah. And where were they gathering? What land were they occupying? New York State! [254] The land where Moroni dwelt at the end. The land of Cumorah!

Was there a meeting? Was there a transfer of information? Was this the Lord's way of providing valuable teachings and symbols from the ancient Book of Mormon people to the Gentiles who would one day inherit the land? Gentiles (Founding Fathers) who would need the information well before the plates came forth out of Cumorah? After all, these Gentiles, these American settlers, were seen and recorded in that Book of Mormon. They were very much a part

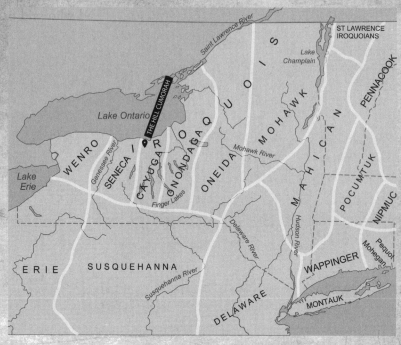

Iroquois Tribes in New York City

of the narrative from the beginning. In fact, Moroni's father, Mormon, prophesied that "the Lord hath reserved their [the Nephites'] blessings, which they might have received in the land, for the Gentiles who shall possess the land" (Mormon 5:19). We might assume that his son understood this and was already thinking ahead about how to transfer gospel principles and ensure that the covenant knowledge would reach the early Gentiles, who needed it before Joseph Smith delivered the plates.

Did the Iroquois serve as transmitters of information, then, from Manasseh to Ephraim? We can only speculate.

Regardless of symbols and interpretations, and who said or believed what and when, there is one thing we can definitely say about our Pilgrim and Puritan forbearers. They set the standard and the precedent. They introduced the covenant theology that would be carried to future generations.

Great Seal of the United States

Samuel Sewall understood the importance of preserving this theology in order to preserve the nation under God they were striving to create. It permeated every aspect of his life, even to the point that his strange propensity to follow LDS teachings and traditions manifested itself again at the birth of his son. He named him Joseph and made it a point to clarify that he was named Joseph "not out of respect to any relation"; rather, he was named after Joseph of Egypt. He said he chose this name "in hopes of the accomplishment of the prophecy, Ezekiel 37 and such like." This prophecy just happens to be the prophecy Latter-day Saints know to be about the Book of Mormon and the gathering of latter-day Israel. Sewall's biographer clarifies that the Puritan judge sought to hasten the times when the Lord would, according to Ezekiel 37:19–22, "take the stick of Joseph, which is in the hand of Ephraim, and the tribes of Israel . . . and make them one stick . . . I will take the children of Israel from among the heathen . . . I will make them one nation in the land upon the mountains of Israel."[255]

Joseph Sewall did his best to fulfill both the prophecy and his father's desired wishes, becoming a pastor and teaching the covenant principles to the next generation. "No greatness or worldly glory," Joseph Sewall taught, "will be any security against God's destroying judgments if such places go on obstinately in their sins. O let not London! Let not Boston, presume to deal unjustly in the land of uprightness." He continued, "We must believe our Lord Jesus when he says to us, *Except ye repent, ye shall likewise perish.*"[256]

Samuel Sewall's grandson was in that next generation who

> "And now, we can behold the decrees of God concerning this land, that it is a land of promise; and whatsoever nation shall possess it shall serve God, or they shall be swept off when the fulness of his wrath shall come upon them. And the fulness of his wrath cometh upon them when they are ripened in iniquity."
>
> —*Ether 2:9*

Joseph Sewall sought to instruct. This grandson, along with thousands who were faithful to the New Israel, fought and won their independence under George Washington.[257] Indeed, the early American settlers set the precedent for the Revolution and the liberties it brought. A modern study of George Washington's revolutionary generation showed that of all the influential thinkers and philosophers who influenced them in their fight to be free, the sources they used the most and quoted the most were those prophets of the Old Testament.[258]

And the bridge from these first New England settlers expanded further, even past the revolutionary generation and into the generation of the Restoration. Yes, their spiritual and covenant-based theology also laid the foundation for those first

WASHINGTON'S INAUGURATION, APRIL 30, 1789.

"We ought to be no less persuaded," Washington said during his inaugural address, "that the propitious smiles of Heaven, can never be expected on a nation that disregards the eternal rules of order and right, which Heaven itself has ordained." [259]

Upon taking his oath, he placed his hand on a Bible, which was open to Genesis 49. Washington's fingers were touching directly on or near the prophecy in Genesis 49 that, as printed on the page, begins: "Joseph is a fruitful bough, even a fruitful bough by a well; whose branches run over the wall." [260]

Latter-day Saints. Remember, the Pilgrims and Puritans often acknowledged that the reason for the covenant was to facilitate a reformation or restoration of Christ's church. No story illustrates this concept like the story of the Puritan son Robert Mason. Known to the New England community where he lived as "Father Mason," his insights into the Bible and the miracles he performed through faith in Christ caused many to see him as a great spiritual leader.

One day, toward the end of his life, Father Mason approached a certain young man in the community who he had taken a liking to. He had known the young man for many years and had watched him grow through his childhood and adolescence. Over the years, Mason had often spoken of spiritual things with the growing boy and his family. And now Mason had a secret for this boy. As the youth grew into manhood, he became a great diarist, so we have his firsthand account of his and Mason's powerful exchange.

The young man recorded the following: "I will here relate one vision, which he related to me. The last time I saw him he said:"

> I was laboring in my field at mid-day when I was en-wrapped in a vision. I was placed in the midst of a vast forest of fruit trees: I was very hungry, and walked a long way through the orchard, searching for fruit to eat; but I could not find any in the whole orchard, and I wept because I could not find any fruit. While I stood gazing at the orchard, and wondering why there was no fruit, the trees began to fall to the ground upon every side of me, until there was not one tree standing in the whole orchard; and while I was marveling at the scene, I saw young sprouts start up from the roots of the trees which had fallen, and they opened into young thrifty trees

before my eyes. They budded, blossomed, and bore fruit until the trees were loaded with the finest fruit I ever beheld, and I rejoiced to see so much fine fruit. I stepped up to a tree and picked my hands full of fruit, and marveled at its beauty, and as I was about to taste of it the vision closed, and I found myself in the field in the same place I was at the commencement of the vision.

I then knelt upon the ground, and prayed unto the Lord, and asked him, in the name of Jesus Christ, to show me the meaning of the vision. The Lord said unto me: "This is the interpretation of the vision; the great trees of the forest represent the generation of men in which you live. There is no church of Christ, or kingdom of God upon the earth in your generation. There is no fruit of the Church of Christ upon the earth. There is no man ordained of God to administer in any of the ordinances of the gospel of salvation upon the earth in this day and generation. But, in the next generation, I the Lord will set up my kingdom and my Church upon the earth, and the fruits of the kingdom and church of Christ, such as have followed the prophets, apostles and saints in every dispensation, shall again be found in all their fulness upon the earth. You will live to see the day, and handle the fruit; but will never partake of it in the flesh."

Father Mason then prophesied to the young man: "I shall never partake of this fruit in the flesh; but you will, and you will become a conspicuous actor in that kingdom." Father Mason then turned and left. Those were the last words he ever spoke to the young man.

The young man in this story was a future prophet of the Church, Wilford Woodruff. Elder Woodruff continued his account of this experience, writing that Mason "had this vision about the year 1800, and he related it to me in 1830—the same spring that this Church was organized. This vision, with his other teachings to me, made a great impression upon my mind, and I prayed a great deal to the Lord to lead me by his Spirit, and prepare me for his Church when it did come."[261]

In the years between 1620, when the Pilgrims landed, and 1644, when the Puritan migration followed, over 20,000 settlers flooded into America.[263] These laid the foundation for the Restoration. As one author put it, this migration placed into America an overwhelming influx of "people who had entered into a deep covenant relationship with God, through the person of His Son, Jesus Christ."[264] As one second-generation American Puritan, John Higginson, so prophetically explained:

> It hath been deservedly esteemed one of the great and wonderful works of God in this last age, that the Lord stirred up the spirits of so many thousands of his servants . . . to transport themselves . . . into a desert land, in America . . . in the way of seeking first the kingdom of God . . . for a fuller and better reformation of the Church of God, than it hath yet appeared in the world.[265]

◆ ◆ ◆

As I returned home from my trip to New England, I was as deeply inspired as I was troubled. I loved the faith, hope, and miracles I saw in the history of these first New England settlements. I loved how I felt there. I loved the connections between their American covenant and the restored gospel attached to that covenant.

WILFORD WOODRUFF
REMEMBERS HIS MENTOR

Wilford Woodruff wrote that Robert Mason "believed that it was necessary to have prophets, apostles, dreams, visions and revelations in the church of Christ, the same as they had who lived in ancient days; and he believed the Lord would raise up a people and a church, in the last days, with prophets, apostles and all the gifts, powers, and blessings, which it ever contained in any age of the world. . . . He frequently came to my father's house when I was a boy, and taught me and my brothers those principles; and I believed him."

After Woodruff found the Restored church on December 29, 1833, he wrote a letter to Father Mason:

> I informed him that I had found the true gospel with all its bless-
> ings; that the authority of the Church of Christ had been restored
> to the earth as he had told me it would be; that I had received
> the ordinances of baptism and the laying on of hands; that I
> knew for myself that God had established through
> Joseph Smith, the Prophet, the Church of Christ
> upon the earth. He received my letter with great
> joy and had it read over to him many times.
> He handled it as he had handled the fruit in
> the vision. He was very aged and soon died
> without having the privilege of receiving the
> ordinances of the gospel at the hands of
> an elder of the Church. The first opportunity
> I had after the truth of baptism for the dead
> was revealed, I went forth and was baptized
> for him in the temple font at Nauvoo.[262]

But I was also sad. I could not readily recognize in today's America what I saw and felt in early American history. If only people knew the truth, perhaps they would find their roots once again. Perhaps we would worship God as a nation as we once had. Perhaps we would then see more miracles and more conversions to Jesus Christ.

I thought of Leo Martin and his wife in Plymouth, like soldiers alone on the front lines, trying to call the nation back. I worried about them. I worried about the broken roof of the Jenney House—their headquarters and museum. I knew they did not have the funding to fix it. But I also knew their operation needed to be whole. I began scheming. I needed to go back to Plymouth one more time. I needed to help them. I needed them to help me. Besides, I had left the first time before Leo had been able to answer my third question about John Howland and what had become of him in the end.

Yes, I needed to return to Plymouth. Whereas Salem, Boston, and the surrounding areas had grown and commercialized so fast, it was harder to follow the history there. Plymouth was different. Its plantation had not evolved into much of a city. In fact, after setting the spiritual and covenant standard for America and after getting other settlers to come follow that pattern, Plymouth Plantation had sort of just disappeared as its descendants had flocked northward and aligned with the larger body of Christians. I felt it was divine. It was supposed to be that way. God left Plymouth in a purer state so Americans today could go back and more easily witness what had started their America. God made it so we could more easily touch history to remember who we are and what we are supposed to be doing. After all I had learned about the early settlers, I knew I needed one more trip there. I needed a capstone, and Plymouth was the place.

Months later, I made the trip and invited a friend this time. I will call him John. (You will see shortly why I need to hide his identity for this book.) Through my studies of the Pilgrim era, I realized that on my first trip, I had failed to go back far enough. I had gone right to Plymouth. But the Pilgrims had first landed near the point of Cape Cod, about twenty-five miles east, over the harbor by boat from Plymouth Rock, or over seventy-five miles from Plymouth around the scorpion-shaped peninsula by car. I waited months so I could be sure to arrive at Cape Cod precisely on November 27—that was a momentous day for the Pilgrims. I wanted to feel as much as possible what they felt at on that day in 1620.

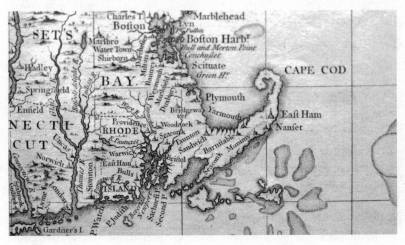

Map of Plymouth, Cape Cod, and Bay

On the freezing afternoon of November 27, John and I stood on the exact piece of Cape Cod beach where the Pilgrims had stood hundreds of years earlier. Wearing at least three layers of clothing, we looked at each other and wondered what we had been thinking. And we had a warm car waiting for us in a nearby parking lot.

I couldn't even imagine what it had been like to land in freezing conditions with nothing warm to run to. No refuge. And in their case, little to no food.

On November 27, 1620, this was the Pilgrim reality. On that day, a small group of Pilgrim explorers left the rest of the group on-board the anchored *Mayflower* and set off in a small boat or shallop in hopes of finding some sort of salvation on this beach. A week earlier, they had been at the beach when someone in the group had noticed an anomaly upon a sand dune. The sand looked softer in a certain place, so the men had approached and begun to dig. They were astonished to find a cache of corn, which they retrieved and took back to the boat. They called this miracle spot Corn Hill. It was something but not quite enough. So they came back to try their luck again. Only this time, on their November 27 trip, temperatures had dropped, and a thick blanket of snow had covered the beaches.

Though desperate, they had their faith. They knew their covenant. With a prayer in their hearts, they went back to Corn Hill. The snow cover did not deter them, for the Lord had already shown them the place. They dug again and found even more corn and dried beans. The food literally saved their lives. "And sure it was God's good providence that we found this corn," Bradford wrote, who was there working with the group at Corn Hill, "for else we know not how we should have done." Bradford also noted the good providence in finding Corn Hill just days earlier, before the snow storm, which snow would have made the discovery impossible and would have likely led to the Pilgrims' deaths.[266] The Pilgrims later identified the Natives whose corn it was. They repaid it and then some once their harvest came.[267]

As John and I walked the beach, we took in the miracle of it all, and the Spirit testified. Then, just over one of the dunes at

Corn Hill, I spotted a very tarnished American flag flying on a pole inside a small courtyard of sorts. From Corn Hill, it looked to be a small makeshift cemetery. The closer we got to it, the more astonished we were at the poor conditions of the place. Whatever it was, nobody cared much for it. When I finally saw what it was, my heart sank. It was a memorial to the miracle at Corn Hill. Its tarnished condition reminded me of how we Americans often behold God and covenant today. Cast aside. Forgotten.

Corn Hill

To make matters worse, I immediately saw something else that troubled me deeply. It was a thin piece of stone leaned up against the memorial that displayed engraved words upon its plaque. The weather, rust, and forgotten condition of the plaque made it almost impossible to read the words, but squinting, I was able to see that the words on the original memorial credited God for the event. The leaning slab of stone also had writing on it, and that writing was loud and clear: "Here, 13 Pilgrims STOLE the corn."

John and I just shook our heads. Before the creation of the United States, tyranny and oppression ran the world. There was little freedom. Misery abounded. Until a group of God-fearing, covenant-making Separatists did what few would do. They risked everything and came to the New World so that a new and free nation could be born, so that all could have a chance at salvation, so that the very people who wrote those disparaging words on the stone slab could have a chance at salvation. The corn that saved the Pilgrims also (ironically) saved those who now disparage the Corn Hill miracle. This is what truth is up against.

As we traveled farther down the shoreline, we came across First Encounter Beach, the place of the second Pilgrim miracle in America. Here, Natives attacked the Pilgrim group while they sat unarmed at their camp. Arrows swarmed the camp. Clothes hanging out to dry were riddled with them, but somehow, not one Pilgrim had even a scratch. "Thus it pleased God," Bradford wrote, "to vanquish our enemies and give us deliverance." He continued, "So after we had given God thanks for our deliverance, we took our shallop and went on our journey."[268]

In our effort to follow their trail, John and I rented a boat. From First Encounter Beach, they made their way across the harbor in search of the land they would eventually call home, and with history books in hand, John and I followed their tracks as best we could.

As they cruised toward what would be their Plymouth colony, a storm took them by surprise. The shallop's mast splintered in three places, rendering it useless. They were at the mercy of the storm, and night had fallen. Fighting through the wind, snow, and waves crashing over the top of them, they were thrust toward an island surrounded only by sharp rocks. All they could do was pray. Then miraculously, as if guardian angels were busy around them, the winds shifted and delivered the small boat safely on a stretch of soft, sandy beach.

The first Pilgrim to hop off the boat was John Clark. The island has ever after been Clark's Island. It was Saturday, December 9.[269]

The next day was Sunday. The storm stopped, and the sun was shining. It was a perfect day to fix the boat and get back to sea. But they would not, for it was the Sabbath. Instead, they worshiped their God and gave thanks for their "deliverances."[270] "Speak thou also unto the children of Israel," the Lord said, "saying, Verily my sabbaths ye shall keep: for it is a sign between me and you throughout your generations" (Exodus 31:13). If ever there was an excuse to skip this command, the Pilgrims had it now. But living as they did by the covenant, they could not afford to take the chance.

As John and I cruised around Clark's Island, we talked about how America used to respect this obligation to its covenant. Our grandparents' generation respected it. They respected the Sabbath day. We determined that if there was one way to turn our national covenant back on, with all the blessings it provides, it would be to once again, as a nation, begin to respect this holy day and give it to God. It would be our sign to Him that we had chosen Him. Then He could once again choose us.

Upon Clark's Island, there is a thirty-ton granite boulder called Pulpit Rock. It is said that the Pilgrim explorer group conducted their Sabbath worship from this rock on that day. Today, you can see engraved into its side the words of William Bradford as he described their short stay on the island: "On the Sabbath Day we Rested."[271]

The next day, Monday, December 11, they repaired and jumped into their shallop and headed west. It was on that Monday after the Sabbath that the Lord showed them their new home, Plymouth, with all its blessed features.[272] Over and over, the Lord proved He would keep His end of the promise.

I recently came across a report of an interesting event that occurred not long ago on Pulpit Rock. In Plymouth, there is a group called the Old Colony Club, which is one of the oldest remaining "gentlemen's clubs" in America. Its purpose is to preserve the truth about the Pilgrims. Its numbers are fading, as younger generations seem to care less and less about America's religious history, but this group of faithful old men reminds me of the three knights in the movie *Indiana Jones and the Last Crusade*, who will stop at nothing to protect the Holy Grail. Pilgrim history is the Holy Grail of the Old Colony Club.

The Hand of the Lord: Why the Pilgrims Came to Plymouth

During a Thanksgiving celebration held at Clark's Island not long ago, one of the eldest among the group, ninety-seven-year-old Harold Boyer, was hoisted to the top of Pulpit Rock so he could declare the following: "[The Pilgrims] were ready to set out the next day, Sunday," he said, "but Sunday was the Sabbath, so they set aside every other thing and worshiped. The first service in the New World." He continued: "My brothers, I may not be here next year with you. So on my last visit to this sacred place, I beg you to remember the words the great prophet said on Mount Nebo. God has promised us this land. He will make the land flow with milk and honey. But we must remember to give him thanks."[273]

THE AMERICAN MOSES SPEECH

American leaders who have wanted their people to remember the covenant have often referenced Moses's great speech as found in Deuteronomy 30. The words have been repeated by the likes of John Winthrop (while standing on the ship that brought the Puritans to America in 1630), by patriots of the American Revolution (particularly after they secured independence), by Martin Luther King Jr. (who repeated these words the night before he was killed in 1968), and by Ronald Reagan (who boldly repeated this covenant language at the base of the Statue of Liberty on its centennial birthday in 1986). In his book, *America's Prophet: Moses and the American Story*, author Bruce Feiler summed up Moses's speech (from Deuteronomy 30:15-20) using the following words:

> See, I have set before you this day life and good, death and adversity. For I command you this day to love the Lord your God, to walk in his ways, and to keep his commandments. But if you turn away, you shall certainly perish; you shall not long endure on the soil that you are crossing the Jordan to enter. I have put before you life and death, blessing and curse. Choose life—that you and your offspring shall live. That you may love the Lord your God, and that you may obey his voice, and that you may cleave unto him: for he is your life, and the length of your days: that you may dwell in the land which the Lord swore unto your fathers, to Abraham, to Isaac, and to Jacob.[274]

These words seemed to echo from Clark's Island as our rented boat turned around and headed back to Plymouth. It was time to check in with Leo.

Once again, we met Leo at his favorite place—the Monument to the Forefathers. And he was dressed head to foot, as always, in his Pilgrim attire (I'm not sure if he owns any other type of clothing). John hadn't been there before, and Leo couldn't stand to know someone was there and had not heard at least part of his lecture on faith and covenants, and John was overjoyed.

As the two circled to the back of the Monument, they caught me staring intently at the engraved words of William Bradford. They joined me. "And as one small candle may light a thousand, so the light here kindled hath shone unto many . . . let the glorious name of Jehovah have all the praise."

"It really did all start here, didn't it, Leo?" I asked, breaking the silence.

He smiled and nodded.

"The history goes on and on and proves and reproves the same covenant formula over and over again. It is so simple. And it's right in front of us."

He knew I was preaching to the choir, but he was kind enough to let me.

"But we don't even need to leave Plymouth to understand it," I continued. "In fact," I said, the passion in my voice growing, "it was all laid out, even in the few days before the Pilgrims landed here at Plymouth. The fulness is spelled out in the antechambers of America: Cape Cod, Corn Hill, Encounter Beach, Clark's Island!" I was out of breath. "It's all there," I concluded. "Make a covenant. Keep a covenant. Reap the blessings. Rinse and repeat."

Leo and John smiled, seemingly amused.

We walked away from the monument in silence and with heavy hearts.

About halfway to the cars, Leo stopped. "Tim, I wish Americans would make the covenant again. But at this point, I would take just any simple act of kindness from one citizen to another."

John and I got into our rental car, and Leo hopped in his car, and we drove the short distance to his Jenney House Museum to say hi to Nancy.

At least, that was the reason I gave John for heading to the old Jenney House. I actually had ulterior motives. You see, John had recently sold his business and was sitting on plenty of cash. I would never ask him to give money away, but I really wanted to see Leo's roof fixed. Admittedly, this was one reason I had invited John on this trip. (I hope we are still friends after he reads this book and learns of my scheming behind his back.)

"Man," I said to John just before getting to the house, "if I ever became a rich man, I'd donate a ton to Leo and Nancy's foundation. They are true warriors of the American covenant."

I wondered if my hint had gone too far. I silently vowed not to say another word.

In the past, I parked my car behind and to the side of the museum house, as it was a closer walk to the entrance and afforded a great view of the old Jenney grist mill. However, you can't see the roof as well from that angle, so I parked across the street in a hotel parking lot, which provided a much better view of the issue at hand.

I prayed a silent prayer as we exited the vehicle.

Within seconds, John said out loud, "Look at the roof! It's a mess!"

I turned my head so John couldn't see my face. And I smiled a huge smile. Triumphant!

Not long after entering the house, John took Leo aside. I inched closer, pretending to be interested in something on the wall near to them. I heard the end of the deal. John was buying Leo and Nancy a new roof!

As I watched the smile grow on Leo's face, I thought of the words he had spoken just ten minutes earlier. *At this point,* he had said, *I would take just any simple act of kindness from one citizen to another.*

Well, it had just happened. It was a start. A good day for Leo. A good day for John. An even better day for America.

Meet Leo Martin: the Modern-Day Pilgrim

◆   ◆   ◆

I couldn't believe it! I was back on a plane, heading home, and I had forgotten again! The emotion of the moment had distracted me once more, and I had forgotten to follow up with Leo on the fate of John Howland.

But Leo had not forgotten.

Several months passed since I had seen Leo last, and I was walking with John on this particular day. We were heading to a meeting in downtown Salt Lake City, taking a short-cut through Temple Square. It was then that John dropped it on me.

"So," he said, "did you know I was with Leo the other day?"

I didn't know.

"I went back to Plymouth with my family to make sure his new roof was put on right."

I smiled and thanked him profusely for his service.

"He brought up your interest in John Howland."

My heart skipped a beat.

"You know John Howland, right?" John asked. "The guy who fell off the boat from England and miraculously survived?"

"Of course!" I said. "Leo was supposed to tell me something about him. He seemed to have something good for me."

"Yeah, well, he told me!" John was beaming from ear to ear.

"And . . . ?"

John was intentionally stalling just to mess with me.

"Does Leo know you're Mormon?" John asked.

"I don't know for sure," I said. "I assume he does. But who cares! Why?"

He chuckled. He sensed I was frustrated, and he enjoyed it a little. I would have done the same were the roles reversed.

"Well," John said, "John Howland ended up marrying Elizabeth Tilley, became one of the most prominent citizens of Plymouth, and fathered ten children."

"Yes," I replied, "I already read all that." I knew there was more.

"Well, the thing Leo wanted to share was who descended directly from Howland's line."

Chills instantly ran through my body. I didn't know how, exactly, but I thought I knew what John would say next. "Wait," I said. "Don't tell me yet."

I pulled out my iPhone. I wanted to participate in this treasure hunt.

As I typed in "direct descendants of John Howland," the chills in my body ran deeper. My mind flashed back to London,

Spykerman, and the heraldry of ancient Israel. I thought of Elder Erastus Snow and the scriptures of the Restoration that teach of Ephraim's migration from Britain to latter-day America. I thought of who we knew scripturally to be the pure and direct descendants of Joseph and Ephraim. I thought of the covenants of Israel and how they were imported to the promised land by those chosen Pilgrims, including Howland himself. I thought of his absolutely miraculous rescue on the high seas, knowing in my heart that he was supposed to make it. He, of all the Pilgrims, *had* to make it. And as my phone was pulling up the results, I knew I was about to confirm exactly why.

The website pulled up, and several photos of famous Howland descendants appeared. And there it was. Just as the image hit my eye, John couldn't contain the message from Leo any longer. He said aloud, "*Joseph Smith!*"

I dug deeper, and I could not believe what I found. It turns out that Joseph Smith's fourth great-grandfather was a man by the

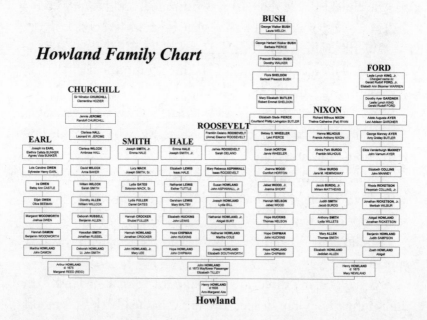

Howland Family Chart

name of John Jr. Emma Smith's fourth great-grandmother was a woman named Hope. John Jr. and Hope were brother and sister. Their parents? John Howland and Elizabeth Tilley![275]

The Miracle That Was John Howland

On the occasion of the Church's centennial in 1930, the First Presidency stated the following regarding those first American settlers of New England:

> They were the advance guard of the army of the Lord, predestined to establish the God-given system of government under which we live, and to make of America, which is the land of Joseph, the gathering place of Ephraim, an asylum for the oppressed of all nations, and prepare the way for the restoration of the Gospel of Christ and the re-establishment of his Church upon the earth.[278]

Are You Related to a Pilgrim? Search Your Family History Here

EMMA SMITH

"I have never seen a woman in my life, who would endure every species of fatigue and hardship, from month to month, and from year to year, with that unflinching courage, zeal, and patience, which she has always done; for I know that which she has had to endure; that she has been tossed upon the ocean of uncertainty; that she has breasted the storms of persecution, and buffeted the rage of men and devils . . . which [would] have borne down almost any other woman."[276]

—*Lucy Mack Smith*

"I would gladly walk from here to you barefoot, and bareheaded . . . to see you and think it great pleasure, and never count it toil . . . . My heart is entwined around yours forever and ever."[277]

—*Joseph to Emma*

CHAPTER 4

The Purchase

The gathering was far from complete. Even after the American settlers commanded the eastern seaboard, the designated lands of the Restoration were still far from the reach of America's New Israelites. The prophesied lands of Missouri, and even the Salt Lake basin, were in the hands of foreign powers even after the United States gained its independence.

And so, from the vantage point of these early Americans, looking West and believing those lands could be theirs should have been an almost impossible idea. Of course, these early Americans knew the impossible could occur in their land of promise, for they had witnessed how the creation of the United States had been a miracle every step of the way. For us looking back on history, these miracles are difficult to refute, especially when the Lord Himself claims credit for the very establishment of the nation. He told the Prophet Joseph that He "established the Constitution of this land, by the hands of wise men whom I raised up unto this very purpose, and redeemed the land by the shedding of blood" (D&C 101:80).

We should not take for granted the fact that the Constitution may be the only political document in history that the Lord has endorsed through scripture. This is remarkable. This is the covenant on the land. But America would eventually need to expand westward so the prophesied lands of the New Jerusalem and the lands where "the mountain of the Lord's house shall be established" (Isaiah 2:2) could come under that covenant. These lands would need to come under the covenant power of the United States so liberty in law could protect their divine development. But how? Like I said, these lands were, in some cases, under the control of foreign superpowers. Further miracles would be required. The word *pilgrim* is defined as "a person who journeys to a sacred place for religious reasons."[279] If ever there was a sacred place, it was these lands to the west. And so the Lord would need a new set of pilgrims to retrieve it.

Most of us have never heard the story of how we got these lands, and yet these lands were larger and, in some ways, even more important than the land secured through war with Britain (the Thirteen Colonies). But the story is a miracle—no less miraculous than the events that brought American independence. Perhaps it's less known because it did not require an American war to secure it. Of course, that fact alone is a miracle unto itself. But the details of how it all happened, particularly as viewed through the lens of the restored gospel, will make your head spin, especially when we discover how the miracles that brought us the designated lands of the New Jerusalem began in the land of the great discoverer, even Christopher Columbus, who predicted the finding of that sacred land in the first place. Indeed, it all began in Hispaniola. But I'm getting ahead of myself.

Before I take you back to that Caribbean island of promise, let me first bring to the scene the man who led the effort to deliver these western American lands. His name was Thomas Jefferson, and as president of the United States, he would be the principal actor in acquiring those prophesied lands. Though many of you are familiar with this power player of American history, let's explore some of his more hidden aspects because it's these things that make it clear to us today that the Lord did indeed raise him up for this very purpose.

Jefferson was a man of many trades: father, husband, businessman, planter, scientist, and statesman. But he is perhaps best known as the Founding Father who wrote most of the Declaration of Independence. Indeed, he wrote those inspired and recognized lines that have anchored America in God's care. "All men are created equal," he wrote. "Endowed by their creator with unalienable rights . . . . And for the support of this declaration, with firm reliance on the protection of Divine Providence, we mutually pledge to each other our lives, our fortunes and our sacred honor."

Outside his immortal words found in the Declaration, Jefferson also declared his belief that Americans should be "acknowledging and adoring an overruling Providence, which by all its dispensations proves that it delights in the happiness of man here and his greater happiness hereafter."[280] Jefferson also warned that if America did not work toward national worthiness, to include efforts toward repenting of its sin of slavery, God would punish them. "For God is just," Jefferson said while commenting on the wickedness of slavery. "His justice cannot sleep forever." [281]

But his knowledge appeared to go even deeper. Appropriately, the man who brought us the lands of the Restoration—even the land whose God is, according to scripture, Jesus Christ Himself (Ether 2:12)—had some interesting thoughts on the Savior. Jefferson deemed himself "a real Christian . . . a disciple of the doctrines of Jesus."[284] He testified, "There is one God, and he all-perfect . . . . that there is a future state of rewards and punishments . . . . that to love God with all thy heart, and thy neighbor as thyself, is the sum of religion."[285]

JEFFERSON AND ISRAEL

Hearkening back to the ancient covenant, Jefferson said during his presidential inauguration, "I shall need, too, the favor of that Being in whose hands we are, who led our forefathers, as Israel of old, from their native land, and planted them in a country flowing with all the necessaries and comforts of life."[282] Promoting a similar message, Jefferson proposed that the official Seal of the United States include a depiction of the "Children of Israel in the wilderness, led by a cloud by day and a pillar of fire by night."[283]

Clearly, such a man fits the mold of one who would be responsible for bringing in and developing the would-be lands of the New Jerusalem.

But Jefferson's thoughts get much more interesting than just this. He recognized a truth rarely acknowledged outside of the LDS faith—namely, that there was a general Apostasy of Christ's true gospel, which would require a general Restoration of it. A restoration that Jefferson believed would be coming soon to the United States of America. Perhaps you are thinking that I must be overinterpreting some obscure thing Jefferson might have said at one time in order to come up with such a seemingly outrageous conclusion. I say "outrageous" because of the implications of bringing Jefferson so close to a doctrine unique to Latter-day Saints, but I'm going off of only his own teachings on the matter. I will now share those particular teachings and allow you to be the judge.

Jefferson routinely pointed out false or misconstrued doctrines Christians of his day taught, which proved to him that there had been an Apostasy. For example, the idea that man's fate is sealed by destiny and that his works and efforts in this life do nothing in connection with God's grace was, according to Jefferson, a false principle. The man who invented such a doctrine, he said, "was indeed an Atheist . . . [who] worshipped a false god."[286]

Jefferson stated: "But a short time elapsed after the death of the great reformer of the Jewish religion before his principles were departed from by those who professed to be his special servants, and perverted into an engine for enslaving mankind, and aggrandizing their oppressors in church and state."[287] Jefferson expressed concern that the Council of Nicaea, and others like it, may have corrupted the more pure doctrines of Christ.[288] Those early attempts to define God were, according to Jefferson, a "mere Abracadabra of the mountebanks calling themselves the priests of Jesus."[289]

Jefferson, of course, has been criticized over the years and accused of not really being much of a Christian. The evidence? Statements such as these, along with his questioning of biblical accounts that he feared might have been translated or interpreted poorly. He believed some things had been lost and didn't know exactly where to draw the line. Without prophets on the earth, it would be difficult to know for sure.

The problem for his critics is that they don't seem to understand concepts such as religious apostasy or gospel restoration. And so, they throw their darts at a man who appears to be fighting Christianity. In fact, he was only fighting distorted or confusing elements and interpretations of mainstream Christianity—elements and interpretations that Joseph Smith also fought. Both men seemed to understand that "they have taken away from the gospel of the Lamb many parts which are plain and most precious; and also many covenants of the Lord have they taken away" (1 Nephi 13:26). But that doesn't make them less Christian, as the critics have alleged. It makes them super Christian.

This is true especially in light of the following words, even prophetic words, of Thomas Jefferson: "The religion-builders have so distorted and deformed the doctrines of Jesus, so muffled them in mysticisms, fancies and falsehoods, have caricatured them into forms so monstrous and inconceivable, as to shock reasonable thinkers . . . . *Happy in the prospect of a restoration of primitive Christianity*, I must leave to younger athletes to encounter and lop off the false branches which have been engrafted into it by mythologists of the middle and modern ages."[290]

And just in case you think Jefferson accidently taught this or that it was taken out of context, let me share another one of his statements on the matter. I especially like this one because of the year in which he gave it. It was 1820—just months after young

Joseph Smith saw God the Father and Jesus Christ, just months after the Restoration had begun its descent into the United States. In the fall of 1820, Jefferson said:

> I hold the precepts of Jesus, as delivered by himself, to be the most pure, benevolent, and sublime which have ever been preached to man. I adhere to the principles of the first age; and consider all subsequent innovations as corruptions of this religion, having no foundation in what came from him . . . If the freedom of religion, guaranteed to us by law in theory, can ever rise in practice under the overbearing inquisition of public opinion, truth will prevail over fanaticism, and the genuine doctrines of Jesus, so long perverted by his pseudo-priests, will again be restored to their original purity. This reformation will advance with the other improvements of the human mind, but too late for me to witness it.[291]

He couldn't have been any clearer on what was about to be built upon the foundation of the US Constitution and its protection of religious freedom. He seemed to know he had been instrumental in laying the foundation for the Restoration he had apparently predicted.

And getting back to our narrative, one of the foundational elements he brought was those sacred lands. He brought them not through war but through negotiation, and it was called the Louisiana Purchase.

◆　◆　◆

As promised, we'll go back to Hispaniola. Christopher Columbus did not choose Hispaniola—Hispaniola seemed to

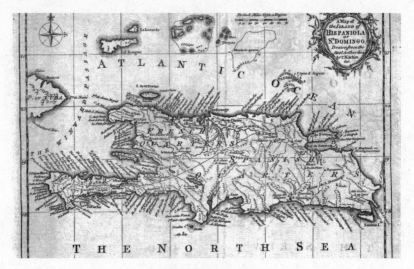

Map of Hispaniola

choose him. Or more likely, God was behind it all. On December 24, 1492, while first exploring the Caribbean islands, one of Columbus's chief crewmen turned control of the ship over to a boy—a deckhand. Night was falling, the sea could not have been calmer, and the experienced sailors took a risk on the boy because they wanted to sleep. In the middle of the night, the inexperienced boy let the ship run into a reef, where it got stuck and then wrecked. The reef just happened to be off the coast of Hispaniola. Instead of getting upset, Columbus, according to his son, determined that the "Lord had caused the ship to stop here, that a settlement might be formed." Thus was born the first European colony in the Americas and the place Columbus would use as basecamp for his New World mission under God.[292]

Just as this island was used as a launching ground to identify the rest of America and the lands of the Restoration, as God loves patterns, so would this island be used over 300 years later to actually acquire the rest of the sacred lands of America through the Louisiana Purchase. Once a promised land, always a promised land.

But before we discuss that stunning narrative, we must look in more depth at the context. You see, the adversary is real. And so, wherever there is a promised land, we can expect to see that evil influence there too, trying to stop God. Indeed, there is a reason America, for all its promises and blessings, also holds the distinction for having one of the worst historical records when it comes to slavery. Because of its divine mandate and mission, Satan was trying to halt America.

This theory is shored up by the fact that of all the American slave territories that dug in the hardest and whose inhabitants brought upon themselves the most hurt and damage over their efforts to preserve this evil practice, Missouri ranks number one. Historian David McCullough explained how the Civil War in Missouri began some seven years before it began in the rest of the country: "It was a war of plunder, ambush, and unceasing revenge. Nobody was safe. Defenseless towns were burned . . . . Neither then nor later did the rest of the country realize the extent of the horrors."[293] There is no doubt Satan had set up camp in Missouri years earlier to stomp out any LDS efforts to build Zion—certainly the devil knew it was a promised land designated for Zion. Just because the LDS people left years before the Civil War doesn't mean the adversary did. As one eyewitness said: "The Devil came to the border [state], liked it, and decided to stay awhile."[294]

Following the pattern, the same can be said of Hispaniola. Though it was a promised land in acting as basecamp for Columbus to carry out his mission, it was constantly under attack. We have already discussed the severe challenges evil ones who had set up their adversarial camps on the island thrust upon

Columbus. But God is always ready to counterstrike in an effort to bring about His purposes. He will not be thwarted in the end. His promised lands will prevail against the evil that seeks to control and destroy.

The foreign dictator who claimed control of both the American lands of the New Jerusalem and the island of Hispaniola could easily be characterized as one who constantly sought control and destroyed those in his way. His name was Napoleon Bonaparte. And by the end of 1801, he was preparing his French fleets to invade the French island colony on western Hispaniola, which was known as Saint-Dominigue (modern-day Haiti). It became the largest French fleet ever sent on an overseas expedition up until that time—nearly forty thousand troops and seventy-four ships. And what was the cause? Something had happened on Hispaniola that had never happened and has yet to happen again in the history of the world. The nearly half a million horribly abused and oppressed slaves under French rule bravely began the process of rebelling, emancipating themselves, raising themselves into an army, and seeking to make themselves a free nation.[295]

Napoleon wasn't about to take that, so he sent a large number of troops to defend this island colony, which was producing more wealth than all the other Caribbean islands. In fact, its exports were greater than Brazil's and Mexico's combined.[296] Looking at the odds, nobody believed it would be difficult for him to reconquer the island from a bunch of former slaves. However, some twenty-five years earlier, in 1776, the British fleets en route to America had similar thoughts. But they, like Napoleon, didn't realize the power of a promised land.

The island rebellion against the French colonial plantation system actually began in 1791, the same year the United States Bill of Rights came into being. (Just a coincidence?) Toussaint

Louverture was the leader who emerged from the movement, a self-educated former slave and son of an African king. At first, the French government, not wanting even more conflict on its hands, sought to legitimize Toussaint, hoping he would assimilate and work together with the motherland. The French even appeared to, or pretended to, support his abolitionist movement. But then Toussaint went too far. In July 1801, without French permission, he instituted a constitution of self-rule for the island colony, which included amendment three: "There can exist no slaves in this territory, where servitude is forever abolished and all men are born, live, and die free." Napoleon did not like this bold move and implied threat of independence, so he turned his armies on Toussaint and sought to re-enslave and exploit the island for himself. That was when he sent in the massive fleet.[297]

But Napoleon's war plan extended beyond the island. He also had his eye on North America. Years earlier, after Britain had beaten the French in the Seven Years' War (also known as the French and Indian War), the French preemptively deeded the sacred lands in North America to their Spanish allies so Britain couldn't claim it as spoils of war. Since Britain didn't see Spain as a threat, they did nothing about it. But since that time, much had changed; Britain had lost her Thirteen Colonies to the Americans, and now Bonaparte wanted to take those western lands back from Spain. In fact, before he sent his fleets to Hispaniola, the deal with Spain had been inked—Napoleon would soon be in control of those scriptural lands America was to possess. His plan was straightforward. After conquering the island, his fleet would continue on to America and take over the Louisiana territory.

Thomas Jefferson and his band of American heroes looked on in horror. It was one thing for Spain to be in possession of the territory, because the Spanish were in decline and posed no threat. But France was different. "France placing herself in that door assumes to us the attitude of defiance," Jefferson said. "Spain might have retained it quietly for years . . . . Not so can it ever be in the hands of France. The impetuosity of her temper, the energy and restlessness of her character, placed in a point of eternal friction with us . . . render it impossible that France and the US can continue long friends."[298] He knew that should Napoleon grab those lands, he would make himself America's "natural and habitual enemy" and a terrifying war would loom on the horizon.[299]

This was a difficult thing for Jefferson to say when he had always loved France, but he was a dreamer and a visionary, and he knew he was supposed to acquire those lands for his country. In fact, beginning in 1793, he was the one who sent two separate expeditions into the American west (the most successful one being the Lewis and Clark expedition) to begin that exploration and eventual acquisition. Again, for a man with inspiration connected to gospel truths, to include the thought of a pending restoration of Christ's church to take place on the continent, such a vision as he possessed for these western lands seems appropriate, if not likely. He would begin to plan a way to persuade Napoleon to sell America the land rather than to come and occupy it.

But Jefferson's ability to persuade the Frenchman would largely come down to the happenings on Hispaniola. If Napoleon, by some miracle, could be stopped there, perhaps he would lose motivation for North America. After all, of the two lands, the only wealth-generating one at the time was the island. For the French dictator, the only immediate and obvious benefit of the American territory (mostly just wilderness) was its potential role as a means to support and protect his commercial enterprise at Hispaniola.

Few today recognize what was at stake during this tense time in the Caribbean. Would the sacred lands of the Garden of Eden, even Adam-ondi-Ahman, and the New Jerusalem, where so much was to happen soon concerning the Restoration,

> "After the waters had receded from off the face of this land [America] it became a choice land above all other lands, a chosen land of the Lord; wherefore the Lord would have that all men should serve him who dwell upon the face thereof . . . . Behold, Ether saw the days of Christ, and he spake concerning a New Jerusalem upon this land."
>
> —Ether 13:2,4

end up in the hands of a foreign dictator? Or would Thomas Jefferson prevail in bringing those lands into the protective arms of the United States, the nation the Savior spoke of as the place where latter-day Americans "should be established . . . and be set up as a free people by the power of the Father . . . that the covenant of the Father may be fulfilled which he hath covenanted with his people, O house of Israel" (3 Nephi 21:4)?

Who knew that while the African prince and former slave Toussaint Louverture stood his ground on a Caribbean island, waiting for one of the most powerful forces on the planet to attack him, so much weighed in the balance? Renowned American historian Henry Adams (grandson and great-grandson to two American presidents) understood very well the situation: "Before Bonaparte could reach Louisiana, he was obliged to crush the power of Toussaint," he wrote. "If he and his blacks should succumb easily to their fate, the wave of French empire would roll on to Louisiana and sweep far up the Mississippi; if

St. Domingo should resist, and succeed in resistance . . . America would be left to pursue her democratic destiny in peace."[300]

Jefferson, in the meantime, refused to comply with the French trade embargo placed upon Toussaint and rejected any idea of prohibiting American merchants from supplying the island revolution.[301] Beyond that, all America could do was pray.

Toussaint knew he could never expect to win a front-on confrontation with the powerful French, so instead, he led his armies into the thick, forested mountains of the island, where the French would have to come to them and confront the terrifying prospect of guerilla warfare. The French found little success. And then, as could be expected in a conflict over promised lands, Mother Nature took over. And she took over in the form of Yellow Fever—Toussaint's most powerful ally. Nearly half of the first wave of French soldiers immediately died from the disease.[302]

But even with those odds, the French were eventually able to capture Toussaint and send him to rot and die in a prison in France, which opened the way for other Haitian leaders who, unfortunately, in the name of revolution, committed horrible and unnecessary atrocities against innocent colonial civilians. Nevertheless, in the end, Toussaint's martyrdom only raised the morale of his freedom-fighting countrymen, who now dug in harder against the French. His people would forever remember the words he spoke as the French carried him away in chains: "In overthrowing me," he yelled, "you have cut down in Saint Domingue only the trunk of the tree of liberty; it will spring up again from the roots, for they are numerous and they are deep."[303]

His words proved prophetic as the French continued losing ground on the island. Desperate, the French command issued genocidal orders: all men and woman, including teenagers

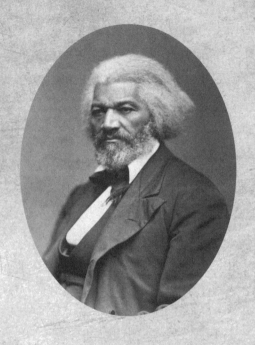

FREDERICK DOUGLASS ON HAITI

The great American abolitionist Frederick Douglass said: "I can speak of her, not only words of admiration, but words of gratitude as well. She has grandly served the cause of universal human liberty. We should not forget the freedom you and I enjoy . . . the freedom that has come to the colored race the world over, is largely due to the brave stand taken by the black sons of Haiti . . . I regard her as the original pioneer emancipator of the nineteenth century."[306]

(everyone twelve years old and older), must be murdered. They even brought three hundred starving bloodhounds and let them loose on the island to help with the mass murder. But the islanders could not be subdued. They would pay any price to remain free from slavery.

After more than forty thousand French soldiers perished, and after the former slaves continued to fight back, gaining more and more ground against the invaders, the French finally quit and went home. Needless to say, their great plans to move on to North America were foiled.

On January 1, 1804, the island freedom fighters officially established their new independent nation, which they named *Haiti*, a word from the island's indigenous language, which means "land of high mountains." Haiti became the first and only nation in history to be formed and led by former slaves after they successfully revolted against their masters, one of the very first nations on the planet to officially abolish slavery, and the second in the Western Hemisphere (after the United States) to achieve independence from the monarchs and dictators of the Old World. [304]

The Haitian Revolution ended up inspiring abolitionist movements in other parts of the world. For example, the revolutionary Simon Bolívar, who led rebellions for independence throughout Latin America, included abolitionism as part of his platform as a result of the Haitian Revolution.[305]

With the final punch landed in Haiti, it seemed that the land of the Restoration would ultimately find safety under America and her covenant, where it always belonged.

◆　◆　◆

The story of what happened next to Napoleon, Jefferson, and the lands of the New Jerusalem is not quite finished. More amazing things were to follow, things that finalized the land deal. And we will get to that shortly. However, I can't quite drop Haiti yet. There is still too much to discuss about this miracle island.

As discussed earlier, my team of operators has spent much time on the island. I can hardly step foot on that piece of land without considering how the one and only slave rebellion in history to birth a free and independent nation governed by the former slaves was also the catalyst to achieving important gospel work pertaining to sacred American lands. And I wonder if that could be just a coincidence.

Then, when I consider the following, I'm certain it was not: Columbus, a man prophesied of in 1 Nephi 13, "accidently" landed on this very island (out of hundreds of Caribbean islands) and made it his basecamp while identifying the New World lands as the lands of the Garden of Eden and the New Jerusalem— something the Book of Mormon itself confirms as a correct identification (see Ether 13:2–8). Then, 1 Nephi 13 goes on to identify another generation of people to follow Columbus, a people who would fight and build a nation under God, even the United States of America (1 Nephi 13:16–19). One of the principal leaders of that movement, Thomas Jefferson, predicted a restoration of the gospel (something equally predicted at the end of 1 Nephi 13) and sought out those very lands that Columbus had pointed to. And then, knowing how God works in patterns, this stunning fact closes the prophetic loop of visions and history: of the many, many lands and islands Jefferson could have looked to for a solution to his France problem, he looked to Columbus's Hispaniola, which then delivered the New World sacred lands into his hands and into God's prophesied nation, even the United States.

Are we going to sit back and call this a big, fat coincidence? Or should we look deeper into this island to see what it has to teach us?

The first operator I hired to specifically conduct missions in Haiti, a former LDS missionary who had served in Haiti, told me: "Tim, Haiti is a land of miracles." At first, this was hard to believe. Haiti ranks among the poorest, most crime-ridden, most miserable, and most corrupt nations on the planet. But then I remembered there were times when the early Latter-day Saints or the American slaves of the nineteenth century could have described America exactly that way. It is because of the meaning that lies at the core of such nations that evil attacks them so relentlessly. And this is when, instead of giving up on your land, you seek for light, you seek for miracles.

And that's what I found in Haiti. I don't believe it is a coincidence that Hispaniola is perhaps the only island on the planet (or perhaps the only small island on the planet, depending on your definition of *island*) that has not one but *two* temples. The Santo Domingo Dominican Republic Temple was the first temple in the Caribbean, dedicated on September 17, 2000, by President Gordon B. Hinckley. And the Port-au-Prince Haiti Temple was dedicated on September 1, 2019, by Elder David A. Bednar.

I have found much power and solace visiting the island's two temples, as well as the two sites where Apostles dedicated the land—Elder M. Russell Ballard in Santo Domingo in 1978 and President Thomas S. Monson in Port-au-Prince in 1983. My team has enjoyed preoperational prayer meetings around these sacred spots. And I will never forget the time, early in my foundation's career, when we contemplated for weeks whether or not we should launch an operation on the island where the intelligence was only good enough to give us about a fifty-fifty chance for success. At a time when money was especially tight and we could not afford to be wrong, it was an especially tough decision. But after much fasting and prayer, we decided it was right to move on it. So we got on a plane.

LUGAR DE DEDICACION DE LA
REPUBLICA DOMINICANA
PARA LA PREDICACION DEL EVANGELIO
POR EL ELDER
M. RUSSELL BALLARD
DICIEMBRE 7 DE 1978
LA IGLESIA DE
JESUCRISTO
DE LOS SANTOS
DE LOS ULTIMOS DIAS

Dedicatory Plaque for the Preaching of the Gospel to The Dominican Republic

The day before the operation, we held a prayer meeting at the spot in a beautiful park where Elder Ballard had dedicated the land, then most of the team worshipped in the Santo Domingo Temple. When I walked out of the temple, I turned on my cell phone, and there was an urgent message waiting for me from my Chief Financial Officer, who had no idea exactly where we were or what we were doing that day.

"Tim, you won't believe this," the message stated. "Today we just received three unexpected checks, which not only will completely cover your current operation on the island but would cover it twice over!" The operation turned out to be a success.

And that wasn't the only miracle. I remember going undercover as an American trafficker into one of the darkest places on the island. For operational security purposes, I can't reveal too many details, but it was a house of sorts where children were being sold. The youngest was but an infant, and the oldest was about thirteen. There were a couple dozen of these children, and they were *all* for sale. Traffickers would come to this place to buy them as sex slaves, labor slaves, or possibly even for the grotesque purpose of organ harvesting. It was an awful site. We were able to infiltrate the network and, working with police, conduct a sting operation where I ended up "buying" some of the children in my undercover capacity. This gave the police the evidence they needed, and they took the place down. All the children were rescued and placed in rehabilitation homes where specialists could help undo the damage.

It is our policy to regularly visit the rehab shelters where the children we rescue are placed, so about a year after this particular rescue, we were visiting our liberated children to see how they were doing. I spotted the oldest survivor of the group, who was now fourteen. I will call her Isabel. I remembered seeing Isabel at the dark house a year earlier, and I remembered being impressed with how she loved the younger children and cared for them in their captivity. She was the only source of love many of them had ever had.

Knowing she would not recognize me, as I had been disguised a year earlier when I had first seen her, I approached her with care and asked her how she was doing.

"I am so happy," she said, her face beaming and her eyes aglow.

"Why is that?" I asked excitedly, trying to match her enthusiasm.

"Because I am training to be a missionary for the new church I found after I moved to this home."

"Wow!" I replied. "Tell me about it."

"Well," Isabel stated, "every Tuesday night, I go to my church, where they teach me about Jesus and His gospel and get me excited for when I can be a missionary. I also go on Sundays."

My heart began to beat fast as my mind focused in on more specific questions I could ask. This was sounding very familiar to me.

"Who teaches you?"

"Two missionaries," she replied with a shy smile, "just like the kind I want to be when I turn nineteen."

I was breathless. "Isabel, what's the name of your new church?"

"The Church of Jesus Christ of Latter-day Saints," she said boldly and happily.

With tears in my eyes, I thought of how great the Lord is. I thought of the gathering of Israel and of the New Testament scripture (John 10:16) Columbus quoted as pertaining to his work on the very island upon which I now stood. "And other sheep I have that are not of this fold: them also I must bring. And they shall hear my voice: and there shall be one fold and one shepherd."[307] "I feel persuaded, by the many and wonderful manifestations of Divine Providence," Columbus once said to Amerigo Vespucci, future namesake of America, "that I am the chosen instrument of God in bringing to pass a great event—no less than the conversion of millions who are now existing in the darkness."[308]

Another story I must tell you about this island is that of a Haitian man, an LDS bishop, named Guesno Mardy. I first learned of Guesno when working as a special agent for the US government. I found his story reported in a local news outlet, and it broke my heart. His son Gardy, just shy of three years old, had been kidnapped and trafficked, taken right out of the Port-au-Prince church parking lot where the family had recently finished their ward sacrament meeting. When I learned very little was being done to help him and his wife recover their child, I flew him up to meet me in the United States.

We sat at a restaurant, and I cut right to the chase, asking him what was being done to find his son.

He looked me in the eyes and asked, "Do you have children, Tim?"

"Yes," I replied.

"Could you get in bed and sleep at night, knowing that one of your children's beds was empty?"

I knew the answer was no, but I couldn't get the words out. Too emotional to speak, I just shook my head.

"I don't sleep, Tim," Guesno said. "I haven't slept since they took my Gardy."

He then explained how every sleepless night he picked a random street in Port-au-Prince and walked all night, hoping to hear his son cry.

I was still speechless.

"Please help me," he pled.

That short but powerful conversation marked the true beginning of Operation Underground Railroad. I would soon learn that I could do very little for him as a US agent, due to the fact that the crime against him had occurred outside the US—outside any jurisdiction we had—so it was not long after my conversation with Guesno that I retired from the government, recruited a team of specialists, and headed to Haiti.

Rescue Operations in Haiti

When we got to the island, the Haitian police welcomed us in and opened the Gardy Mardy case file. We confirmed what Guesno had previously suspected: that Gardy's kidnapping was somehow attached to suspects who ran an orphanage in downtown Port-au-Prince. We researched the place and did surveillance of its premises. It was a large compound made up of four large cement walls. Inside was a yard and some old, decrepit outbuildings. We were alarmed to find out that the place was not a registered orphanage and could not facilitate adoptions. So what were these people doing with the twenty-eight kids, from toddlers to teenagers, that we had identified inside the compound?

We now knew what it was. A shell "orphanage" that opened its doors for innocent but desperate people to bring children into—people who somehow found themselves with children they could not care for. But it was a trap. The children would soon join the ranks of the millions of others who would be sold for a number of nefarious purposes. We had to act fast. Gardy could be in there. That was our hope. It was Guesno's dream.

The Haitian police sent in me and my team. We once again posed as American traffickers and knocked on the door of the compound. We were let in and our cover stories worked beautifully. Within minutes, the thugs who worked for the criminal organization told us the children were all for sale, starting at ten thousand American dollars each. Per the instructions the Haitian authorities had given us, we negotiated a deal and, after several meetings and visits, eventually carried out the "purchase" of children. Our undercover body cameras captured it all. We had more than enough evidence for police to then raid the place, arrest the culprits, and liberate the children.

Guesno had waited out the entire operation at a nearby hotel, praying desperately that Gardy would be found among the twenty-eight kids. But as the dust settled, it became clear that Gardy was not there. It was a bittersweet experience for all of us. On the one hand, twenty-eight children had been liberated from captivity. On the other, Gardy was still missing.

After the operation was complete, I made my way to the hotel where Guesno was waiting.

We sat at a table.

I couldn't say anything, but I didn't need to. Guesno could tell by the look on my face that we had not recovered his son. He wept. I fought back tears.

Finally, he broke the silence. "Tell me the truth, Tim," he said. "They already sold him, didn't they?"

I nodded and looked away. I couldn't force myself to look into Guesno's eyes. The pain was too severe.

Guesno allowed himself to mourn the bad news for only a moment. Then he popped his head up as a warm smile, which appeared to melt his tears away, formed across his face. "But you rescued the twenty-eight kids, right?" he exclaimed.

"Yes, of course," I responded, confused by his emotion.

"Tim, don't you see what happened? Those kids would never have been saved were it not for Gardy. If he had never been kidnapped, you and your team would never have come here. Those twenty-eight kids would still be slaves!"

I just looked at him, astonished. Then he said perhaps the most profound thing anyone has ever said to me.

"Tim, if I have to give up my son so that these twenty-eight kids can be set free, then that's a burden I'm willing to bear. I will make that sacrifice."

The parallels to God's love in sacrificing His own Son for the salvation of others was not lost on me. I just looked at Guesno, speechless, wishing I were a better man, knowing I would not have been able to say what he had just said were our roles reversed.

Then, proving that he meant what he said, he marched down to the police station the very next day and volunteered to take in any of the children we had just rescued in the name of his son. He volunteered to care for them as his own. Eight of the children were promptly delivered to his home, and he is now their father.

To this day, we work closely with Guesno, still looking for his son and still hoping and believing that we are closer than ever. In the meantime, Guesno has become a very active participant in our operations, helping us rescue more and more children every year.

I tell you these stories about what I still call the "Miracle Island" because there is a message to it all. There is always light within the darkness of God's nations. Because of their divine missions, promised lands are especially vulnerable to this darkness. And even with America's past, it's quite possible that this nation's darkest days are still ahead. As darkness increases, there may even come a time when people begin questioning whether America was ever a promised land, just like many today question Hispaniola's status. This is when we remember the miracles that have built our nations. This is when we acknowledge that those living in a promised land are still encouraged to look to God and are still allowed to be miracle chasers. Only then will we see the light—see the Isabels and the Guesnos among us—and turn to our temples, which Columbus and other pilgrims fought so long and so hard to make possible. We will remember the words of Toussaint Louverture and know that even though our enemies have "cut down . . . the trunk of the tree of liberty; it will spring up again from the roots, for they are numerous and they are deep." In the end, that light will grow and grow until it has chased out every shadow.

On Sunday morning, September 1, 2019, I sat quietly in the back row of the small celestial room of the Port-au-Prince Haiti Temple. Elder David A. Bednar approached the stand and began to deliver the dedicatory prayer. I thought of little Gardy and the Mardy family as Elder Bednar prayed, "We thank Thee, our Holy Father, for Thy plan of salvation and happiness which makes possible immortality and eternal life for Thy sons and daughters. We love and worship Thee as our Eternal Father."

And I thought of Haiti as the Apostle prayed, "Heavenly Father, we pray that this holy temple will be a beacon of light and truth to the nation of Haiti. Please bless the people of this land with peace, with an appreciation for their legacy of liberty . . . . By the power of Thy holy priesthood and the influence of Thy Spirit, may order arise out of chaos and opportunity emerge from calamity."[309]

Interview with Bishop Guesno Mardy

◆ ◆ ◆

As Napoleon and Jefferson were watching the former slaves of Haiti land one blow after another to the humiliated French armies, they each played their next move. Jefferson didn't skip a beat. He sent his best American statesmen to France (Robert Livingston, who had helped write the Declaration of Independence, and James Monroe, future US president) to make an offer to purchase the town of New Orleans, the only real, tangible asset in the vast western region. Jefferson would have loved to purchase all of the Louisiana territory, but that would be too costly for the still-small republic. And anyway, why would Napoleon want to give up valuable land that was four times larger than France itself? But Jefferson hoped that his offer, in conjunction with the French defeat at Hispaniola and France's need for more money to fight its war with

Britain, would fully incentivize Napoleon to abandon the western hemisphere altogether. To initiate the negotiation, Jefferson laid $2 million before the French dictator.

But Napoleon had already made a decision in a different direction and halted all negotiations. In the summer of 1802, he organized a completely separate fleet of nearly one hundred ships upon the Dutch river Scheldt. Frustrated at his inability to easily conquer the Haitians, he was sending this new, enormous fleet directly to New Orleans, bypassing Hispaniola altogether this time, to finally take control of his longed-for American territory. From there, he would set up his stronghold in America, then deal with whatever else needed dealing with in Hispaniola.

Just before Napoleon's fleet was about to leave for America, something unusual happened. The river froze over and trapped the ships where they were anchored. The sailors were forced to wait it out and consumed all the provisions that had been set aside for the trip. Months passed before spring came and melted the ice. Again, the fleet was about to launch their expedition when a ferocious storm hit them, causing them further delay. Weeks passed again before they restocked the ships and were ready to try one more time. Finally, they set sail. But just before clearing the estuary and entering the open sea, a courier stopped them in their tracks. Orders from Paris commanded the ships to return. Napoleon had just sold the Louisiana lands to the United States.

The Miracle Island

What exactly had turned in Napoleon's heart and mind that allowed him to sell the land is somewhat of a mystery. It seems almost certain to me that the Lord was working on him—first through the failures in the Caribbean, then through the bewildering delays forced upon his fleet on the river Scheldt. Did he wonder if the universe was telling him something?

The moment of final decision apparently came to him on Easter Sunday 1803 (coincidentally or not, just a few days after Toussaint Louverture died a martyr in a French prison). After worshipping in church, Napoleon came home and pondered and discussed the idea with his advisors. He went to bed and woke up resolute: "I renounce Louisiana," he said. "It is not only New Orleans that I will cede, it is the whole colony without any reservation. I know the price of what I abandon . . . . I renounce it with the greatest regret. But to attempt obstinately to retain it would be folly."[310] America had asked for only New Orleans. Napoleon was now offering the entire territory.

Perhaps he had learned something the day before in church about the further consequences that awaited him should he pursue a land meant for another nation. We will likely never know because he didn't give much of an explanation for his decision and likely didn't feel he needed to. However, many of his closest friends and advisors saw it as a ridiculous giveaway. After all, he was offering to sell 529,920,000 acres for only three cents an acre. Napoleon made sure he gave America a deal it could afford. Even in today's market, it would be like selling all that land for around forty-one cents an acre.[311] It truly was unthinkable. Furthermore, it was valuable land. As historian Paul Johnson pointed out, "If Bonaparte had used France's legitimate rights to its American territory to explore and create an enormous dominion across the Atlantic, instead of trying to carve out an illegitimate empire in

Europe, he would have enriched France instead of impoverishing her, [and] provided scope for countless adventurous young Frenchmen instead of killing them in futile battles."[312]

Jefferson learned the news from a dispatch that arrived to him on the night of July 3. It was beautiful timing for the man who wrote the Declaration of Independence and was already getting into a celebratory mood for the next day's festivities. After all, as Horatio Gates, a Revolutionary War hero who had served under Washington, said when learning about the purchase, "It must . . . strike the mind of every true friend to freedom in the United States, as the greatest and most beneficial event that has taken place since the Declaration of Independence . . . it has the air of enchantment."[315]

Jefferson was as happy as Napoleon's brothers had been distraught. All he had ever sought was the town of New Orleans—and that he wanted so he could prevent an American-Franco war. And yet, here he was now, getting one of the happiest, friendliest, greatest, and largest land deals in history—instead of getting war. "I very early saw that Louisiana was indeed a speck in our horizon which was to burst in a tornado," Jefferson stated, "and the public are unapprised how near this catastrophe was."

Instead, miracle followed miracle, and on the eve of Independence Day, the president could sit back and, with a sigh of relief, say, "This removes from us the greatest source of danger to our peace."[316] It was like a gift from heaven. Alexander Hamilton said of the deal, "Let us then, with all due humility, acknowledge this as another of those signal instances of the kind interpositions of an overruling Providence."[317] This reflected the general sentiments of that faithful generation of Americans. As author Charles Cerami noted in his book *Jefferson's Great Gamble: The Remarkable Story of Jefferson, Napoleon and the Men Behind the Louisiana Purchase,* "To have been given such an imperial gift as

EMPEROR IN THE BATH

When Napoleon's brothers heard what he was about to do, they marched
into Napoleon's bathroom, interrupting his bath. They were irate. They told
their brother that if he didn't reverse his decision on America, they would rally
the public against him and force him to renege. Napoleon was incredulous
at their audacity. He stood up in his bath and let his brothers have it. "You
will have no need to lead the opposition," he screamed, red in the face, "for I
repeat there will be no debate, for the reason that the project . . . conceived
by me, negotiated by me, shall be ratified and executed by me, alone. Do you
comprehend me?"[313] The emperor slammed his fist against a nearby snuffbox
and broke it into pieces. Then he hurled himself back into the tub, perhaps
like a child performing a cannonball dive, and soaked one of his brothers who
dared to get that close.[314]

the Louisiana Territory must have convinced many of the seriously faithful that nature's design for the planet included a special role for America."[318]

In the end, the purchase brought us what today we would recognize as Iowa, Arkansas, Oklahoma, Kansas, Nebraska, Montana, South Dakota, part of North Dakota, part of Wyoming, part of Colorado, part of Minnesota, part of New Mexico, part of Texas, and part of Louisiana. And, of course, *all* of Missouri—the Center Place, Adam-ondi-Ahman, the Garden of Eden, the New Jerusalem. The American Zion.

It was an awesome miracle, from the unlikely events in the Caribbean to the strange Dutch ice to the mysterious mental shifting of the dictator. "But without . . . the miscalculation of an emperor, and a trick of the climate, Louisiana might long have remained foreign soil," the Harvard historian Oscar Handlin wrote. "Thanks to the ice that had formed across the waters of a remote Dutch harbor, the advancing host of American settlers moving westward towards the Pacific at a turning point in our history now found the way open before them."

And who were those American settlers? Eventually, when the time was right, they would include the pilgrims and prophets of the latter-day gathering. Indeed, soon enough, they would be westward bound to establish the American Zion. As Andrew Jackson wrote to Jefferson concerning the newly acquired lands, "Every face wears a smile, and every heart leaps with joy."

Another wise observer wrote the president: "The [purchase] is new in the annals of the world. The great matter now is to make the wonderful event a blessing to the human race."[319]

They did not know how correct, even prophetic, they were.

CHAPTER 5

The Patriots

It was about three o'clock in the morning as I drove my rental car down a small, dark, winding road in a suburb of Boston. It was near zero degrees outside and was snowing lightly. The GPS in the car had lost its signal, and I had no idea where I was. I was having a hard time seeing out the window through the darkness and the snowdrifts, especially as I fidgeted with the map. I panicked. I wasn't afraid of being temporarily lost; I was afraid I was going to miss the opportunity I'd sought that morning. It was the reason I'd risen at 2:00 a.m.

I had landed in Boston fewer than forty-eight hours earlier. I'd had a brief assignment in the area that had left me no time to see the site I was now looking for. I had an early flight home that very morning, so the only chance I was going to have to catch a glimpse of the place was to get up way too early.

Not sure whether I had missed a turn or not, I continued to drive down the road, praying I would see it. Praying I had not missed it.

Suddenly, the darkness disappeared to my left and was replaced by a soft glow. The moonlight was bouncing off the untouched snow that lay over the garden to my left and reflecting on the house. At first, the soft light entered only peripherally through the driver's-side window. I could spare only a quick glance, as I didn't want to take my eyes off the iced-over road. *That's it!* I thought. Though I had never been there before, I knew instantly I had arrived. A bit overwhelmed, I pulled the car over to catch my breath as I stared at the three-story colonial/country-style house, once surrounded by hundreds of acres of farmland. It was the home of John and Abigail Adams.

I pictured John at work, plowing the fields and getting his hands dirty. And this scene played out in my mind as though it were *after* his presidency, back in the days when public servants retired from public office without a lifetime pension. Adams was made to work by the sweat of his brow in retirement, even until his dying day. He was still young when he walked away from his professional aspirations as planter and lawyer in order to serve the cause of liberty. He gave up the personal fortune easily within his reach and sacrificed it for God and country. I love that about John Adams.

I also pictured another historical figure standing on the street where I was parked—John Marston. He is mostly an unknown man in history, but he happened to witness something outside the Adams' house one summer evening in 1826 that has deeply intrigued me over the years and was the compelling factor that got me up that morning to see the house.

There are only a few places I have visited that overwhelm me with spiritual feelings. The Lincoln Memorial is one. The Adams home is another. The only other place that causes such sensations in me is the temple. And there is a reason. You see, the event Marston witnessed at the Adams home was connected to the temple in a powerful way.

In the introduction of this book, the doctrines of Christ are spelled out clearly regarding the purpose of the gathering of Israel—the temple. The Lord brings in His Israel so He can create Zion, a place where the priesthood can be restored, where temples can be built, and where families can be sealed and placed on the path of eternal life. "For behold," the Lord said, "this is my work and my glory—to bring to pass the immortality and eternal life of man" (Moses 1:39).

During the length of this book, we have witnessed the early participants in this gathering, the forerunners of the Restoration—discoverers, explorers, Pilgrims, Puritans, and presidents—and each points us to this same divine end: to the national covenants of Israel, which lay the political foundation for temples. They point us to the restoration of these covenants in the land, which lead to the planning of temples; they point us to the acquisition of sacred soil, which leads to the building of temples; they point us to the reconstitution of Zion and the New Jerusalem, which leads to the protection and sustainability of temples.

And now I bring you back to the Founding Fathers, the last generation who bridged the gap between early American history and the Restoration. These patriots have one more story to tell in their epic saga to bring to pass the will of the Father, to seal their sacrifice to God and country, and to point us one last time to the temple.

That this final story occurred in New England should be of little surprise. So much of America's early history takes place there, and there are few areas within the promised land of America that are foreseen as much and have seen as many prophecies fulfilled as New England. The renowned Puritan Jonathan Edwards stated:

> And if we may suppose that this glorious work of God
> shall begin in any part of America, I think, if we consider
> the circumstances of the settlement of New England,
> it must needs appear the most likely, of all American

colonies, to be the place whence this work shall princi-
pally take its rise. And, if these things be so, it gives us
more abundant reason to hope that what is now seen in
America, and especially in New England, may prove the
dawn of that glorious day; and the very uncommon and
wonderful circumstances and events of this work, seem to
me strongly to argue that God intends it as the beginning
or forerunner of something vastly great.[320]

Edwards wrote this in his work titled "The Latter-Day Glory
Is Probably to Begin in America." Prophetic. The patriots of New
England were indeed forerunners to the Restoration of Christ's
gospel. And no single event illustrates this idea better than that
which John Marston, a friend and neighbor to the Adams family,
witnessed outside the John Adams home on that summer evening
in 1826.

Since this story is ultimately about temples, it is naturally a
love story. Fittingly, the lead characters in this story, John and
Abigail Adams, were deeply in love. If anyone desired and deserved an eternal marriage, it was them. And because John spent
so much time away, working on behalf of the country, they had
ample opportunity to write each other. Today, we have more than
twelve hundred letters they wrote to each other as a witness of
their profound love.[321] But that's just the beginning of their love
story, which, as I've suggested, eventually connects to the gospel,
to the temple, and to the event John Marston witnessed that day
outside of their house.

Before the Revolution really heated up, John and Abigail
were doing their best to raise their small children and run their
New England farm. John had toyed with the idea of following
his father into the ministry but, instead, had become a successful attorney in and around Boston. Throughout their twenties

THE LOVE OF JOHN AND ABIGAIL: EXCERPTS FROM THEIR LETTERS TO EACH OTHER

Miss Adorable,

By the same token that the bearer hereof sat up with you last night I hereby order you to give him, as many kisses, and as many hours of your company after 9 o'clock as he shall please to demand and charge them to his account [322] —John

John,

All my desires and all my ambition is to be esteemed and loved by my partner, to join with him in the education and instruction of our little ones, to sit under our own vines in peace, liberty, and safety.[323] — Abigail

Oh my dear girl,

I thank Heaven that another fortnight will restore you to me—— after so long a separation. My soul and Body have been both thrown into Disorder, by your Absence, and a Month or two more would make me the most insufferable Cynick, in the World. . . . But you who have always softened and warmed my Heart, shall restore my Benevolence as well as my health and Tranquility of mind.[324] ——John

My Dearest Friend,

Look—(is there a dearer Name than Friend; think of it for me;) Look to the date of this Letter—and tell me, what are the thoughts which arise in your mind? Do you not recollect that Eighteen years have run their annual Circuit, since we pledged our mutual Faith to each other, and the Hymeneal torch was Lighted at the Alter of Love. Yet, yet it Burns with unabating fervour, old ocean has not Quenched it, nor old Time smoothered it . . . . It cheers [me] in the Lonely Hour, it comforts [me] even in the gloom which sometimes possesses [my] mind [325] — Abigail

(after three years of separation, John serving as Foreign Minister overseas)

Dearest Friend,

Should I draw you the picture of my Heart, it would be what I hope you still would Love; tho it contained nothing New; the early possession you obtained there, and the absolute power you have ever maintained over it, leaves not the smallest space unoccupied. I look back to the early days of our acquaintance, and Friendship, as to the days of Love and Innocence, and with an undescribable pleasure I have seen near a score of years roll over our Heads, with an affection heightened and improved by time-nor have the dreary years of absence in the smallest degree effaced from my mind the Image of the dear untitled Man to whom I gave my Heart. [326] — Abigail and thirties, John and Abigail found themselves managing a successful law practice, farming their land, watching their children grow, and getting involved in local politics. In 1774, on the eve of turning forty, Adams was elected by his countrymen to represent them in Philadelphia at the Continental Congress, which had been designed as a national venue to discuss, among other things, the emerging conflict with Britain.

Though Adams arrived at Philadelphia as unassuming and as normal as any of the other delegates, he found himself—much by the influence and encouragement of his dear wife—rising to his feet and taking the floor of the congressional convention so powerfully and so often that he soon made a name for himself. His speeches in favor of independence from Britain have been recognized as some of the most persuasive and powerful in the history of Congress. They have even been described as being spiritually moving. And this was important. Because the cause for American independence seemed to require the irrational act of pitting America's citizen-soldiers up against the world's superpower, it was not all that popular. Indeed, to many (often to the majority), seeking independence from Britain seemed the work of a madman. Only with spiritual eyes could one grasp the eternal necessity of this revolution. And so, it was by a spiritual vessel that the Lord would touch the hearts of the delegates.

This point cannot be overstated. Yes, it is true that John Adam served as a US foreign minister, the first US vice president, and the second US president, but nothing he did was more important than securing independence. If he had not done that, his other positions would not have existed. More importantly, the Restoration would not have had a foundation of liberty upon which to grow.

It was July 1, 1776. The delegates convened one last time to debate and vote on whether the Declaration of Independence should be signed and executed. The highly respected delegate John Dickinson stood and made one final plea, with plenty of reason on his side, to stop the madness of declaring independence. To go forward with the declaration, he warned, would be "to brave the storm in a skiff made of paper." Aware of his logic, the delegates sat in silence as Dickinson took his seat.

John Adams stood. This was it. Besides nominating George Washington to the field of battle, this would be his most important moment. No doubt he felt Abigail's influence. She was never quiet about the fact that God required American independence. He likely thought of what she had told him not long before: "Your task is difficult," she wrote. "Heaven direct and prosper you."[327] Abigail had always been faithful about the American cause. "I feel no anxiety at the large armament designed against us," she once said. "The remarkable interpositions of heaven in our favor cannot be too gratefully acknowledged. He who fed the Israelites in the wilderness, who clothes the lilies of the field and who feeds the young ravens when they cry, will not forsake a people engaged in so righteous a cause, if we remember His loving kindness."[328]

It seems John Adams did remember as he stood before the delegates on July 1 and delivered what historian David McCullough called "the greatest speech of Adams's life."[329]

Strangely, little is known about the precise content of this improvised speech, as nobody recorded it. Yet it was called his greatest, based on the reaction it produced. One delegate observed that though the speech was neither "graceful nor elegant," Adams delivered it "with a power of thought and expression that moved us from our seats." Adams himself testified that he had been "'carried out in spirit' as enthusiastic preachers sometimes express themselves." So powerful was the speech that upon finishing, he was asked to stand and give it again.[330]

He set the tone of the day and made converts to the cause. Joseph Hewes of North Carolina, who up until that point had opposed independence, was one of many who was overcome. As Adams later recorded, Hewes "started suddenly upright, and lifting up both his hands to Heaven, as if he had been in a trance, cried out, 'It is done! And I will abide by it.'"[331] The following day, July 2, 1776, the delegates voted to declare independence. "It was John Adams," according to McCullough, "more than anyone, who had made [independence] happen."[332] Adams would appropriately become known as the Voice of Independence.

With Washington having already left Philadelphia for the battlefield, Adams would need all the support he could get from Congress. And there was one who rose to the occasion. If Adams was the Voice of Independence, Thomas Jefferson was the Pen. Together, they sat on the committee that drafted the Declaration of Independence: "And for the support of this declaration, with firm reliance on the protection of Divine Providence, we mutually pledge to each other our lives, our fortunes and our sacred honor." So concluded that precious document.

In the previous chapter, we discussed the spiritual profundity of Jefferson as he invoked the national covenant, recognized the gospel apostasy that filled the world in which he lived, and predicted a restoration of Christ's doctrines. Adams could not have asked for a better partner.

Like Jefferson, Adams also believed in the covenant. He once said that America would win the war only if "we fear God and repent our sins."[333] Immediately after the Declaration was signed, he called for Americans to protect the document's divinity and integrity through offerings to God. Independence Day, he predicted, "will be celebrated by succeeding generations as the great anniversary festival." He then described how the day should be celebrated: "Pomp and Parade, with Shows, Games, Sports,

Guns, Bells, Bonfires and Illuminations from one End of this Continent to the other from this Time forward forever more."[334] But he had a more profound point here. For he then instructed those succeeding generations that "it ought to be commemorated as the Day of Deliverance by solemn acts of devotion to God Almighty."[335] A lesson for us all as we celebrate July the Fourth.

But what of the gospel? Believing in the national covenant foundation is one thing, but what did one of the most important players in the rolling out of the Declaration of Independence think about the crowning achievement that God would place upon that foundation? Firstly, like Jefferson, Adams was a Christian. Adams's regular scripture study, church attendance, and regular Sabbath observance (including a reluctance to travel on Sunday)[336] are evidence of his spiritual character. He said of Christianity that it is "the brightest of the glory and the express portrait of the character of the eternal, self-existent, independent, benevolent, all powerful, and all merciful creator, preserver, and father of the universe."

Abigail completed Adams's personal religion. He remembered the testimony she bore to him on the day they met: "Men and woman are here to serve God and humanity. . . . We are made in the image of God, and we must fulfill our promise or we are a blasphemy to God. An hour wasted is an hour's sin." Said Adams of Abigail, "She makes me so happy . . . her Christian beliefs make her ever a joy to know."[337]

It appears John Adams's testimony of the gospel, like that of Jefferson's, went deep. For example, like Jefferson, Adams perceived that he lived in some sort of a religious apostasy, where the fulness of the gospel had been taken from the earth. He was a light seeker and sought after true gospel doctrines that the Restoration would shortly bring. For example, the idea that predestination was the rule of heaven and that our earthly efforts had no bearing on our eternal progression and salvation was, according to Adams, "detestable" and "hurtful." He further expressed disdain for the false doctrine that mankind was inherently punished for Adam's transgressions.[338]

Another doctrinal problem Joseph Smith and the Restoration would have solved for Adams (but at the time locked him in a state of disappointment and frustration) was the popular theological proposition that if one does not accept Christ in mortality, even if not given the opportunity, he or she is consigned to hell for eternity. In a letter to Jefferson, Adams explained that nine-tenths of the world had not heard of Christ and would, according to that doctrine, thus suffer forever. Adams rhetorically asked why God would create "innumerable millions to make them miserable, forever." He explained that the only answer churches could give him as to why God would do this was "For his Own Glory," which, for Adams, was an unacceptable and sickening explanation. "Is he vain?" Adams asked. "Tickled with Adulation? Exulting and triumphing in his Power and the Sweetness of his Vengeance? Pardon me, my Maker, for these Aweful Questions. My Answer to them is always ready: I believe no such Things."[339]

Indeed, the Voice and the Pen of Independence were special. They seemed to know their work for God and country was leading to something more grand. The opening of America represented, according to Adams, "the Opening of a grand scene and Design in Providence, for the Illumination of the Ignorant."[340] Adding to this sentiment, Adams said in the middle of the devastations of the Revolutionary War that "through all the Gloom I can see the Rays of ravishing Light and Glory. I can see that the End is more than worth all the Means."[341] Adams also stated, "I must study politics and war, that my sons may have liberty to study mathematics and philosophy."[342] He might have added just as well that he studied politics and war that the Prophet Joseph might have the liberty to bring forth God's gospel. The idea, after all, is similar. Adams, Jefferson, and their colleagues, indeed, laid the groundwork of liberty upon which the gospel would flourish.

As astonishing as their gospel knowledge appeared to be, even while living in a world still suffering the effects of the Apostasy, what if I told you Adams's and Jefferson's knowledge was about to extend even further, that they were about to reach the very core of the restored gospel? I take you to the end of their lives.

At the time, both were retired from public life and lived privately with their families in their respective homes—Adams in the home outside of Boston that I had so enthusiastically visited that freezing morning, and Jefferson in his sprawling estate in Virginia.

Sadly, Adams and Jefferson, once best friends, had not spoken or written to each other in many, many years. In fact, they wondered whether they were friends at all anymore. After working so hard together to secure independence and set in motion the building of the nation, they parted ways. And not peacefully. The two could not agree on what the new country should look like. Adams favored a strong federal government, while Jefferson argued that a strong federal government would take away too many rights from the individual states. They ended up running against each other in two of the most vitriolic, mudslinging presidential elections ever recorded in US history. Adams won the first, Jefferson the second. They said awful things about each other for political gain and became enemies.

What made the bitter separation so difficult, especially for the two families, was how close they had been at one time. They had become the best of friends after meeting as delegates at the Continental Congress. The quiet Jefferson was in his early thirties when he showed up in Philadelphia. Before that, he had spent most of his days as a planter, lawyer, husband, father, and perpetual student of anything and everything. Adams was the one who nominated Jefferson to write the Declaration of Independence, after which they drew it up together, with the help of Benjamin Franklin.[343] Soon after, they served together as ambassadors to France, seeking European support for their Revolution. At one point, the Adams and Jefferson families lived under one roof in France. Adams even conceded to Jefferson that Adams's son John Quincy "was as much your son as mine."[344]

When the Adamses departed France to fulfill a diplomatic assignment in Britain, Jefferson confessed he was "in the dumps" and that "my afternoons hang heavily on me." Then, when the Adams family finished that assignment and returned home to America, leaving Jefferson alone on his side of the Atlantic, Jefferson despaired, "I now feel widowed."[345] So when these bonds were broken years later, it produced deep sorrow, indeed. These two old men, retired from public life, would sadly think often about each other without ever reaching out.

But then something happened. Something that would have eternal consequences and leave us with a witness from heaven about America and its godly purposes. It began with a fellow signer of the Declaration of Independence, Benjamin Rush. Rush had stayed close to both Adams and Jefferson in their old age and was deeply pained by the silence between the two. He wanted to do something but did not know what. And then the Lord intervened. He sent Rush a dream. And Rush couldn't get it out of his head.

Rush approached Adams because he had to tell him what had been revealed. He explained that in the dream, he had seen a history book—a history book of the future that told the story of

John Adams and Thomas Jefferson. The book told of their tumultuous relationship but then reached a happy ending. According to the book, the two old patriarchs at last reconciled at the end of their lives. The book told of how "Mr. Adams addressed a short letter to his friend Mr. Jefferson . . . with assurance of his regard and good wishes for his welfare." Then, according to the dream book, "Mr. Jefferson replied to this letter and reciprocated expressions of regard and esteem." What followed, according to the book, was a "correspondence of several years" that offered "many precious aphorisms [truths]," the hope of which being that "the world will be favored with the sight of them."[346]

"A dream again!" Adams replied to Rush's recounting of his vision. "It may be prophecy."[347] Adams thought long and hard. Would he help the prophecy be fulfilled? He would. He pulled out pen and paper on New Year's Day 1812. Just as the dream predicted, Jefferson responded enthusiastically. "A letter from you," Jefferson responded, "calls up recollections very dear to my mind. It carried me back to times when, beset with difficulties and dangers, we were fellow laborers in the same cause, struggling for what is most valuable to man."[348]

Dozens of letters were exchanged. They spoke of the Revolution, philosophy, religion. Even trivialities: "I walk every fair day," Adams wrote to Jefferson, "sometimes three and four miles." It is clear from the handwriting in these letters that Adams's feeble, shaking hands made writing difficult. But it was so good to have his friend back. To Rush, he wrote, "Your dream is out . . . You have wrought wonders!"[349]

Of all the wonders Rush wrought through this experience, there is one that sits ahead of the rest. When Rush predicted that precious truths that would benefit the world would be offered through the letters, he was not kidding. Perhaps the greatest of all

these truths is a revelation found in the letter exchange that connects directly to the fullest gospel purposes of America. It all came
about as a result of a tragic event that occurred at the Adams
home on October 28, 1818.

◆　◆　◆

Nearly two centuries later, I got out of my parked rental car
that early, predawn, winter morning and approached the home.
It was so cold, the snow still gently falling, that I could not feel
my hands. It was silent. Completely still. It seemed I was the only
creature stirring within a multimile radius. I was calmed, not only
by the quiet but by the beautiful glow of the moonlight reflecting
off the newly fallen snow on the Adamses' lawn. I knew nobody
was home, as the property was now a historical park for tourists,
but still, I was careful not to make noise (just in case). I immediately walked to the left side of the house and stood under the
second-story window, where John and Abigail's bedroom was. I
thought of that tragic scene on that dreary day in October 1818.
I could almost hear the uncontrollable sobbing of John Adams.
His Abigail, who had been fighting typhoid fever for two weeks,
had succumbed to it. She was one month shy of being seventy-four. John was eighty-three.[350]

"I wish I could lie down beside her and die too," the grief-
stricken Adams bemoaned as he left her bedside in tears. "I cannot bear to see her in this state."[351] Politically, Adams's career had
been successful but difficult. He had regularly been betrayed and
rarely knew whom to trust or whom to confide in. But Abigail
had always been there, the only one who had stood true every
step of the way. Adams once referred to their fifty-four years of
marriage as a "love feast."[352] And she clearly felt the same way
toward him. "When he is wounded, I bleed," she once told a

friend.[353] Understandably, the old man Adams was inconsolable upon the death of his lifelong partner.

Jefferson learned of Abigail's passing in the papers. He was reminded of the death scene of his own wife, Martha, when he was only thirty-nine. She had died shortly after giving birth to their sixth child. At the moment of her death, he had, according to his daughter, fallen into "a state of insensibility" and fainted. For weeks, he hardly uttered a word but wandered aimlessly through the countryside and woods. His daughter remembered the sad time and was herself a witness to "many a violent burst of grief" from the poor widower.[354]

Jefferson, though young, promised the love of his life on her deathbed that he would never remarry.[355] He never did. Instead, he waited for the day he would be with Martha again. He knew the gospel secret. He alluded to it in the words he placed upon Martha's tombstone: "In the melancholy shades below, The flames of friends and lovers cease to glow, Yet mine shall sacred last; mine undecayed. Burn on through death and animate my shade."[356]

Like Jefferson, did Adams know, notwithstanding the contrary teachings of the churches in their day, that marriage could be eternal? Jefferson pulled out his pen and wrote to Adams.

> Tried myself, in the school of affliction, by the loss of every form of connection which can rive the human heart, I know well, and feel what you have lost, what you have suffered, are suffering, and have yet to endure . . . . altho' mingling sincerely my tears with yours, will I say a word more, where words are vain, but that it is of some comfort to us both that the term is not very distant at which we are to deposit, in the same cerement, our sorrow and suffering bodies, and to ascend in essence to an ecstatic meeting with the friends we have loved and lost

and whom we shall still love and never lose again. God bless you and support you under your heavy affliction.[357]

"I always loved Jefferson, and still love him,"[358] the elderly Adams said of his old friend. No doubt this letter improved upon his sentiments.

Adams returned his own feelings and thoughts of that glorious eternity that was rapidly approaching. His mind still upon his recently deceased Abigail, Adams wrote the following to Jefferson:

> I know not how to prove physically that we shall meet and know each other in a future state; nor does revelation, as I can find give us any positive assurance of such a felicity. My reasons for believing it, as I do, most undoubtedly, are . . . [that] I cannot conceive that such a being . . . as the human merely to live and die on this earth. If I did not believe [in] a future state, I should believe in no God . . . And, if there be a future state, why should the Almighty dissolve forever all the tender ties which unite us so delightfully in this world?[359]

Notwithstanding what the doctors of religion said at the time (their cold words of "until death do you part" cankering almost any soul), Adams knew better. In the wake of Abigail's death, he reaffirmed his faith in this yet-to-be-officially-revealed gospel doctrine in a letter to his son John Quincy: "The separation [from your mother] cannot be so long as twenty Separations heretofore. The Pangs and the Anguish have not been so great as when . . . I embarked for France in 1778."[360] In other words, as he himself was nearing the end of mortality, he expected to meet her sooner in heaven than he might have expected to see her again after leaving for Europe. That was his faith. The separation of the veil was no more distant than an ocean. He would be with her again very soon.

Then it happened—one of the greatest miracles of American history: John Adams died. In and of itself, that fact of history seems obvious and unimportant. But in context, it is anything but. You see, he died on the very same day that his friend Thomas Jefferson died. That was more than interesting to Americans, in that they were two of the very last signers of the Declaration of Independence still living (only the eighty-eight-year-old Charles Carroll of Maryland also survived). Not to mention they were the two most important signers. But it gets even more amazing. Their deaths—which occurred for reasons unrelated to each other and which took effect at their respective homes some five states away from each other—happened on a most remarkable day. They both died on July 4, 1826: the fiftieth anniversary of the Declaration of Independence. Adams was ninety. Jefferson was eighty-two.[361]

Two revolutionaries dying on the same day might be a curiosity. But two revolutionaries who were so connected with God and His national covenant and who were the most prominent in achieving independence—even the *Voice* and *Pen* of the Declaration of Independence—dying on the same day of unrelated causes is more than that; indeed, it is more than mere coincidence. And finally, that this all happened on the fiftieth anniversary of the Declaration of Independence, that document they jointly brought to the world, only seals the entire event as a singular act of God. It seals and symbolizes their joint sacrifice in His work.

Have you ever read scriptural accounts and marveled at the signs and wonders described therein? Like Noah's rainbow, the Nephites' days without darkness, or the star over Bethlehem? Have you ever wondered why we don't see such manifestations today?

FINAL THOUGHTS FOR POSTERITY

A year before his death, Jefferson left these final words of advice to younger travelers along the weary trail: "Adore God. Reverence and cherish your parents. Love your neighbor as yourself, and your country more than yourself. Be just. Be true. Murmur not at the ways of Providence. So shall the life into which you have entered be the portal to one of the eternal and ineffable bliss."[362]

Adams also had his final say for posterity: "He who loves the Workman [the Lord] and his work," the old patriarch said, "and does what he can to preserve and improve it, shall be accepted of Him." He wanted his family to know: "Do justly. Love mercy. Walk humbly. This is enough."[363]

Perhaps we would see if we knew where to look. The entirety of American history is filled with such manifestations, and this one may be the capstone of them all. It is nothing short of God testifying to us what He had already stated in the Book of Mormon: America was His. And He had a plan for it.

John Quincy Adams (at the time serving as president of the United States) wrote in his diary that the miraculous nature of the twin deaths of his father and Jefferson was a "visible and palpable mark . . . of Divine favor, for which I would humble myself in grateful and silent adoration before the Ruler of the Universe."[364] Another leading statesman of the day, Daniel Webster, eulogized Adams weeks after his death. He echoed John Quincy, declaring the Adams-Jefferson miracle to be "proof" from the Almighty "that our country, and its benefactors, are objects of His care."[365]

After I finished pondering Abigail's death outside her bedroom window, I walked to the other side of the house and looked up at the second-story windows that sat above me there. I was looking at John Adams's study. It is believed that he died in that room. Reportedly, it was difficult for him to sleep in the bedroom where Abigail had died, so he had a cot moved into his study. I thought of how badly he'd wanted to see his Abigail. I pictured him pining away for that day in the upstairs room. Someone once suggested to him that it would be nice if we could relive life. Adams shot back: "I had rather go forward and meet whatever is to come."[366]

I pondered the details of Adams's death, which reveal so much more about the miracle. Days before his death, he was asked what message he might have to be read as a toast for his town's upcoming Fourth of July celebration. "I will give you," Adams replied, "Independence forever." When asked if he wanted to add anything to his brief comment, he simply replied, "Not a word."[367]

Then, on the day of his death, even in the final moments leading up to his death, a semiconscious Adams shifted in his sleep and, in a voice strong enough for several witnesses present to understand, said, "Thomas Jefferson survives."[368] Adams then passed away; the time was approximately six twenty in the evening. Just hours earlier, at approximately one o'clock in the afternoon, Thomas Jefferson had passed away at his Virginia estate.[369]

My mind went back to the prophetic dream Benjamin Rush had reported, which led to the letter-writing campaign that had given Adams and Jefferson the opportunity to bear testimony of life after death and eternal marriage, and I thought of another prophecy from the dream that had been fulfilled. The dream history book of the future had also predicted that the two national patriarchs, after rekindling their great friendship and revealing powerful truths for posterity, "sunk into the grave nearly at the same time, full of years and rich in the gratitude and praises of their country."[370]

Speaking of prophecies being fulfilled by this event, I take you back to the prediction Jefferson made in 1820 (cited in the previous chapter). You will recall that he stated, "The genuine doctrines of Jesus . . . will again be restored to their original purity . . . but too late for me to witness it."[371] *Too late for him to witness it*, he said. He made that statement some six years before his miraculous death, and just four years after his death, The Church of Jesus Christ of Latter-day Saints was established within the protective nation he and Adams had helped build.

Standing outside the window where the death scene had taken place, I thought intently about the final words Adams had spoken. There has been much speculation as to why he would have expressed the words "Thomas Jefferson survives" as his dying refrain. Seems quite bizarre. But then I remembered that Brigham Young's dying words were, "Joseph! Joseph! Joseph!" Zina Young,

Brigham's daughter, witnessed the event and stated that her father's final words, together with "the divine look in his face seemed to indicate that he was communicating with his beloved friend, Joseph Smith, the Prophet."[372]

Is it not reasonable to assume that just as Joseph picked up Brigham and took him home, Jefferson, who had passed away a few hours earlier, might have swung by the Adams estate to accompany his old friend home? Were Adams's final words as he lay there dying a declaration that he had seen and identified the spirit of Jefferson? Daniel Webster might have approved of such an interpretation, because he said that "on our fiftieth anniversary . . . while their own names were on all tongues, [Jefferson and Adams] took their flight together to the world of spirits."[373] John Quincy added that while "the mortal vestments" of his father and Jefferson were "sinking into the clod of the valley, their emancipated spirits were ascending to the bosom of their God!"[374]

With this beautiful imagery flowing through my mind, I turned and looked back at the street, where my rental car was parked. I pictured John Marston once again. He had been sitting with John just hours earlier, saying his good-byes, and now he was standing there looking to the heavens at the violent thunderstorm that had marked this fateful day—"The artillery of Heaven," as some later called it.[375] Then something very strange happened. With a final clap of thunder, the rain and storm immediately ceased, and the sun broke through the clouds. According to Marston, the sunlight began "bursting forth . . . with uncommon splendor."[376]

I tried to imagine the final clap of thunder, followed by the stunning sunburst breaking through the rain clouds. According to Marston, this strange weather event occurred exactly "at the moment of [Adams's] exit . . . with a sky beautiful and grand beyond description."[377] I imagined Adams and Jefferson passing together into the world of spirits at that splendid moment.

The Adams Home

◆ ◆ ◆

Usually, the story would end here. But in the case of Adams and Jefferson, it does not. For they are two of the very few in history whose activities in the afterlife have been documented. Remember, these two were light seekers. They had identified the Apostasy; they had sought a restoration. Most importantly, they had looked forward to the blessings of eternal marriage that would be made possible only in the forthcoming temples of God. They had laid the foundation for these temples to come to earth. And the temples did come. And one in particular plays a significant role in our story—the St. George Utah Temple.

August 1877.

The temple president was Apostle Wilford Woodruff, who received a stunning revelation. Along with George Washington, the signers of the Declaration of Independence appeared to Elder Woodruff in the temple. He recorded the following:

> Two weeks before I left St. George, the spirits of the dead gathered around me, wanting to know why we did not redeem them. Said they, "You have had the use of the

Endowment House for a number of years, and yet nothing has ever been done for us. We laid the foundation of the government you now enjoy, and we never apostatized from it, but we remained true to it and were faithful to God." . . . I straightway went into the baptismal font and called upon Brother McAllister to baptize me for the signers of the Declaration of Independence, and fifty other eminent men.[378]

On the same day these ordinances were performed . . . Sister Lucy Bigelow Young went forth into the font and was baptized for . . . seventy (70) of the eminent women of the world.[379]

In an effort to express that the above event was not some invention of mind or a formalistic rite of passage, Elder Woodruff recorded that he spoke with these individuals (he uses the word *argued*) and that they "pled" to him that their ordinances be done "as a man pleading for his life." Later, upon performing the baptisms, Elder Woodruff noted that it seemed as if "the room was filled as with flaming fire."[380]

Elder Woodruff recorded in his journal, as well as in the annals of the St. George Temple, the names of these people whose work was done pursuant to the heavenly visitation. I saw the list. And when I did, four names jumped out at me as if they had been written in bold print: *John* and *Abigail Adams. Thomas* and *Martha Jefferson.*[382]

It appears as though they received what they sought, what they deserved, what they built. They had fulfilled their roles as gatherers of Israel and forerunners of the Restoration and were now receiving their just reward.

A PROPHET'S TESTIMONY

More than two decades after the St. George Temple vision, Wilford Woodruff, now President of the Church, stood at the April 1898 general conference and made one final declaration about what had happened: "Another thing I am going to say here, because I have a right to say it," the prophet stated. "Every one of those men that signed the Declaration of Independence, with General Washington, called upon me, as an Apostle of the Lord Jesus Christ, in the Temple at St. George, two consecutive nights, and demanded at my hands that I should go forth and attend to the ordinances of the House of God for them."[381]

◆　◆　◆

My heart was full that quiet morning, standing alone outside the Adams home. I considered one final thought John had had on his last day in mortality. When someone mentioned to the semi-conscious man that it was the Fourth, he smiled and answered clearly, "It is a great day. It is a *good* day."[383] For him, it certainly was. He was about to reunite for the final time with the love of his life. Never to part again. A sign near the house identified a fact that I had forgotten but that matched that Fourth of July perfectly. It also matched what I was feeling that morning. The Adams had named their estate *Peacefield*.

I thought I had seen everything I had come to see that morning, but I decided to walk around the entire house, just in case. Moments later, I bumped into what I thought most certainly was a tomb. That was what it looked like standing very near the main house. Upon closer examination, though, I learned it was a library. As a lover of books, I was deeply intrigued. I wanted to go inside. *Perhaps there is a window open*, I thought. *Perhaps I can just sneak in for a peek.* I quickly realized that if caught, the newspaper headline wouldn't read "Author Innocently Sneaks into Library to Peek at Old Books"; rather, it would read "Government Agent Breaks into Adams Home to Steal State Secrets." I would just have to come back.

It wasn't long after that trip that I was standing in that library (in the middle of the day this time) on a tour led by an Adams House docent. Built by John Quincy in 1873, after his parents had passed, the library houses some fourteen thousand volumes belonging to John Quincy and his father. I learned these facts standing inside the structure and admiring the two levels (a ladder takes the reader to the upper deck) of old, awesome-looking books.

After the brief presentation, someone in the tour group raised a hand and asked the guide, "What is the most fascinating book in this collection?"

Without hesitation, the guide turned and picked up the book that sat at the head of the large reading table that served as the centerpiece of the library. "I would say it is this one," the guide replied, holding it up.

Were my eyes deceiving me? Nope. As I lived and breathed, I was looking at an early edition copy of the Book of Mormon. I looked around at the tour group, wanting to share this amazing moment with someone. No one else seemed much impressed. I adjusted my position to see the faces of the few LDS friends who had traveled with me to Peacefield that day.

Good, I thought, *I'm not the only one wide-eyed and jaw-dropped.*

"Mormon founder Joseph Smith," the guide stated, "signed and gifted this copy of the Book of Mormon to John Adams's grandson Charles Francis Adams, who then placed the book here."

She opened to the front of the book and showed us the prophet's signature. I asked her why she thought that was the most interesting book in the library. She did not know. She said it was just intriguing to her. Apparently, it was intriguing to other docents as well. Of the thousands of books in the library, only one sat at the head of the main table (at least on the day I visited). It was the Book of Mormon—the stick of Joseph.

The docent allowed us to take a closer look at the book. I confirmed that it was an 1841-edition copy of the Book of Mormon, signed by Joseph Smith, with a date of May 15, 1844. Curiously (and for reasons unexplained), the spine of the book had a name printed on it: *Emma Smith*. Under Joseph's signature was the following inscription:

THE ADAMS HOUSE BOOK OF MORMON

In May 1844, just weeks before Joseph Smith was murdered, the famed statesman Charles Francis Adams, grandson to John Adams, visited Nauvoo. He wanted to meet the so-called prophet who was running for the US presidency at the time. Adams was accompanied by his cousin—and one-time mayor of Boston—Josiah Quincy. Adams described Joseph as "unshaved and in clothes neither very choice nor neat."

Joseph was anxious to teach the visitors about the restoration of the gospel. He showed them the mummies he possessed, which he explained carried the words of Abraham, and as it rained outside, he also took them in his carriage to visit the temple, still under construction. Adams described the temple as "original" and "curious." "The prophet," he later wrote, "seems to have drawn his ideas largely from the Jewish system."

When Adams listened to the prophet and others talk of the persecution the Saints had suffered, he described it as "one of the most disgraceful chapters in the dark history of slavery in the United States."

When his long visit with the prophet was over, Adams was left surprised and confused. The usually overly verbose grandson of the second president was left largely speechless. "There is a mixture of . . . knowledge and ignorance,"

The Book of Mormon Given to Charles Francis Adams, May 15, 1844

Adams wrote, "of wisdom and folly in this whole system of this man that I am somewhat at a loss to find definitions for it."

Josiah Quincy concurred, writing that if one did not know what to make of Smith, "I myself stand helpless before the puzzle."

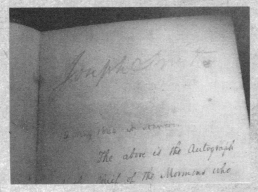

Joseph Smith's Signature inside Adams's Copy of the Book of Mormon

As the visitors left to board their ferry, Joseph accompanied them to the landing, where he gave Adams the copy of the Book of Mormon.

"You have too much power to be safely trusted to one man," Quincy barked at Joseph.

With a smile on his face, Joseph replied that he agreed that one man should not have the power he possessed. Then he confidently said, "I am the only man in the world whom it would be safe to trust with it. Remember, I am a prophet!"[384]

"The above is the autograph of the Chief of the Mormons who gave me this book at Nauvoo in Illinois on the 15th of May 1844. —C. F. Adams."

As we exited the library, I immediately recognized how fitting it was that the Book of Mormon held a place of honor at the Adams home. I thought of the angel Moroni, that prominent character in the book who supported, helped, and guided the American cause. According to the Apostle Orson Hyde, the "angel [Moroni] was with Columbus, and gave him deep impressions, by dreams and by visions, respecting this New World."[385] Elder Hyde also stated that Moroni was "in the camp of Washington."[386] Not coincidentally, both Columbus's discovery of the New World and Washington's fight for independence are recorded as prophecies in that same Book of Mormon sitting in the Adams library (see 1 Nephi 13). I wondered if Adams, Jefferson, and the others also felt his influence. I thought about the fact that as Adams and Jefferson were dying, the Prophet Joseph had already begun his regular tutorials on the Hill Cumorah from the same angel Moroni, or "Prince of America," as the Apostle called him.[387]

The angel Moroni had passed the torch—instead of tutoring national covenant makers, he was now preparing priesthood covenant makers. Instead of tutoring pilgrims, he was now preparing prophets. The Restoration was coming! Temples were coming!

The Adams House Book of Mormon

◆ ◆ ◆

On December 22, 1820, during the bicentennial celebration of the founding of the Mayflower Compact, statesman Daniel Webster (that same Webster who so eloquently eulogized John Adams) gave a speech in which he famously invoked the American covenant. He emphasized the covenant's promised blessings, even "those principles of civil and religious liberty," which he concluded had come to America only through the early settlers' great sacrifice and endurance. He then exhorted his fellow Americans "to transmit the great inheritance unimpaired" that all in the future might enjoy these same blessings.[388] And finally, he acknowledged that this national covenant was brought to us by and through Jesus Christ (even He whom Latter-day Saints recognize was crowned long before by God the Father as the "God of the land [America]" [Ether 2:12]). Webster concluded:

> Finally, let us not forget the religious character of our origin. Our fathers were brought hither by their high veneration for the Christian religion. They journeyed by its light, and labored in its hope. They sought to incorporate its principles with the elements of their society, and to diffuse its influence through all their institutions, civil, political, or literary. Let us cherish these sentiments, and extend this influence still more widely; in the full conviction, that this is the happiest society which partakes in the highest degree of the mild and peaceful spirit of Christianity.[389]

One of the sons of these God-fearing, Christ-loving New England settlers was John Adams. And John *knew* it. He knew he had sprung from America's first settlers. He carried their blood in his veins, their legacy in his mind, and their spirit in his heart. He said of Webster's speech that "if there be an American who can read it without tears, I am not that American. . . . It ought to be read at the end of every . . . year, for ever and ever."[390]

John Adams, Son of the Pilgrim Fathers

Conclusion

Provincetown, Cape Cod, Massachusetts

What does all this mean? What's the point? What's the application?

I have a tendency to feverishly plow through stories, evidence, and documents, excited to make historical connections, excited about the questions I have gathered in my studies. But eventually, I come up for air, take a breath, internalize, and seek to answer my questions.

I have found that the most effective way to do this is to look toward my children. After all, they are the next generation. They are the future torchbearers. If our children can't answer these questions, we have all failed, and it will have all been for naught. And if ever there was a time to share these stories and convert the next generation to the applied principles of these stories, it's now.

A recent study revealed the rather depressing fact that 59 percent of millennials raised in a church (any church) have since fallen away from that religion. With only 20 percent of this next generation (Americans under 30) believing church is worthwhile, our national faith is at an all-time low.[391] If we don't turn this trend around, the power of the national covenant—the very thing that built the nation and provided the foundation for the gospel that grew out of this nation—will only grow weaker and weaker. Indeed, since our national covenant is powered by the national faith that is in decline, our ability as a nation and a church to assist God in gathering Israel, bringing them to the temple, and opening the portals to eternal life will only become more and more difficult.

This is why I am compelled to share these stories with my children. I need to answer these questions and explain the application of this history with them. Show them. Teach them. Until *they* get it. Until *we* get it together.

As I was finishing the manuscript for this book, I took my fourteen-year-old son, Jimmy, to New England. At daybreak, we set out: Plymouth, Cape Cod, First Encounter Beach, and Corn Hill. It was late at night and dark when we finally reached land's end, the tip of the cape, at the quaint little town appropriately called Provincetown. It was here where the *Mayflower* first dropped anchor until eventually finding Plymouth across the bay.

We found a memorial park that sat against the western shore of the cape, facing the bay—Pilgrims' First Landing Park—which hosted an old plaque that read, "The First Landing Place of the Pilgrims, Nov. 11, 1620. The map in *Mourt's Relation* [that book we discussed earlier, written by Bradford and Winslow, that served as a recruiting tool for other settlers] shows that near this spot the Pilgrims first touched foot on American Soil. Erected by the Research Club of Provincetown 1917."

As I wandered through the small park, I looked up, and Jimmy was gone. Always the extreme explorer, he often wandered off, and I was very used to losing sight of him. As I scanned the landscape through the dark of night, I spotted him near the beach, looking at a flashing light that seemed to be streaming from a source miles away, out in the bay. I walked up to him, my eyes also fixed on the light.

"Has that light moved?" I asked Jimmy. "Is it a boat?"

"If it's a boat," he responded, "it's anchored out there, because that light is not moving."

He then pointed to a jetty made of large rocks that led out in the direction of the light. "Let's go see what it is," he said, already on the move. His mind was made up, and I was too tired to argue.

Before I knew it, we were running and jumping from rock to rock as we made our way into Provincetown Harbor. With nothing but the flashlight on my iPhone, I recognized the obvious danger of moving so rapidly over wet rocks. It was also a bit unsettling that we could see only a few feet in front of us as we made our way. But Jimmy was undeterred; I had to keep up with him.

"I think I know what the light is," I yelled up to Jimmy, out of breath. We had been going straight for about ten minutes, and I was having a hard time matching his energy.

"I think it's the *Mayflower*," I said. "Maybe in its ghost form."

Jimmy looked back at me, rolled his eyes, and kept moving.

"But really, Jim," I said, "you should know the *Mayflower was* docked right out here." I was trying to make some application in this moment.

Ten minutes turned into twenty. Twenty into thirty. The flashing light didn't seem to be getting any closer as we continued to skip over rocks and boulders, falling down from time to time but getting back up and continuing our trek.

"Stop!" I yelled ahead to Jimmy. I didn't want to put an end to this adventure, but I had walked over dozens of ocean breakwaters in my life and had never seen anything like this. I quickly calculated in my mind and determined that we had been hiking across this strange land bridge for close to a mile. And the tide seemed to be rising. I turned around and saw the lights of

Provincetown—our safety. It was so far away. I looked at my cell phone. No service. All of a sudden, I felt alone. I felt concerned.

"What are we doing?" I asked Jimmy, a hint of nervousness in my voice. "What is this place?"

Jimmy just shrugged and smiled, not worried at all. Then he turned his gaze longingly to the west, toward the light.

We were exhausted by the time we got back to Boston around 2:00 a.m. By 7:00 a.m., we were fast asleep on a home-ward-bound plane.

Over the next several months, I thought about my trip with Jimmy, especially our ill-conceived jetty adventure. I decided not to tell him (or my wife) how ill-conceived the adventure had *really* been. My post-trip research told me what I hadn't known that night. The jetty we were on is known as the Provincetown break-water, and it runs almost one-and-a-half miles, bridging the harbor from Provincetown to a piece of marshy land called Long Point (if Cape Cod were a scorpion, Provincetown would be the base of the curved tail, the marshy land the very tip of the stinger). The "stinger" is home to a one-hundred-plus-year-old lighthouse—pre-sumably the light I had pretended was the *Mayflower*.

The bad news: I found posts and articles about how danger-ous the jetty is. People, including children, have found them-selves trapped on the jetty as the tide has risen unexpectedly, and drowning or freezing to death, according to what I learned, was a very real possibility out there. Oops. The good news: this in-formation provided me a perfect teaching opportunity, full of parallels and analogies, to help Jimmy and my other children understand the purpose of this book. (And it helped me better understand too.)

"Remember that light we were chasing at Cape Cod?" I asked Jimmy as he was driving my car. Months had passed since our trip. He was now fifteen years old and had his driver's permit. He was stuck in a seatbelt next to me, and he had no choice but to listen. I *had* him. "It was a lighthouse! Isn't that cool? Built in 1827—seven years after Joseph Smith's first vision" (I was trying to prepare his mind for gospel talk).

"Katherine," I said to my wife, who was sitting in the backseat. "What's that hymn about a lighthouse?"

I hadn't discussed any teaching strategy with her before the car ride, but I knew she would know the hymn. (She knows all of them.) I knew she would sing it. And I knew it would make my point.

"Brightly beams our Father's mercy," she sang, as if on cue, in her beautiful soprano voice.

From his lighthouse evermore
But to us he gives the keeping
Of the lights along the shore.
Let the lower lights be burning;
Send a gleam across the wave.
Some poor fainting, struggling seaman
You may rescue, you may save.

"What's the song about?" I asked Jimmy.

"Missionary work," he replied immediately.

I went in for the kill. "Jim, do you know what I discovered through all that Pilgrim research? It is the story of the gathering of Israel. It was God moving people into place. Bringing Columbus from Spain to the New World. The Pilgrims from Britain to Holland to New England. The pioneers from New England to the West—to the Center Place in Missouri and on to the Rocky Mountains. The Lord gathering His chosen ones from distant lands so that He could build Zion and bring us the Restoration. Bring us the temple!"

I then went on to explain to him how a lot of those physical movements, the physical parts of the gathering I discuss in this book, while not necessarily completed, have largely run their course.

"But that doesn't mean the gathering has ended!" I said, "There is a *spiritual* element to it that we have been called to. And the purpose is always the same, whether physical or spiritual. Whether you are an American Pilgrim in 1620 or a Church member 400 years later. The purpose is still to gather people. To begin a process that will lead them to the temple."

"So, what's the gathering today, for you?" I asked him.

"It's missionary work," he replied. "It's the lighthouse."

He got it!

"Send forth the elders of my church unto the nations which are afar off; unto the islands of the sea; send forth unto foreign lands; call upon all nations" (D&C 133:8). "And they shall fish them . . . and they shall hunt them from every mountain, and from every hill, and out of the holes of the rocks."
—Jeremiah 16:16

As we drove, I reminded Jimmy of an experience we'd had a few weeks before our trip to New England. We were exploring and doing research in Philadelphia when it happened. We were staying in a bed-and-breakfast hotel—an old house dating back to the American colonial period—across the street from Philadelphia's City Tavern, an eighteenth-century pub (still active) where Washington, Adams, Jefferson, and other revolutionary heroes had dined and schemed. The hotel manager informed us that these same revolutionary characters had almost certainly visited the very house where we were residing.

It was past midnight, and I was sound asleep when Jimmy hopped onto my bed and woke me up.

"Dad! Remember this scripture?" He had his triple combination open. "As I was reading my scriptures tonight, I was thinking about what I need to start preparing for . . . and I just opened right to it."

As I slowly awoke to full consciousness, I began to remember clearly. I took out my own set of scriptures and turned to the scripture reference, which I had committed to memory some six years earlier, when Jimmy had been only eight years old. As I opened to the designated page, I saw where I had written *Jimmy* in the margin, right next to the relevant scripture verses so I would not forget what had happened all those years ago.

Katherine and I had just put the younger kids to bed and were enjoying that brief yet wonderful window of opportunity all young couples long for, when the house—usually filled to capacity with the constant noise (laughs, cries, contentions, etc.) of small children and babies—was completely still. That was when Jimmy, my eight-year-old towhead, walked into our home library, where I was sitting.

In his cute, raspy little voice, he said, "Dad! I was praying just now. I asked Heavenly Father if the Church was true. And if it was true, what I should do about it."

He had my undivided attention.

"Then," he said excitedly, "I saw the numbers 1, 5, 3 in my mind."

"What do you think that means?" I asked him.

He shrugged his shoulders.

"Maybe it's a scripture," I said. "Let's look in your new triple combination." (He had just received it as a gift for his baptism.)

We turned directly to Doctrine and Covenants 15:3. I read aloud: "And I will tell you that which no man knoweth save me and thee alone—" I continued reading to the next verses: "For many times you have desired of me to know that which would be of the most worth unto you . . . And now, behold, I say unto you, that the thing which will be of the most worth unto you will be to declare repentance unto this people, that you may bring souls unto me, that you may rest with them in the kingdom of my Father, Amen" (verses 4, 6).

That night, I told Jimmy the same thing I would tell him over six years later as we drove together, talking about our Pilgrim expedition. "Please," I begged him, "never forget this experience Heavenly Father blessed you with the very year you were baptized."

Indeed, this is our mission. To gather Israel. It's the same mission the historical men and women in this book were called to. Yes, the tactics have changed a bit, from an emphasis on the physical gathering to a more spiritual gathering, which I was exploring with Jimmy in the car, but the overall strategy is the same. The goal is the same. The key for us is to take the energy, passion, devotion, and commitment of these early American settlers and patriots and apply them to our shared mission today. To take the torch they have given us and honor their sacrifice by serving that same God who called us all.

In more than one place, the scriptures of the Restoration seem to encourage us to bridge the gap between those historical heroes and us. We have discussed in this book the profound content in 1 Nephi 13. The angel in this account begins by showing Nephi (and us) the Great Apostasy (verses 1–9), then takes him on a prophetic journey to the Restoration. Nephi sees the discoverers (verses 12), settlers (verses 13–16, 20–23), and revolutionaries (verses 17–19) we have discussed in this book as they build the foundation for freedom. The chapter then ends with the

Restoration—it ends with us!—where the fulness of the gospel abides (verses 34–42). And it is here in the chapter where the Lord, through Nephi, leaves us, his readers, in the here and now, with a clear and direct call to action: "And blessed are they who shall seek to bring forth my Zion at that day . . . and whoso shall publish peace, yea, tidings of great joy, how beautiful upon the mountains shall they be" (1 Nephi 13:37). From them to us. One mission under God.

There is something else interesting about this book of Nephi. As we know, this book came to us as a contingency plan. After Joseph Smith lost the 116 pages of the Book of Mormon manuscript, the Lord made it known that among the gold plates, there existed this separate book of Nephi that would fill in that which was lost. In Doctrine and Covenants 10 (one of the very first times we see the Lord provide commentary on the content of the Book of Mormon), we learn why the Lord was desirous for the book of Nephi to come out.

"Behold," the Lord said, "there are many things engraven upon the plates of Nephi which do throw greater views upon my gospel." The Lord explained that the Nephites' "faith in their prayers was that this gospel should be made known also, if it were possible that other nations should possess this land; and thus they did leave a blessing upon this land in their prayers, that whosoever should believe in this gospel in this land might have eternal life; yea, that it might be free unto all of whatsoever nation, kindred, tongue, or people they may be" (D&C 10:45, 49–51).

The Lord then opened Joseph's mind to his day and generation, stating, "And now, behold, according to their [the Nephites'] faith in their prayers will I bring this part of my gospel to the knowledge of my people. Behold, I do not bring it to destroy that which they have received, but to build it up . . . Now I do not say

this to destroy my church, but I say this to build up my church"
(D&C 10:52, 54).

The pattern from 1 Nephi 13 is repeated: A blessed and
choice land. A free land to all those who possess it. And then the
fulness of the gospel, even the Restoration. This revelation was
given in 1828, two years after Adams and Jefferson died. Two
years *before* the Church was established. So what church was the
Lord referring to that was already in existence, which church
would not be destroyed but would now be added upon and built
up? I can't help but think of those forerunners of the Restoration.
That group, that church of religious adherents—the discoverers,
the settlers, the patriots. They fulfilled the prayers and prophecies
of the Nephites. They came to the promised land under God, and
they laid the covenant foundation that brought us the fulness of
the gospel—temples in the land. The Lord has now called us to
add our history to theirs.

"I am the light which shineth in darkness," the Lord said
just a few verses later, "and the darkness comprehendeth it not"
(D&C 10:58).

The light.

My mind often goes back to the light Jimmy and I were
running to as we slipped and stumbled over the wet and rocky
Provincetown breakwater. My focus is on Jimmy and the next
generation. Like the pilgrims and pioneers before him, I see him
on his trek toward the light. Like them, I see him making the
commitment to take the journey. I see him march way beyond
the safety and security of the town, leaving behind the material
things. Those comfortable lights become smaller and smaller on
that distant shore. This is difficult. It's scary at times. I see him
fall, then get back up, trusting in the Lord and His miracles. I
see him trekking over the rocks, dressed in a white shirt and tie.

A missionary badge. I see him later, farther down the breakwater, dressed in white, an eternal companion at his side. Further on, I see him running behind his own child, who has now set out on the trek.

Walking, running, falling, then getting up again. Enduring. Sometimes only able to see the next couple steps ahead. But always moving toward the goal, like the *Mayflower*. Moving toward that light. That mission. That calling. Reaching for what the Pilgrims and prophets reached for—God's covenants.

A Call to Action: What Is Your Mayflower?

Notes

Contents

1 *Oxford Dictionaries*, s.v. "Pilgrim," https://en.oxforddictionaries.com/definition/pilgrim.

Foreword

2 Rebecca Frasier, *The Mayflower: The Families, the Voyage, and the Founding of America* (New York: St. Martin's Press, 2017), 64.

3 The full account is given in the Editorial Preface of Bradford, *History of Plymouth Plantation*; see also Francis B. Dedmond, "A Forgotten Attempt to Rescue the Bradford Manuscript," *The New England Quarterly* 58. No. 2 (June, 1985): 242–252; Thomas R. Turner and Jennifer A. Turner, "Abraham Lincoln and the Plymouth Forefathers Monument," *The Bridgewater Review* 22, Issue 2 (December 2003).

Introduction

4 Sewall proposed the place of the New Jerusalem using a trajectory from New England toward Mexico. Depending on what Sewall understood about the vast territories of "Mexico" at the time, such a trajectory would likely include, in Sewall's mind, territory over the middle of North America, perhaps directly over Missouri itself. Samuel Sewall, and Reiner Smolinski, "*Phaenomena Quaedam Apocalyptica Ad Aspectum Novi Orbis Configurata. Or, Some Few Lines*

towards a Description of the New Heaven (1697) 32, 43," DigitalCommons@ University of Nebraska – Lincoln, accessed September 23, 2019, https://digitalcommons.unl.edu/cgi/viewcontent.cgi?article=1025&context=etas. See Eve LaPlante. *Salem Witch Judge* (New York: HarperCollins, 2008), 207–208. More on this, including how the "revelation" came to Sewall, will be discussed in chapter 4.

5 D&C 28; 42:8–9, 34–36; 45:66–67; 52:2, 42–43; 57:1–5; 58:7, 44–58; 84:2–5

6 *The Encyclopedia of Mormonism,* Vol. 2, Daniel Ludlow, ed. (New York: Macmillan Publishing Company, 1992), 536.

7 Joseph Smith, "History, 1838–1856, volume D-1 [1 August 1842–1 July 1843], Page 1572," *The Joseph Smith Papers*, accessed September 03, 2017, http://www.josephsmithpapers.org/paper-summary/history-1838-1856-volume-d-1-1-august-1842-1-july-1843/217.

8 Ezra Taft Benson, "A Message to Judah from Joseph," The Church of Jesus Christ of Latter-day Saints, May 2, 1976, https://www.churchofjesuschrist.org/study/ensign/1976/12/a-message-to-judah-from-joseph?lang=eng.; N. Eldon Tanner. "If They Will But Serve the God of the Land." The Church of

Jesus Christ of Latter-day Saints, April 3, 1976. https://www.churchofjesuschrist.org/study/general-conference/1976/04/if-they-will-but-serve-the-god-of-the-land?lang=eng.

9   *Gospel Principles* (Salt Lake City: The Church of Jesus Christ of Latter-day Saints, 2009), 248.

10 For declarations in the Book of Mormon that the Nephites were from Joseph, see 2 Nephi 3:4–5; Jacob 2:25; Alma 10:3; Alma 26:36; Alma 46:24; 3 Nephi 15:12.

11 To learn more regarding both the scriptural and historical evidence that the referenced "Stick of Joseph" or "Stick of Ephraim" is in fact the Book of Mormon, read Matthew Brown, *All Things Restored: Evidences and Witnesses of the Restoration* (American Fork: Covenant Communications, 2000), 186–190.

12 Examples include Isaiah 50–53; Jeremiah 3; 18; Ezekiel 6:8–10; 11–12; 36 and many others.

13 Examples include 2 Nephi 10; Jacob 5, and many others.

14 Prophesies of the latter-day gathering include 1 Kings 22:17; Jeremiah 31:7–12; 32:37–40; Ezekiel 36:24, and many others.

15 Joseph Smith, "History, 1838–1856, volume E-1 [1 July 1843–30 April 1944]," *The Joseph Smith Papers*, accessed September 3, 2017, https://www.josephsmithpapers.org/paper-summary/history-1838-1856-volume-e-1-1-july-1843-30-april-1844/354.

16 Abraham Lincoln, "Abraham Lincoln 16th President of the United States: 1861–1865 Second Annual Message," The American Presidency Project. UC Santa Barbara, December 1, 1862, https://www.presidency.ucsb.edu/documents/second-annual-message-9.

17 Erastus Snow, "Journal of Discourses, 23:186–187, May 6, 1882," BYU Digital Collections, Brigham Young University, 2004, https://contentdm.lib.byu.edu/digital/collection/JournalOfDiscourses3/id/1534/rec/23.

18 Russell M. Nelson, "A Treasured Testament," *Ensign,* July 1993.

19 Rabbi Ken Spiro, "The Impact of the Bible #3: In God We Trust," Aish.com, March 18, 2000, https://www.aish.com/jl/jnj/jn/48925797.html.; Ryan S. Gardner, "A History of the Concepts of Zion and New Jerusalem in America from Early Colonialism to 1835 with a Comparison to the Teachings of Joseph Smith," ScholarsArchive, Brigham Young University, September 2002, https://scholarsarchive.byu.edu/cgi/viewcontent.cgi?article=5705&context=etd. p.38,45; Robert Cushman, "The Sin and Danger of Self-Love," The Project Gutenberg eBook of *The Sin and Danger of Self-Love Described, in a Sermon Preached at Plymouth, in New-England, 1621,* Gutenberg.org, October 30, 2013, http://www.gutenberg.org/files/44071/44071-h/44071-h.htm#FNanchor_A_2.

Chapter 1

20 Ibid.

21 Gordon B. Hinckley stated: "That verse from Nephi's vision states: 'And I looked and beheld a man among the Gentiles, who was separated from the seed of my brethren by the many waters; and I beheld the Spirit of God, that it came down and wrought upon the man; and he went forth upon the many waters, even unto the seed of my brethren, who were in the promised land' (1 Ne. 13:12). We interpret that to refer to Columbus. It is interesting to note that the Spirit of God wrought upon him. After reading that long biography, a Pulitzer winner of forty years ago, titled *Admiral of the Ocean Sea*—I have no doubt that Christopher Columbus was a man of faith, as well as a man of indomitable determination." Gordon B.

Hinckley, "Building Your Tabernacle," General Conference, The Church of Jesus Christ of Latter-day Saints, accessed August 03, 2017, https://www.lds.org/general-conference/1992/10/building-your-tabernacle.p52?lang=eng.

22 Salvador de Madariaga, *Christopher Columbus: Being the Life of the Very Magnificent Lord Don Cristobal Colón* (London: Hollis & Carter, 1949), 16.

23 Delno C. West and August Kling, *The Libro de las profecías of Christopher Columbus* (Gainesville: University of Florida Press, 1991), 105.

24 West and Kling, *Libro de las profecías,* 3.

25 Laurence Bergreen, *Columbus: The Four Voyages, 1492-1504* (New York: Penguin Books, 2012), 61.

26 Kirkpatrick Sale, *The Conquest of Paradise: Christopher Columbus and the Columbian Legacy* (New York: Plume, 1992), 67.

27 Dan Carlinsky, "Christopher Confusion," *Modern Maturity*, February–March 1992, 52.

28 West and Kling, *Libro de las profecías*, 105.

29 Kay Brigham, *Christopher Columbus's Book of Prophecies: Reproduction of the Original Manuscript with English Translation* (Ft. Lauderdale: Libros CLIE, 1991), 180.

30 Bartolomé De Las Casas, *The Diario of Christopher Columbus's First Voyage to America, 1492–1493*, trans. Oliver Dunn and James E. Kelley, Jr. (Norman, OK: University of Oklahoma Press, 1988), 144.

31 De Las Casas, et al., *The Diario of Christopher Columbus's First Voyage to America*, 291.

32 Charles Edwards Lester and Andrew Foster, *The Life and Voyages of Americus Vespuccius with Illustrations Conerning the Navigator, and the Discovery of the New World* (New Haven, CT: H. Mansfield, 1853), 87–88.

33 West and Kling, *Libro de las profecías,* 111.

34 Peter Marshal and David Manual, *The Light and the Glory* (Grand Rapids: Revell, 2009), 45.

35 As quoted in Bergreen, *The Four Voyages*, 83.

36 Bergreen, *The Four Voyages*, 77, 80.

37 Kathleen Deagan and José María Cruxent, *Columbus's Outpost among the Taínos* (New Haven: Yale University Press, 2002), 16–19.

38 Bergreen, *The Four Voyages,* 148.

39 Deagan and Cruxent, *Columbus's Outpost among the Taínos,* 53–61.

40 Bergreen, *The Four Voyages*, 204, 212.

41 Edward Everett Hale, *The Life of Christopher Columbus: From His Own Letters and Journals* (Chicago, IL: G.L. Howe & Co., 1891), 64–65.

42 Bergreen, *The Four Voyages*, 133–135, 140, 167.

43 Samuel Eliot Morrison, *The Great Explorers: The European Discovery of America* (New York: Oxford University Press, 1978), 454.

44 Hugh Nibley, *Temple and Cosmos: Beyond This Ignorant Present* (Salt Lake City: Deseret Book Company, 1992), 31.

45 Carol Delaney, "Columbus's Ultimate Goal: Jerusalem," in *Comparative Studies in Society and History* 48 (Cambridge, UK: Cambridge University Press, 2006): 261, 287.

46 Leonard Sweet, "Christopher Columbus and the Millennial Vision of the New World," *The Catholic Historical Review* 72, no. 3 (1986): 381.

47 In General Conference, April 1843, Joseph Smith prophesied that before the coming of the Lord, the temple at Jerusalem would be restored. See *History of the Church*, 1:196; from "History of the Church" (manuscript), book A-1, 137, Church Archives.; "Discourse, 6 April 1843–B, as reported by Willard Richards, Page 75," *The Joseph Smith*

Papers, accessed September 03, 2017, http://www.josephsmithpapers.org/paper-summary/discourse-6-april-1843-b-as-reported-by-willard-richards/12. That a temple will be built in the New Jerusalem in America is prophesied, among other places, in D&C 84:4–5, D&C 57:3.

48 Joseph Fielding Smith, *The Progress of Man* (Salt lake City: Deseret News Press, 1936), 258.

49 Kay Brigham, *Book of Prophecies*, 17; West and Kling, *Libro de las profecías*, 85.

50 West and Kling, *Libro de las profecías*, 49, 105.

51 West and Kling, *Libro de las profecías*, 229.

52 West and Kling, *Libro de las profecías*, 111.

53 Arnold K. Garr, "Christopher Columbus: Man of Destiny," Religious Studies Center, Brigham Young University, 2005, https://rsc.byu.edu/archived/window-faith-latter-day-saint-perspectives-world-history/columbus-man-destiny.

54 John Boyd Thacher, *Christopher Columbus: His Life, His Work, His Remains as Revealed by Original Printed and Manuscript Records Together with an Essay on Peter Martyr of Anghera and Bartolomé De Las Casas, the First Historians of America, Vol. III* (New York and London: G.P. Putnam's Sons & The Knickerbocker Press, 1904), 456–457.

55 "Chart of Juan De La Cosa: The First Known Map of America—Google Arts & Culture," *Google*, accessed October 2, 2019, https://artsandculture.google.com/story/IgJCiowwoJqZIQ.

56 West and Kling, *Libro de las profecías*, 111.

57 West and Kling, *Libro de las profecías*, 217.

58 Isaiah 2:2–3; During the Idaho Falls dedicatory prayer, George Albert Smith prayed the following: "We thank thee that thou hast revealed to us that those who gave us our constitutional form of government were wise in thy sight and that thou didst raise them up for the very purpose of putting forth that sacred document . . . We pray that kings and rulers and the peoples of all nations . . . may be constrained to adopt similar governmental systems, thus to fulfill the ancient prophecy of Isaiah and Micah that "out of Zion shall go forth the law and the word of the Lord from Jerusalem." George Albert Smith, "Idaho Falls Temple Dedicatory Prayer," *Improvement Era*, October 1945, 564; "1 Kings–Malachi," in *Old Testament Student Manual* (Salt Lake: The Church of Jesus Christ of Latter-day Saints, 2003), 138–139.

59 West and Kling, *Libro de las profecías*, 67–68.

60 D&C 116:1, 84:1–5.

61 West and Kling, *Libro de las profecías*, 18.

62 West and Kling, *Libro de las profecías*, 68.

63 West and Kling, *Libro de las profecías*, 60.

64 *Encyclopedia of Mormonism*, Vol. 3, Daniel Ludlow, ed. (New York: Macmillan Publishing, 1992), 1009.

65 Bruce R. McConkie, "Lesson 151: Ether 13–15," *Book of Mormon Seminary Teacher Manuel*. The Church of Jesus Christ of Latter-day Saints, accessed December 27, 2019. https://www.churchofjesuschrist.org/study/manual/book-of-mormon-seminary-teacher-manual-2013-obs/ether/lesson-151?lang=eng.

66 Frank Graziano, *The Millennial New World* (New York: Oxford University Press, 1999), 28; reference to Isaiah 65 quoted in West and Kling, *Libro de las profecías*, 183.

67 West and Kling, *Libro de las profecías*, 165.

68 Harold B. Lee, "Strengthen the

Stakes of Zion," The Church of
Jesus Christ of Latter-day Saints, accessed August 13, 2017, https://
www.lds.org/ensign/1973/07/
strengthen-the-stakes-of-zion?lang=eng.

69 *Old Testament Student Manual*,
191–200.

70 *Old Testament Student Manual*, 83–87.;
"Zion—The Guide to the Scriptures."
LDS Gospel Library. The Church of
Jesus Christ of Latter-day Saints, accessed December 22, 2019. https://
www.churchofjesuschrist.org/study/
scriptures/gs/zion?lang=eng.

71 Bergreen, *The Four Voyages*, 26.

72 Joseph Smith—History 1:40–41.

73 Delno C. West and Jean M. West,
*Christopher Columbus: The Great
Adventure and How We Know about It*
(New York: Atheneum, 1991), 1–3.

74 Bergreen, *The Four Voyages*, 61–63.

75 West and Kling, *Libro de las profecías*,
25–27.

76 De Las Casas, et al., *The Diario of
Christopher Columbus's First Voyage to
America*, 41.

77 De Las Casas, et al., *The Diario of
Christopher Columbus's First Voyage to
America*, 59.

78 Ferdinand Columbus, *The Life of the
Admiral Christopher Columbus by his Son
Ferdinand*, trans. Benjamin Keen (New
Brunswick: Rutgers University Press,
1959), 59.

79 Washington Irving, "The Life and
Voyages of Christopher Columbus," *The
Works of Washington Irving* 6 (New York:
Peter Fenelon Collier, 1866), 264–266.

80 E. D. Partridge, "The Three Nephites,"
The Improvement Era, June 1909,
621–624.

81 Ferdinand Columbus, *The Life of the
Admiral*, 91.

82 Ferdinand Columbus, *The Life of the
Admiral*, 92.

83 Christopher Columbus, *The Log of
Christopher Columbus*, trans. Robert H.
Fuson (Camden, ME.: International

Marine Publishing Company, 1992),
174.

84 Ferdinand Columbus, *The Life of the
Admiral*, 91, 97.

85 Peter Marshall and David Manual, *The
Light and the Glory: 1492–1793* (Grand
Rapids, MI: Revell, 2009), 49–53.

86 Ferdinand Columbus, *The Life of the
Admiral*, 91, 98.

87 Francesco Tarducci, *The Life of
Christopher Columbus*, trans. Henry F.
Brownson (Detroit: H. F. Brownson,
1890), 231.

88 Bergreen, *The Four Voyages*, 113.

89 Bergreen, *The Four Voyages*, 251–252.

90 Bergreen, *The Four Voyages*, 275–277.

91 Bergreen, *The Four Voyages*, 282.

92 Bergreen, *The Four Voyages*, 301–303.

93 Ferdinand Columbus, *The Life of the
Admiral*, 228–229.

94 "DNA Verifies Columbus' Remains
in Spain, Spanish Bones Linked to
Explorer, but Dominican Claim Could
Still be Valid," *NBC News Report*,
May 29, 2006, accessed September
2, 2017, http://www.nbcnews.com/
id/12871458/ns/technology_and_sci-
ence-science/t/dna-verifies-colum-
bus-remains-spain/#.WP4gSpF1oUU;
Bergreen, *The Four Voyages*, 363–364.

95 Tad Walch, "In Jerusalem, Mormon
apostles and Jewish leaders like
Joe Lieberman remember Orson
Hyde prayer," DeseretNews.
com, October 28, 2016, accessed
August 03, 2017, http://www.de-
seretnews.com/article/865665842/
In-Jerusalem-Mormon-apostles-and-
Jewish-leaders-like-Joe-Lieberman-
remember-Orson-Hyde-prayer.html.
"Orson Hyde's 1841 mission to
Jerusalem to dedicate this land for the
return of the Jews and for Jerusalem to
be its capital city was an important moment in the latter-day Jewish return to
their homeland," Elder Holland said at
the event. "We believe the work of Elder

Orson Hyde has played a key role in God choosing Jerusalem again."

96 Orson Hyde, in *Journal of Discourses*, 6:368. This was given in a speech on July 4, 1854 in the Tabernacle at Temple Square. In the speech, Elder Hyde makes it abundantly clear that he is referring to the Angel Moroni. Elder Hyde describes Columbus' angel as the same "that appeared unto Joseph Smith, and revealed to him the history of the early inhabitants of this country."

97 West and Kling, *Libro de las profecías*, 54; D&C 20:1.

98 West and Kling, *Libro de las profecías*, 54–55.

99 Hyde, in *Journal of Discourses*, 7:108. The quote here is from a speech Elder Hyde gave on July 4, 1853. Though Hyde doesn't mention Moroni by name in this speech, instead referring to "the Spirit Angel," we know he is referring to Moroni through another speech he gave on the same subject on July 4, 1854. That speech is documented in *Journals of Discourses*, 6:368.

100 Ezra Taft Benson, "God's Hand in Our Nation's History," BYU Speeches, Brigham Young University, March 28, 1977, https://speeches.byu.edu/talks/ezra-taft-benson/gods-hand-nations-history/.

101 Truman G. Madsen, *Presidents of the Church: Insights into Their Lives and Teachings* (Salt Lake City: Deseret Book Publishing, 2004), 104–105.

102 Brian H. Stuy, "Wilford Woodruff's Vision of the Signers of the Declaration of Independence," *Journal of Mormon History* 26, No. 1 (Spring 2000): 71–72.

103 See also D&C 115:5–6.; Boyd K. Packer, "A Defense and a Refuge," General Conference, The Church of Jesus Christ of Latter-day Saints, October 8, 2006, https://www.churchofjesuschrist.org/study/general-conference/2006/10/a-defense-and-a-refuge?lang=eng.; Patrick Kearon,

"Refuge from the Storm," General Conference, The Church of Jesus Christ of Latter-day Saints, April 3, 2016. https://www.churchofjesuschrist.org/study/general-conference/2016/04/refuge-from-the-storm?lang=eng.

104 Bergreen, *The Four Voyages*, 30, 114.

105 Robert Alexander González, *Designing Pan-America: U.S. Architectural Visions for the Western Hemisphere* (Austin, TX: University of Texas Press, 2011), 102–147.

106 West and Kling, *Libro de las profecías*, 53–54.

107 West and Kling, *Libro de las profecías*, 111; see West and Kling, *Libro de las profecías*, 31, for more on the Abbot Joachim.

108 Bergreen, *The Four Voyages*, 193, 185, 280–281.

109 Bergreen, *The Four Voyages*, 287.

110 Bergreen, *The Four Voyages*, 338, 294, 306, 333.

111 As quoted in Bergreen, *The Four Voyages*, 363, 185.

112 West and Kling, *Libro de las profecías*, 41.

113 Ferdinand Columbus, *The Life of the Admiral*, 284.

114 Discourse by Elder George Q. Cannon, delivered in the Tabernacle, Salt Lake City, August 15, 1869. Reported by David W. Evans, *Journal of Discourses*, 14:55.

Chapter 2

115 Rod Gragg, *The Pilgrim Chronicles: An Eyewitness History of the Pilgrims and the Founding of Plymouth Colony* (Washington, DC: Regnery History, 2014), 87–98.

116 Nick Bunker, *Making Haste from Babylon: The Pilgrims and Their World, A New History* (New York: Alfred A. Knopf, 2010), 218–221.

117 Bunker, *Making Haste From Babylon*, 212,215.; William Bradford, Bradford's History of Plymouth Plantation:

1606-1646, ed. by William T. Davis (New York: Charles Scribners Sons, 1908), 64. https://books.google.com/books?id=uVIWAAAAYAAJ&pg=PA39#v=onepage&q&f=false.

118 Ellen Mackay Hutchinson and Edmund Clarence Stedman, *A Library of American Literature from the Earliest Settlement to the Present Time: in eleven volumes. Vol. 1.* (New York, NY: Charles L Webster & Co., 1892), 130.

119 Rebecca Fraser, *The Mayflower: The Families, the Voyage, and the Founding of America* (New York: St. Martins Press, 2017), 16–18, 28.

120 Gragg, *The Pilgrim Chronicles*, 96–101.; William Bradford, Bradford's History of Plymouth Plantation: 1606-1646, ed. by William T. Davis (New York: Charles Scribners Sons, 1908), 64. https://books.google.com/books?id=uVIWAAAAYAAJ&pg=PA64#v=onepage&q&f=false.; Bunker, Making Haste From Babylon, 230–231.

121 Bunker, 23–24.

122 Patricia Scott Deetz and James Deetz, "Population of Plymouth Town, Colony & County, 1620–1690," Historical Archaeology and Public Engagement Department of Anthropology, The University of Illinois at Urbana-Champaign, accessed December 18, 2019, http://www.histarch.illinois.edu/plymouth/townpop.html.

123 Hutchinson and Stedman, *Library of American Literature*, 131.

124 Paget, *History of the Plymouth Settlement*, 27–28.

125 Bradford, *History of Plymouth Plantation*, 167, 382, 416.

126 "Farefell Letter from John Robinson at Delfshaven August 1620," *American History Told by Contemporaries, Volume 1. Era of Colonization 1492–1689*, ed. Albert Bushnell Hart (New York: Macmillan, 1908), 187.

127 Paget, *History of the Plymouth Settlement*, 66.

128 Paget, *History of the Plymouth Settlement*, 63.

129 Paget, *History of the Plymouth Settlement*, 75–76.

130 John Robinson, *The Works of John Robinson: Pastor of the Pilgrim Fathers, Vol. 2,* ed. Robert Ashton (London: John Snow, 1851), 304.

131 Rebecca Fraser, *The Mayflower*, 16.

132 John Winthrop, "A Model of Christian Charity," The Winthrop Society: Descendants of the Great Migration, April 8, 1630, https://www.winthropsociety.com/doc_charity.php.

133 William Bradford, *History of Plimoth Plantation*, ed. Charles Deane (Boston: Privately printed, 1856), 29.

134 Paget, *History of the Plymouth Settlement*, 17.

135 Edward Winslow and William Bradford, "Primary Sources for 'The First Thanksgiving' at Plymouth," Pilgrim Hall Museum, accessed August 1, 2017, http://www.pilgrimhallmuseum.org/pdf/TG_What_Happened_in_1621.pdf.

136 Barney Kasdan, *God's Appointed Times*, (Maryland: Lederer Books/Messianic Jewish Publishers, 2007), 92.

137 William Bradford, *History of Plymouth Plantation*, ed. Charles Deane (Boston: Privately printed, 1856), xiv.

138 Stephen Birmingham, chapter 10 in *The Jews in America Trilogy* (New York: Open Road Media, 2016), eBook.

139 Cotton Mather, "Life of William Bradford from: *Cotton Mather's Magnalia Christi Americana: or, the Ecclesiastical History of New-England* (Originally Published 1702)," Pilgrim Hall Museum, accessed October 10, 2019, https://pilgrimhall.org/pdf/William_Bradford_Mathers_Magnalia_Christi.pdf.

140 Randy J. Forbes, "H.Res.397—111th Congress (2009–2010): Affirming the Rich Spiritual and Religious History of Our Nation's Founding and

Subsequent History and Expressing Support for Designation of the First Week in May as 'America's Spiritual Heritage Week' for the Appreciation of and Education on America's History of Religious Faith." Congress.gov, Library of Congress, May 4, 2009, https://www.congress.gov/bill/111th-congress/house-resolution/397/text.

141 Ibid.

142 Ibid.

143 Sheldon Rubenfeld, *Medicine After the Holocaust: From the Master Race to the Human Genome and Beyond* (New York: Palgrave Macmillan, 2010), 5.

144 Robinson, *The Works of John Robinson*, xliv.

145 Paget, *History of the Plymouth Settlement*, 1–2.

146 As quoted in Bruce Feiler, *America's Prophet: Moses and the American Story* (New York: William Morrow, 2009), 24.

147 Frazier, *The Mayflower*, 18.

148 Paget, *History of the Plymouth Settlement*, 63.

149 Nathaniel Philbrick, *Mayflower: A Story of Courage, Community, and War* (USA: Viking Penguin, 2007), 356.

150 Nick Bunker, *Making Haste from Babylon: The Mayflower Pilgrims and Their World: A New History* (Great Britain: The Bodley Head, 2010), 59.

151 Paget, *History of the Plymouth Settlement*, 63.

152 Erastus Snow, *Journal of Discourses* 23:186–187, May 6, 1882.

153 Ibid.

154 "A Family Meeting in Nauvoo," *The Utah Genealogical and Historical Magazine*, January 1919, 107; Brigham Young, *Journal of Discourses* 2:269.

155 "Joseph Smith's Family Tree," *Liahona*, December 2005, lds.org/liahona/2005/12/joseph-smiths-family-tree?lang=eng.

156 Daniel Ludlow, "Of the House of Israel," *Ensign*, January 1991, lds.org/ensign/1991/01/0f-the-house-of-israel?land=eng.

157 See 2 Kings 17; "Kingdom of Israel—LDS Bible Dictionary," The Church of Jesus Christ of Latter-day Saints, accessed November 16, 2019, https://www.churchofjesuschrist.org/study/scriptures/bd/israel-kingdom-of?lang=eng&clang=eng#p1.

158 Joseph Fielding McConkie and Donald W. Parry, *A Guide to Scriptural Symbols* (Salt Lake City, UT: Bookcraft, 1990), 45. McConkie and Parry also point out that often "the east wind is a destructive wind" God uses to rebuke his people. Interestingly, the tribe of Ephraim had been rebuked for breaching their covenant, which is why they were pushed out of ancient Israel in the first place, theoretically in a westerly direction (the same direction as an east wind).

159 See *Apocrypha*, 2 Esdras 13:39–47.

160 George Reynolds, *Are We of Israel?* (Salt Lake City, UT: Deseret Sunday School Union, 1948), 10–11.

161 See Terry Blodgett, "Tracing the Dispersion," *Ensign*, February 1994, https://www.lds.org/ensign/1994/02/tracing-the-dispersion?lang=eng#footnote18–94902_000_032. Additional evidence that supports an Israelite migration into Europe is found within this article.

162 Flavius Josephus, *The Antiquities of the Jews* (Book XI, 5:2), trans. William Whiston, accessed November 14, 2019, http://www.gutenberg.org/files/2848/2848-h/2848-h.htm#link112HCH0005.

163 Robert L. Millet and Joseph Fielding McConkie, *Our Destiny: The Call and Election of the House of Israel* (Sandy, UT: Leatherwood, 2006), 136.

164 Deane, *History of Plymouth Plantation*, 29.

165 *LDS Bible Dictionary*, s.v. "Gentile."

166 "Proposal for the Great Seal of the United States," National Archives

and Records Administration, accessed November 16, 2019, https://founders.archives.gov/documents/Franklin/01-22-02-0330.; Martin, Russell. "Seal of the United States." Monticello - Thomas Jefferson Encyclopedia, June 6, 1989. https://www.monticello.org/site/research-and-collections/seal-united-states.

167 Evidence that supports British-Israelitism goes much deeper than we can discuss here. It includes written records, ancient folklore, artifacts (to include grave-markers), and even DNA. There are also scholars who oppose the idea. The pros and cons to the argument can all be studied and vetted out in scholarly works written by respected modern historians and geneticists. Such works include Dr. David Goldstein's, *Jacob's Legacy: A Genetic View of Jewish History;* genealogist Donald Yates's, *When Scotland Was Jewish: DNA Evidence, Archeology, Analysis of Migrations, and Public and Family Records*; geneticist A. E. Mourant's, *The Genetics of the Jews*; historian Jon Entine's, *Abraham's Children: Race, Identity, and the DNA of the Chosen People*; J. H. Allen, *Judah's Scepter and Joseph's Birthright*; E. Raymond Capt, *King Solomon's Temple: A Study of Its Symbolism* and *Jacob's Pillar: A Biblical Historical Study*; Steven M. Collins, *The Lost Ten Tribes of Israel, Found*; and Yair Davidy, *Lost Israelite Identity* and *Hebrew Ancestry of Celtic Races.*

168 To corroborate Spykerman, see Vaughn E. Hansen, *Whence Came They? Israel, Britain, and the Restoration* (Springville, UT: Cedar Fort, 1993), 74–75.

169 Leslie Pearson Rees, *Ye Have Been Hid: Finding the Lost Tribes of Israel* (Salt Lake City, UT: Digital Legend Press and Publishing, 2011), 254.

170 Rees, *Ye Have Been Hid*, 260.

171 Terry Blodgett, "Tracing the Dispersion," *Ensign*, February 1994, https://www.lds.org/ensign/1994/02/tracing-the-dispersion?lang=eng#footnote18–94902_000_032.

172 Vern Grosvenor Swanson, *Dynasty of the Holy Grail: Mormonism's Sacred Bloodline* (Springville, UT: Cedar Fort, Inc., 2006), 139–140; Rees, *Ye Have Been Hid*, 142–143; Edward Odlum, *God's Covenant Man: British-Israel* (London: Robert Banks and Sons, 1916), 73–74.

173 Edward Odlum, *God's Covenant Man*, 73–74.

174 W. H. Bennett, "The Story of Celto-Saxon Israel," Evangelistic Two-House Information Center, accessed August 17, 2017, http://www.israelite.info/book-excerpts/storyofceltosaxonisrael.html.; Raymond F. McNair, "The Origin of the Saxons," Hope of Israel Ministries, http://www.hope-of-israel.org/saxonorigins.html.

175 Rees, *Ye Have Been Hid*, 142–143.

176 Hansen, *Whence Came They?*, 126–127.

177 "The Convert Immigrants," *The Trek West*, The Church of Jesus Christ of Latter-day Saints, August 1, 2013, https://history.lds.org/article/pioneer-story-the-convert-immigrants-?land=eng.; Douglas F. Tobler, "Truth Prevailing: The Significance of the Nineteenth-Century LDS Experience in Britain," The Church of Jesus Christ of Latter-day Saints, July 1987. https://www.churchofjesuschrist.org/study/ensign/1987/07/truth-prevailing-the-significance-of-the-nineteenth-century-lds-experience-in-britain?lang=eng.

178 Heber C. Kimball, *Journal of Discourses*, 5:22.

179 John Whitmer, "John Whitmer, History, 1831–circa 1847, Page 27," *The Joseph Smith Papers*, Church History Department of The Church of Jesus Christ of Latter-day Saints, accessed November 15, 2019, https://www.josephsmithpapers.org/paper-summary/

john-whitmer-history-1831-circa-1847/31.

180 "Doctrine and Covenants 133:1–35" in *Doctrine and Covenants and Church History Seminary Teacher Manual*, The Church of Jesus Christ of Latter-Day Saints, accessed December 18, 2019, https://www.churchofjesuschrist.org/study/manual/doctrine-and-covenants-and-church-history-seminary-teacher-manual-2014/section-7/lesson-141-doctrine-and-covenants-133-1-35?lang=eng.

181 Hansen, *Whence Came They?*, 92–93.

Chapter 3

182 Nick Bunker, *Making Haste from Babylon: The Pilgrims and Their World, A New History* (New York: Alfred A. Knopf, 2010), 47.

183 Rebecca Fraser, *The Mayflower: The Families, the Voyage, and the Founding of America* (New York: St. Martin's Press, 2017), 39.

184 Bunker, *Making Haste from Babylon*, 31.

185 Fraser, *The Mayflower*, 39.

186 William Bradford, *Bradford's History of Plymouth Plantation: 1606–1646*, ed. William T. Davis (New York: Barnes & Noble, 1946), 95.

187 Bradford, *History of Plymouth Plantation*, 92–96.

188 Bunker, *Making Haste from Babylon*, 31.

189 The full account is given in the Editorial Preface of Bradford, *History of Plymouth Plantation*; see also Francis B. Dedmond, "A Forgotten Attempt to Rescue the Bradford Manuscript," *The New England Quarterly* 58. No.2 (June, 1985): 242–252; Thomas R. Turner and Jennifer A. Turner, "Abraham Lincoln and the Plymouth Forefathers Monument," *The Bridgewater Review* 22, Issue 2 (December 2003).

190 Turner and Turner, "Plymouth Forefathers Monument."

191 Deetz, Patrica, and James Deetz. "The Plymouth Colony Archive Project."

Mayflower Passenger Deaths, 1620–1621. The University of Illinois at Urbana-Champaign. Accessed February 20, 2020. http://www.histarch.illinois.edu/plymouth/Maydeaths.html.

192 Philbrick, *Mayflower*, 119.

193 Edward Winslow, *Mourt's Relation, or Journal of the Plantation at Plymouth, With an Introduction and Notes by Henry M. Dexter*, ed. Henry Martyn Dexter (Boston: J. K. Wiggin, 1865), 83–85.

194 Winslow, *Mourt's Relation*, 59–64.

195 Paget, *History of the Plymouth Settlement*, 80; Fraser, *The Mayflower*, 66–67.

196 Gragg, *The Pilgrim Chronicles*, 252–253.

197 Philbrick, *Mayflower*, 96.

198 Gragg, *The Pilgrim Chronicles*, 252.

199 Marshall and Manual, *The Light and the Glory*, 168.

200 Philbrick, *Mayflower*, 115–116.

201 Alexander Young, *Chronicles of the Pilgrim Fathers of the Colony of Plymouth: 1602–1625* (Boston: Freeman & Bolles, 1841), 408.

202 Edward Winslow, *Good News from New England: A True Relation of Things Very Remarkable at the Plantation of Plimoth in New England* (Bedford, MA: Applewood Books, 1996), 32–37.

203 Fraser, *The Mayflower*, 95.

204 Fraser, *The Mayflower*, 84–86.

205 Fraser, *The Mayflower*, 112.

206 Philbrick, *Mayflower*, 66, 91; Karen Ordahl Kupperman, "The Puzzle of the American Climate in the Early Colonial Period," *The American Historical Review* 87, no. 5 (December 1982): 1262–289.

207 Young, *Chronicles of the Pilgrim Fathers*, 347–350.

208 Gragg, *The Pilgrim Chronicles*, 274–276.

209 As quoted in Matthew S. Holland, *Bonds of Affection: Civic Charity and the Making of America—Winthrop, Jefferson, and Lincoln* (Washington D.C.: Georgetown University Press, 2007), 1–2.

210 John Winthrop, *The Journal of John Winthrop: 1630–1649*, eds. Richard S.

Dunn and Laetitia Yeandle (Cambridge, MA: Belknap Press, 1996), 9.

211 Winthrop, *The Journal of John Winthrop*, 10.

212 Ibid.

213 Edward Johnson, *Wonder-working Providence: 1628–1651*, ed. by J. Franklin Jameson (New York: Charles Scribner's Sons, 1910), 47.

214 Winthrop, *The Journal of John Winthrop*, 10–11.

215 Winthrop, *The Journal of John Winthrop*, 9.

216 John Cotton, *God's Promise to His Plantations* (London: John Bellamy, 1630), 13–15.

217 Sacvan Bercovitch, "'Nehemias Americanus': Cotton Mather and the Concept of the Representative American." *Early American Literature* 8, no. 3 (1974): 220–238.

218 Samuel Sewall, *Diary of Samuel Sewall: 1674–1729. Vol 1.* (Boston: Massachusetts Historical Society, 1878), 58.

219 John Winthrop, "Reasons for the Plantation in New England," The Winthrop Society: Descendants of the Great Migration, accessed August 03, 2017, http://winthropsociety.com/doc_reasons.php.

220 Jonathan Edwards, *The Works of Jonathan Edwards, Vol. I–III*, ed. Anthony Uyl (Woodstock, ON: Devoted Press, 2017), 35.

221 Perry Miller, *Errand into the Wilderness* (Cambridge, MA: The Belknap Press of Harvard University Press, 1956), 11.

222 Fraser, *The Mayflower*, 120.

223 Fraser, *The Mayflower*, 133

224 William Cullen Bryant, ed., *Picturesque America, or the Land We Live In: A Delineation by Pen and Pencil of the Mountains, Rivers, Lakes,* (New York: D. Appleton, 1872), 502.

225 Jeffrey R. Holland, "Prophets, Seers, and Revelators," *Ensign,* November 2004. The Cotton Mather statement is from *Magnalia Christi Americana; or, The Ecclesiastical History of New-England, from Its First Planting, in the Year 1620, unto the Year of Our Lord 1698 in seven books, Vol. 2* (Hartford, Silas Andrus, 1820), 432.

226 LaPlante, *Salem Witch Judge,* 133; Jess Blumberg, "A Brief History of the Salem Witch Trials," Smithsonian.com, Smithsonian Institution, October 23, 2007, accessed December 16, 2019, https://www.smithsonianmag.com/history/a-brief-history-of-the-salem-witch-trials-175162489.

227 LaPlante, *Salem Witch Judge,* 207–208; Sewall, *Diary of Samuel Sewall,* 53.

228 Ibid.

229 See D&C 28; 42:8–9, 30–42; 45:66–67; 52:2, 42–43; 57:1–5; 58:7, 44–58; 84:2–5.

230 LaPlante, *Salem Witch Judge,* 220, 222; Sewall, *Diary of Samuel Sewall,* 94.

231 Harold B. Lee, "Teach the Gospel of Salvation," The Church of Jesus Christ of Latter-day Saints, accessed August 03, 2017, https://www.lds.org/general-conference/1972/10/teach-the-gospel-of-salvation?lang=eng.

232 Samuel Sewall, "The Selling of Joseph," Libraries at University of Nebraska-Lincoln, http://digitalcommons.unl.edu/etas/26.

233 Samuel Sewall, *Phaenomena quaedam Apocalyptica ad aspectum Novi Orbis configurata,* ed. Reiner Smolinski Evans, Early American Imprint Collection, Libraries at University of Nebraska-Lincoln, http://digitalcommons.unl.edu/etas/25/.

234 Samuel Macpherson Janney, *The Life of William Penn* (Philadelphia, PA: Friend's Book Association, 1882), 246.

235 Sewall, *Phaenomena quaedam Apocalyptica.*

236 Sewall, *Diary of Samuel Sewall,* 318.

237 W. H. Bennett, *Symbols of Our Celto-Saxon Heritage* (Windsor, Ontario: Herald Press Limited, 1995), 29.

238 David Ovason, *The Secret Architecture of Our Nation's Capital*, 218.

239 Ovason, *Secret Architecture*, 218–221.

240 John Adams, "Online Library of Liberty," *The Works of John Adams, vol. 2 (Diary, Notes of Debates, Autobiography)*, Online Library of Liberty, accessed August 08, 2017, http://oll.libertyfund.org/titles/2100#lf1431-02_footnote_nt_328_ref.

241 Lewis R. Harley, *The Life of Charles Thomson: Secretary of the Continental Congress and Translator of the Bible from Greek* (Philadelphia: George W. Jacobs & Co., 1900), 49.

242 Harley, *The Life of Charles Thomson*, 49.

243 Gary A. Warrick, "The Precontact Iroquoian Occupation of Southern Ontario," ed. Jordan E. Kerber, *Archeology of the Iroquois* (Syracuse: Syracuse University Press, 2007), 124.

244 Moroni finished the Book of Moroni, as part of the Book of Mormon, around 421 AD. See Moroni Chapter 10.

245 Morris K. Udall, "H.Con.Res.331—100th Congress (1987–1988): A Concurrent Resolution to Acknowledge the Contribution of the Iroquois Confederacy of Nations to the Development of the United States Constitution and to Reaffirm the Continuing Government-to-Government Relationship between Indian Tribes and the United States Established in the Constitution." govinfo. U.S. Government Publishing Office, October 21, 1988. https://www.govinfo.gov/content/pkg/STATUTE-102/pdf/STATUTE-102-Pg4932-2.pdf.

246 Ibid.

247 From the Iroquois Constitution, quoted in Arthur C. Parker, *The Constitution of the Five Nations* (Albany: New York State Museum Bulletin, 1916), 8–9.

248 Parker, *Constitution of the Five Nations*, 9.

249 Parker, *Constitution of the Five Nations*, 30.

250 Horatio Hale, *Hiawatha and The Iroquois Confederation: A Study in Anthropology* (Salem, MA: Salem Press, 1881), 9–13.

251 Parker, *Constitution of the Five Nations*, 9–11.

252 See 2 Samuel 2:4; 1 Chr. 29:22; for the dismissal of a leader, see 2 Chr. 10:16; for the people's approval and consent of new legislation, see Exodus 19:8. Furthermore, the government under Moses boasted of separate branches of government, as explained in Feiler, *America's Prophet*, 94. In 1788, while the Constitution was being debated for final ratification, colonial leaders, including Samuel Langdon and Benjamin Franklin, pointed out how God, through the Constitution, had resurrected the government of ancient Israel in modern America, as explained in Feiler, *America's Prophet*, 94–95.

253 Moroni finished the Book of Moroni, as part of the Book of Mormon, around 421 AD. See Moroni Chapter 10.

254 Gary A. Warrick, "The Precontact Iroquoian Occupation of Southern Ontario," ed. Jordan E. Kerber, *Archeology of the Iroquois: Selected Readings and Research Sources* (Syracuse: Syracuse University Press, 2007), 124.

255 LaPlante, *Salem Witch Judge*, 99.

256 LaPlante, *Salem Witch Judge*, 273.

257 LaPlante, *Salem Witch Judge*, 271.

258 Feiler, *America's Prophet*, 92–93.

259 George Washington, "Washington's Inaugural Address of 1789," National Archives and Records Administration, accessed December 6, 2019, https://www.archives.gov/exhibits/american_originals/inaugtxt.html.

260 Hilary Parkinson, "On Exhibit: George Washington's First Inaugural Address and Bible," A blog of the U.S. National Archives, National Archives and Records Administration,

January 9, 2017, accessed December 18, 2019. https://prologue.blogs.archives.gov/2017/01/09/on-exhibit-george-washingtons-first-inaugural-address-and-bible/.

261 Wilford Woodruff, "Leaves from my Journal," *Millennial Star*, May 23, 1881, 334–335.

262 Ibid. Wilford Woodruff heard his first sermon from an LDS missionary on December 29, 1833; see "Chapter 4: Wilford Woodruff: Fourth President of the Church," in *Presidents of the Church Student Manual*, The Church of Jesus Christ of Latter-day Saints, accessed December 6, 2019, https://www.churchofjesuschrist.org/study/manual/presidents-of-the-church-student-manual/chapter-4?lang=eng.

263 "The Great Migration of Picky Puritans, 1620-40," New England Historical Society, November 18, 2019, http://www.newenglandhistoricalsociety.com/the-great-migration-of-picky-puritans-1620-40/.

264 Marshall and Manual, *The Light and the Glory*, 186.

265 Cotton Mather and John Higginson, *Magnalia Christi Americana: or, The Ecclesiastical History of New-England, from Its First Planting, in the Year 1620, Unto the Year of Our Lord 1698* (London: Printed for Thomas Parkhurst, 1702), 7–8.

266 William Bradford and Edward Winslow, "Mourt's Relation: A Journal of the Pilgrims at Plymouth, 1622, Part I," The University of Illinois at Urbana-Champaign, January 1, 1970, accessed December 18, 2019, http://www.histarch.illinois.edu/plymouth/mourt1.html.

267 Deane, *History of Plymouth Plantation*, 82–83.

268 Bradford and Winslow, "Mourt's Relation, Part 1."

269 William T. Davis, *Ancient Landmarks of Plymouth. Part I. Historical Sketch and Titles of Estates. Part II. Genealogical Register of Plymouth Families, Vol.1–2* (Boston: A. Williams & Co., 1883), 150.

270 Johnson, *Of Plymouth Plantation*, 120–121.

271 Johnson, *Of Plymouth Plantation*, 468.

272 Gragg, *The Pilgrim Chronicles*, 224.

273 Feiler, *America's Prophet*, 7–9, 24–25.

274 Feiler, *America's Prophet*, 26; Ronald Reagan, "Remarks at the Opening Ceremonies of the Statue of Liberty Centennial Celebration in New York, New York,: Ronald Reagan Presidential Library—National Archives and Records Administration," Ronald Reagan Presidential Library & Museum, National Archives and Records Administration, July 4, 1986, https://www.reaganlibrary.gov/research/speeches/70386d.; John Winthrop, "A Model of Christian Charity." The Winthrop Society: Descendants of the Great Migration, April 8, 1630, https://www.winthropsociety.com/doc_charity.php.; Martin Luther King, Jr., "I've Been to the Mountaintop." American Rhetoric, April 3, 1968, https://www.americanrhetoric.com/speeches/mlkivebeentothemountaintop.htm.; Deuteronomy 30:15–20.

275 See "Howland Family Chart," Family Search, https://familysearch.org/wiki/en/images/4/4c/Howland_Chart.pdf.

276 "Lucy Mack Smith, History, 1845," p. 190, *The Joseph Smith Papers*, accessed December 6, 2019, https://www.josephsmithpapers.org/paper-summary/lucy-mack-smith-history-1845/198.

277 "Letter to Emma Smith, 12 November 1838," p. [2], *The Joseph Smith Papers*, accessed December 6, 2019, https://www.josephsmithpapers.org/paper-summary/letter-to-emma-smith-12-november-1838/2.

278 Heber J. Grant in *One Hundredth Annual Conference of The Church of Jesus Christ of Latter-day Saints* (Salt Lake

City, UT: Deseret Book Company, 1930), 8.

Chapter 4

279 *Oxford Dictionaries*, s. v. "Pilgrim,» https://en.oxforddictionaries.com/ definition/pilgrim.

280 Thomas Jefferson, "Thomas Jefferson First Inaugural Address," Avalon Project - Yale Law School, accessed August 04, 2017, http://avalon.law.yale.edu/19th_century/jefinau1.asp.

281 Thomas Jefferson, "A Bill for Establishing Religious Freedom, 18 June 1779," National Archives and Records Administration, accessed December 17, 2019, https://founders.archives.gov/ documents/Jefferson/01-42-02-0203

282 Thomas Jefferson, "Second Inaugural Address March 4, 1805," Avalon Project - Yale Law School, accessed August 04, 2017, http://avalon.law.yale.edu/19th_century/jefinau2.asp.

283 Thomas Jefferson, "Jefferson's Proposal, 20 August 1776," National Archives and Records Administration, accessed August 04, 2017, https:// founders.archives.gov/documents/ Jefferson/01–01-02–0206–0002.

284 Thomas Jefferson, "Thomas Jefferson to Charles Thomson, 9 January 1816," National Archives and Records Administration, accessed August 04, 2017, https://founders.archives.gov/ documents/Jefferson/03–09-02–0216.

285 Thomas Jefferson, "From Thomas Jefferson to Benjamin Waterhouse, 26 June 1822," National Archives and Records Administration, accessed August 04, 2017, https:// founders.archives.gov/documents/ Jefferson/98–01-02–2905.

286 Thomas Jefferson, "From Thomas Jefferson to John Adams, 11 April 1823," National Archives and Records Administration, accessed August 04, 2017, https://founders.archives.gov/ documents/Jefferson/98–01-02–3446.

287 Thomas Jefferson, "Thomas Jefferson to William Baldwin (Draft), 19 January 1810," National Archives and Records Administration, accessed August 04, 2017, https:// founders.archives.gov/documents/ Jefferson/03–02-02–0124–0002.

288 Thomas Jefferson, "From Thomas Jefferson to Thomas Cooper, 14 August 1820," National Archives and Records Administration, accessed December 17, 2019, https://founders.archives.gov/ documents/Jefferson/98-01-02-1453.

289 Thomas Jefferson, "Thomas Jefferson to Francis Adrian Van der Kemp, 30 July 1816," National Archives and Records Administration, accessed August 04, 2017, https://founders.archives.gov/ documents/Jefferson/03–10-02–0167.

290 Thomas Jefferson, as quoted by Tad Callister, *The Inevitable Apostasy* (Salt Lake: Deseret Book, 2006), 217–218; Thomas Jefferson, "From Thomas Jefferson to Timothy Pickering, 27 February 1821," National Archives and Records Administration, accessed August 04, 2017, https:// founders.archives.gov/documents/ Jefferson/98–01-02–1870.

291 Jefferson, as quoted in Callister, *The Inevitable Apostasy and the Promised Restoration* (Salt Lake City: Deseret Book, 2006), 105–106, emphasis added. Jefferson, Thomas. "From Thomas Jefferson to Jared Sparks, 4 November 1820," National Archives and Records Administration, accessed August 04, 2017, https://founders.archives.gov/ documents/Jefferson/98–01-02–1628.

292 Christopher Columbus, *The Journal of Christopher Columbus (During His First Voyage, 1492–93)*, trans. Clements R. Markham (London: The Hakluyt Society, 1893), 137.

293 David McCullough, *Truman* (New York: Simon and Schuster, 1992), 28.

294 McCullough, *Truman*, 28.

295 Bob Corbett, "Napoleon's West Indian

Policy and the Haitian 'Gift' To The United States," Haiti: Revolution Part 4, Webster University, September 1991, http://faculty.webster.edu/corbetre/haiti/history/revolution/revolution4.htm.; Edward E. Baptist, "The Ironic, Tragic History of the Louisiana Purchase That Your Teacher Never Told You," *Slate Magazine*, Slate, August 6, 2015. https://slate.com/human-interest/2015/08/the-most-successful-slave-rebellion-in-history-created-an-independent-haiti-and-secured-the-louisiana-purchase-and-the-expansion-of-north-american-slavery.html.

296 Ibid.

297 Ibid.

298 Thomas Jefferson, "From Thomas Jefferson to Robert R. Livingston, 18 April 1802," National Archives and Records Administration, accessed August 04, 2017, https://founders.archives.gov/?q=%E2%80%9C-France%20placing%20herself%20in%20that%20door%20assumes%20to%20us%20the%20attitude%20of%20defiance%2C%E2%80%9D%20&s=1111311111&sa=&r=1&sr=

299 Ibid.

300 Henry Adams, *History of the United States of America* (New York: Charles Scribner's Sons, 1889), 390–391.

301 Bob Corbett, "Napoleon's West Indian Policy and the Haitian 'Gift' To The United States," Haiti: Revolution Part 4, Webster University, September 1991, http://faculty.webster.edu/corbetre/haiti/history/revolution/revolution4.htm.; Edward E. Baptist, "The Ironic, Tragic History of the Louisiana Purchase That Your Teacher Never Told You," *Slate Magazine*, Slate, August 6, 2015. https://slate.com/human-interest/2015/08/the-most-successful-slave-rebellion-in-history-created-an-independent-haiti-and-secured-the-louisiana-purchase-and-the-expansion-of-north-american-slavery.html.

302 Corbett, "The Haitian 'Gift' to the United States"; Baptist, "The Louisiana Purchase."

303 As quoted in Michele Wucker, *Why the Cocks Fight: Dominicans, Haitians, and the Struggle for Hispaniola* (New York: Hill and Wang, 1999), 80.

304 Bob Corbett, "Napoleon's West Indian Policy and the Haitian 'Gift' To The United States," Haiti: Revolution Part 4, Webster University, September 1991, http://faculty.webster.edu/corbetre/haiti/history/revolution/revolution4.htm.; Edward E. Baptist, "The Ironic, Tragic History of the Louisiana Purchase That Your Teacher Never Told You," *Slate Magazine*, Slate, August 6, 2015. https://slate.com/human-interest/2015/08/the-most-successful-slave-rebellion-in-history-created-an-independent-haiti-and-secured-the-louisiana-purchase-and-the-expansion-of-north-american-slavery.html.

305 Bob Corbett, "Napoleon's West Indian Policy and the Haitian 'Gift' To The United States," Haiti: Revolution Part 4, Webster University, September 1991, http://faculty.webster.edu/corbetre/haiti/history/revolution/revolution4.htm.; Edward E. Baptist, "The Ironic, Tragic History of the Louisiana Purchase That Your Teacher Never Told You," *Slate Magazine*, Slate, August 6, 2015. https://slate.com/human-interest/2015/08/the-most-successful-slave-rebellion-in-history-created-an-independent-haiti-and-secured-the-louisiana-purchase-and-the-expansion-of-north-american-slavery.html.

306 Frederick Douglass, "Lecture on Haiti," American Memory from the Library of Congress, accessed August 04, 2017, https://www.loc.gov/item/mfd.25020.

307 West and Kling, *Libro de las profecías,* 229.

308 Lester C. Edwards and Andrew Edwards Foster, *The Life and Voyages of Americus Vespucius: with Ilustrations Concerning the Navigator, and the Discovery of the New World* (New Haven: H. Mansfield, 1855), 87–88.

309 Dedicatory Prayer for the Port-Au-Prince Haiti Temple, September 1, 2019, available at Churchofjesuschrist.org/church/news/dedicatory-prayer-for-the-port-au-prince-haiti-temple?lang=eng

310 As quoted in Jon Meacham, *Thomas Jefferson: The Art of Power* (New York: Random House, 2013), 387.

311 Michael Medved, *The American Miracle: Divine Providence in the Rise of the Republic* (New York: Crown Forum, 2017), 140.

312 Richard Kluger, *Seizing Destiny: How America Grew from Sea to Shining Sea* (New York: Vintage Books, 2008) 279.

313 Henry Adams, *History of the United States of America, during the First Administration of Thomas Jefferson* (New York: Scribner, 1909), 36.

314 Harriss, Joseph A. "How the Louisiana Purchase Changed the World." Smithsonian.com. Smithsonian Institution, April 1, 2003. https://www.smithsonianmag.com/history/how-the-louisiana-purchase-changed-the-world-79715124/.

315 Meacham, *The Art of Power,* 387–388.

316 Meacham, *The Art of Power,* 387, 389.

317 "Purchase of Louisiana, [5 July 1803]," Founders Online, National Archives, accessed September 29, 2019, https://founders.archives.gov/documents/Hamilton/01-26-02-0001-0101. [Original source: The Papers of Alexander Hamilton, vol. 26, 1 May 1802–23 October 1804, Additional Documents 1774–1799, Addenda and Errata, ed. Harold C. Syrett. New York: Columbia University Press, 1979, pp. 129–136.]

318 Charles Cerami, *Jefferson's Great Gamble: The Remarkable Story of Jefferson, Napoleon and the Men behind the Louisiana Purchase* (Naperville: Sourcebooks, 2003), 277.

319 As quoted in Meacham, *Thomas Jefferson: The Art of Power,* 388.

Chapter 5

320 Sereno Edwards Dwight, Edward Hickman, and Jonathan Edwards, *The Works of Jonathan Edwards* (United Kingdom: Westley and Davis, 1835), 383.

321 Joseph Ellis, *First Family: Abigail & John Adams* (New York: Alfred A. Knopf, 2010), 5.

322 John Adams, "Letter from John Adams to Abigail Smith, 4 October 1762," masshist.org, Massachusetts Historical Society, accessed December 19, 2019, https://www.masshist.org/digitaladams/archive/doc?id=L17621004ja&bc=/digitaladams/archive/browse/letters_1762_1773.php.

323 Abigail Adams, "Abigail Adams to John Adams, 29 August 1776," National Archives and Records Administration, accessed December 18, 2019, https://founders.archives.gov/documents/Adams/04-02-02-0071.

324 John Adams, "John Adams to Abigail Smith, 30 September 1764," National Archives and Records Administration, accessed December 18, 2019, https://founders.archives.gov/documents/Adams/04-01-02-0038.

325 Abigail Adams, "Founders Online: Abigail Adams to John Adams, 25 October 1782," National Archives and Records Administration, accessed December 18, 2019, https://founders.archives.gov/documents/Adams/04-05-02-0013.

326 Abigail Adams, "Abigail Adams to John Adams, 23 December 1782," National Archives and Records Administration, accessed December 18, 2019, https://

founders.archives.gov/documents/
Adams/04-05-02-0030.

327 Abigail Adams, "Abigail Adams to John
Adams, 15 August 1774," National
Archives and Records Administration,
accessed December 18, 2019, https://
founders.archives.gov/documents/
Adams/04-01-02-0092.

328 Abigail Adams, "Abigail Adams to
John Adams, 17 June 1776," Founders
Online, accessed December 18,
2019, https://founders.archives.gov/
documents/Adams/04-02-02-0009.

329 David McCullough, *John Adams* (New
York: Simon & Schuster, 2004), 127.

330 David McCullough, *John Adams*.

331 The details and background of this great
speech of Adams, to include the quotes
used in this book to describe it, can be
found in McCullough, *John Adams*,
126–129.

332 McCullough, *John Adams*, 129.

333 McCullough, *John Adams*, 160.

334 Ellis, *First Family*, 53.

335 McCullough, *John Adams*, 130.

336 McCullough, *John Adams*, 41.

337 John C. McCollister, *God and the Oval
Office: The Religious Faith of Our 43
Presidents* (Nashville: W Publishing
Group, 2005), 11–12.

338 John Adams, "From John Adams
to Samuel Quincy, 22 April 1761,"
National Archives and Records
Administration, accessed August 16,
2017, https://founders.archives.gov/
documents/Adams/06-01-02-0039.

339 John Adams, "John Adams to Thomas
Jefferson, 14 September 1813," National
Archives and Records Administration,
accessed August 16, 2017, https://
founders.archives.gov/documents/
Jefferson/03-06-02-0389.

340 John Adams, "The Diary of John
Adams, February 1765," National
Archives and Records Administration,
accessed August 16, 2017, https://
founders.archives.gov/documents/
Adams/01-01-02-0009-0002.

341 John Adams, "John Adams to Abigail
Adams, 3 July 1776," Founders
Online, National Archives and Records
Administration, accessed December 17,
2019, https://founders.archives.gov/
documents/Adams/04-02-02-0016.

342 Charles Francis Adams, *Familiar Letters
of John Adams and His Wife Abigail
Adams During the Revolution: With a
Memoir of Mrs. Adams* (New York, NY:
Hurd and Houghton, 1876), 381.

343 McCullough, *John Adams*, 119–120.

344 Ellis, *First Family*, 115.

345 Ellis, *First Family*, 121, 136.

346 McCullough, 600; Joseph J. Ellis,
*Founding Brothers: The Revolutionary
Generation* (New York: Alfred A. Knopf,
2000), 220; Rush, Benjamin, *Letters of
Benjamin Rush*, L. H. Butterfield, editor
(Princeton: The American Philosophical
Society, 1951), Vol. II, 1021–1022, to
John Adams on October 17, 1809.

347 McCullough, *John Adams,* 600; Adams,
John. "From John Adams to Benjamin
Rush, 25 October 1809," National
Archives and Records Administration,
accessed August 16, 2017, https://
founders.archives.gov/documents/
Adams/99-02-02-5454.

348 McCullough, *John Adams,* 603.

349 McCullough, *John Adams,* 603–604.

350 "Abigail Adams (1744 - 1818)," National
Parks Service, U.S. Department of the
Interior, April 30, 2015, https://www.
nps.gov/adam/learn/historyculture/abi-
gail-adams-1744-1818.htm.

351 Ellis, *First Family,* 244.

352 McCollister, *God and the Oval Office,*
13.

353 McCullough, *John Adams*, 262.

354 Henry S. Randall, *The Life of Thomas
Jefferson* (New York: Derby & Jackson,
1858), 382.

355 Meacham, *The Art of Power,* 146.

356 William Eleroy Curtis, *The True Thomas
Jefferson* (Philadelphia: Kessinger
Publishing, LLC., 2007), 35; Jefferson

borrowed these words from Homer's *Iliad.*

357 Thomas Jefferson, "To John Adams from Thomas Jefferson, 13 November 1818," National Archives and Records Administration, accessed August 16, 2017, https://founders.archives.gov/documents/Adams/99-02-02-7026.

358 Thomas Jefferson, "Thomas Jefferson to Benjamin Rush, 5 December 1811," National Archives and Records Administration, accessed August 16, 2017, https://founders.archives.gov/documents/Jefferson/03-04-02-0248.

359 John Adams, "From John Adams to Thomas Jefferson, 8 December 1818," National Archives and Records Administration, accessed August 16, 2017, https://founders.archives.gov/documents/Adams/99-02-02-7039.

360 Amanda A. Mathews, "I Can Do Nothing without You: The 250th Anniversary of John and Abigail Adams," The Beehive, The Official Blog of the MHS, The Massachusetts Historical Society, May 8, 2019, http://www.masshist.org/beehive-blog/2014/10/i-can-do-nothing-without-you-the-250th-anniversary-of-john-and-abigail-adams/.

361 McCullough, *John Adams,* 643.

362 Thomas Jefferson, "From Thomas Jefferson to Thomas Jefferson Smith, 21 February 1825," Founders Early Access, The University of Virginia Press, accessed August 16, 2017, http://rotunda.upress.virginia.edu/founders/default.xqy?keys=FOEA-print-04-02-02-4987.

363 McCullough, *John Adams,* 650.

364 John Quincy Adams, as quoted by Richard Brookhiser, *What Would the Founders Do?: Our Questions, Their Answers* (New York: Basic Books, 2006), 6.

365 Daniel Webster, as quoted in McCullough, *John Adams,* 648. It is worth noting that Daniel Webster, along with John Quincy Adams, fittingly participated in the miracle at the St. George Temple. See Vicki Jo Anderson, *The Other Eminent Men of Wilford Woodruff* (Cottonwood, Zichron Historical Institute, 1994), preface.

366 McCullough, *John Adams,* 642.

367 McCullough, *John Adams,* 645.

368 McCullough, *John Adams,* 646.

369 Ibid.

370 Ellis, *Founding Brothers,* 220.

371 Jefferson, as quoted in Callister, *The Inevitable Apostasy,* 106, emphasis added.

372 Susa Young Gates and Leah D. Widtsoe, *The Life Story of Brigham Young* (Whitefish, MT: Kessinger Publishing, LLC, 2010), 362.

373 Daniel Webster, "Adams and Jefferson, August 2, 1826," *Adams and Jefferson,* Dartmouth College, accessed December 18, 2019, www.dartmouth.edu/~dwebster/speeches/adams-jefferson.html.

374 John Quincy Adams, "December 5, 1826: Second Annual Address," Miller Center, University of Virginia, February 23, 2017, accessed December 19, 2019, https://millercenter.org/the-presidency/presidential-speeches/december-5-1826-second-annual-address

375 McCullough, *John Adams,* 646.

376 McCullough, *John Adams,* 647.

377 Ibid.

378 *Journal of Discourses,* 19:229, September 16, 1877.

379 Thomas E. Daniels, "Has the Temple Work for the Founding Fathers of the United States Been Done?" *Ensign,* October 1991, The Church of Jesus Christ of Latter-day Saints, October 1991, https://www.churchofjesuschrist.org/study/ensign/1991/10/i-have-a-question/has-the-temple-work-for-the-founding-fathers-of-the-united-states-been-done?lang=eng.

380 Madsen, *Presidents of the Church,*, 104–105.

381 Wilford Woodruff, *Conference Report,* April 1898, 89–90.

382 These are but a sample of the more than 190 men and women recorded in church records, including Wilford Woodruff's personal journal at the BYU Special Collections library, to have received their temple baptisms and endowments pursuant to the visitation, as discussed in Anderson, *The Other Eminent Men of Wilford Woodruff*, Preface and Introduction, 1–2.

383 McCullough, *John Adams*, 646.

384 *Diary of Charles Francis Adams (1807–1886)*, for the period May 14, 1844 to May 16, 1844, available at Book of Abraham Project, Brigham Young University, www.boap.org/LDS/EarlySaints/CFA.html; Richard Bushman, *Joseph Smith: Rough Stone Rolling* (New York: Alfred A. Knopf, 2005), 3–7.

385 Hyde, in *Journal of Discourses*, 6:368. This was given in a speech on July 4, 1854, in the Tabernacle at Temple Square. In the speech, Elder Hyde makes it abundantly clear that he is referring to the Angel Moroni. Elder Hyde describes this visiting angel as the same "that appeared unto Joseph Smith, and revealed to him the history of the early inhabitants of this country."

386 Ibid.

387 Orson Hyde (July 4, 1854), as quoted in *Journal of Discourses* 6:368 (Liverpool, England: F. D. and S. W. Richards, 1854–1866), 368.

388 Daniel Webster, *The Speeches and Orations of Daniel Webster: With an Essay on Daniel Webster as a Master of English Style*, ed. Edwin P. Whipple (Boston, MA: Little, Brown, and Co., 1914), 27.

389 Daniel Webster, *Speeches and Forensic Arguments* (Boston: Perkins & Marvin, 1830), 56.

390 Fletcher Webster, ed., *The Private Correspondence of Daniel Webster. Vol. 1* (Boston: Little, Brown, 1857), 318.

Conclusion

391 Sam Eaton, "59 Percent of Millennials Raised in a Church Have Dropped Out," FaithIt.com, accessed December 16, 2019, http://faithit.com/12-reasons-millennials-over-church-sam-eaton/.

Index

IMAGE CREDITS

Jacob Blessing Ephraim and Manasseh, Rembrandt, 1656. Public Domain: 4.

Santo Domingo - Alcázar de Colón, March 2016, part of UNESCO World Heritage Site Ref. Number 526, Martin Falbisoner: 16.

The story of the United States by Marshall, H. E. (Henrietta Elizabeth), b. 1876. Public Domain: 21.

Appendix, Bradford's History "Of Plimoth Plantation." Public Domain: 75.

Jean de Marco, artist, *Moses (c. 1350-1250 B.C.) Hebrew prophet and lawgiver.*, Architect of the Capitol. Public Domain: 77.

Photograph of U.S Supreme Court Building, Washington D.C. by Matthew Cooper: 77.

Mike Haywood, artist, *Pilgrim Overboard*, Painting. http://www.mikehaywoodart.co.uk/images/ Pilgrim-overboard-800.jpg/: 81.

Snow, Erastus Fairbanks, 1818-1888--Portraits; L. Tom Perry Special Collections, Harold B. Lee Library, Brigham Young University: 83.

Map of Europe and Middle East © Mapbox, © OpenStreetMap. http://www.mapbox.com/, https://www.openstreetmap.org/: 90.

Thomas Wallace Knox, *The Pass of Dariel, Caucasus,* 1887. Public Domain: 91

The romanticized woodcut engraving of Flavius Josephus appearing in William Whiston's translation of his works. Public Domain: 92.

Proposal for the official seal of the nation/Originally printed in The New Harper's Magazine, Volume 13, Issue 74, July 1856, page 180, article Great Seal of the United States by Benson J. Lossing. Public Domain: 97.

Westminster Abbey. https://commons.wikimedia.org/wiki/File:Westminster-Abbey.JPG/: 98.

Sodacan, artist, 2010, *Coat of arms of HRH Prince William, Duke of Cambridge (Formerly Prince William of Wales, William Arthur Philip Louis; born 21 June 1982) son of Prince Charles, Prince of Wales and Lady Diana Spencer.* https://commons.wikimedia.org/wiki/File:Coat_of_Arms_of_ William,_Duke_of_Cambridge.svg/: 105.

Yousuf Karsh. Library and Archives Canada, e010751643 / *The Roaring Lion,* 1941. Photograph. Public Domain: 107.

Flag of the United Kingdom. Public Domain: 110.

David Dugan, photographer, monument to the forefathers, front. https://web.archive.org/ web/20161031123622/http://www.panoramio.com/photo/125733132/: 115.

Cover of Manuscript, Bradford's History "Of Plimoth Plantation." Public Domain: 120.

Bryant, William Cullen, 1794-1878 Gay, Sydney Howard, 1814-1888, *A popular history of the United States : from the first discovery of the western hemisphere by the Northmen, to the end of the first century of the union of the states ; preceded by a sketch of the prehistoric period and the age of the mound builders.* Public Domain: 125.

Brooks, Elbridge Streeter, 1846-1902 Daughters of the American Revolution, *The Century book of famous Americans : the story of a young people's pilgrimage to historic homes,* The Institute of Museum and Library Services through an Indiana State Library LSTA Grant: 126.

Bodge, George M. (George Madison), 1841-1914. cn, *Soldiers in King Philip's war; being a critical account of that war, with a concise history of the Indian wars of New England from 1620-1677, official lists of the soldiers of Massachusetts colony serving in Philip's war, and sketches of the principal officers, copies of ancient documents and records relating to the war, also lists of the Narraganset grantees of the united colonies, Massachusetts, Plymouth, and Conneticut; with an appendix, 3d ed., with additional appendix containing corrections and new material,* Allen County Public Library Genealogy Center: 128.

John Winthrop, c. 1800, after an original likeness probably painted in England before 1630. Public Domain: 132.

Engraving from The Providence Plantations for 250 Years, *Welcome Arnold Greene, 1886, Return of Roger Williams from England with the First Charter, 1644. From a painting by C.R. Grant. Engraving from The Providence Plantations for 250 Years, Welcome Arnold Greene,* From a painting by C.R. Grant. Public Domain: 137.

John Smibert, artist, Bequest of William L. Barnard, by exchange, and Emily L. Ainsley Fund, *Judge Samuel Sewall,* 1729, Museum of Fine Arts, Boston. Painting. Public Domain: 141.

Nicholas Gevelot, artist, Sandstone, 1827, Capitol Rotunda, above north door. Architect of the Capitol. Public Domain: 142.

John Mix Stanley, The Trial of Red Jacket, 1869, oil on canvas, Smithsonian American Art Museum, Gift of George M. Stanley (grandson of the artist) and family and museum purchase , 1990.34. Public Domain: 147.

ZooFari, Artist, *Early Indian tribes of the U.S. state of New York,* 2010, Smithsonian Institution. Public Domain: 152.

Ramon de Elorriaga, *George Washington's inauguration as the first President of the United States which took place on April 30, 1789,* c. 1899. Public Domain: 155.

Charles Roscoe Savage (1832–1909), photographer, *Studio portrait of Wilford Woodruff,* Original photograph: ca. 1875 - 1890. Digital version published July 2004 at Brigham Young University.. Public Domain: 159.

Photograph of Corn Hill Monument by Timothy Ballard: 163.

Howland Chart courtesy familysearch.org/: 172.

Joseph and Emma Smith. https://web.archive.org/web/20161019153831/http://www.panoramio.com/photo/60127796/: 174.

From the *The New Harper's Magazine,* Volume 13, Issue 74, July 1856, page 180, article Great Seal of the United States by Benson J. Lossing: 177.

Frederick Douglass, c. 1879. Public Domain: 189.

Photograph of Elder Ballard Dedication by Timothy Ballard: 193.

Gilbert Stuart, Artist, John Adams, [Between c. 1800 and c. 1815], National Gallery of Art. Public Domain: 210.

Gilbert Stuart, Artist, Abigail Smith Adams, [Between c. 1800 and c. 1815], National Gallery of Art. Public Domain: 210.

Rembrandt Peale (1778–1860), Thomas Jefferson, 1800, White House Collection. Public Domain: 225.

Brooks, Elbridge Streeter, 1846-1902, *Charles Francis Adams, Sr., United States Minister to England during the Civil War*, New York Public Library. Public Domain: 234.

Photographs of Adam's family Book of Mormon by Mike Porenta: 235.

Shutterstock/© Pres Panayotov: 100.

iStock.com Images. iStock.com/© bauhaus1000: 53. iStock.com/© bauhaus1000: 72. iStock.com/© sqback: 97, 150. iStock.com/© ZU_09: 100. iStock.com/© Liliboas: 135. iStock.com/© ZU_09: 138. iStock.com/© ChrisGorgio: 147. iStock.com/© t_kimura: 147. iStock.com/© Nosyrevy: 148. iStock.com/© ioanmasay: 148. iStock.com/© AS506: 161. iStock.com/© ZU_09: 167. iStock.com/© GeorgiosArt: 204. iStock.com/© NateAbbott: 231.

Library of Congress Prints and Photographs Division.
Andrews, Joseph, Engraver, and Peter Frederick Rothermel. *Landing of the Pilgrims on Plymouth Rock,/ P.F. Rothermel paintr. ; J. Andrews engravr.* Massachusetts Plymouth Plymouth Rock, ca. 1869. Photograph. https://www.loc.gov/item/2010646064/: 13.

J. & R. Lamb Studios, Designer, and Heinrich Van De Burgh. *Design drawing for stained glass window fanlight atop 4 over 4 pane showing St. Christopher in waist-high water carrying Child giving blessing gesture.*, None. [Between 1900 and 1950] Photograph. https://www.loc.gov/item/2016676816/: 32.

Library of Congress Prints and Photographs Division.
Ferris, Jean Leon Gerome, 1863-1930, artist, *The First Thanksgiving.*, 1621, Painting. http://hdl.loc.gov/loc.pnp/cph.3g04961/: 74.

Lincoln, Abraham. Abraham Lincoln papers: Series 1. General Correspondence. 1833 to 1916: Plymouth Massachusetts Monument Society to Abraham Lincoln, Monday,Receipt for Contribution to Fund. 1861. Manuscript/Mixed Material. https://www.loc.gov/item/mal0908000/: 120.

Hall, Louis, Artist, Vision of Deganawida: confederacy of true humans: Kanonsonnionwe, governed by Gayaneregowa. , None. [Between 1965 and 1980] Photograph. https://www.loc.gov/item/2016648075/: 150.

Sauvage Iroquois. , 1796. Photograph. https://www.loc.gov/item/2002721190/: 151.

Rosskam, E., photographer. Corn Hill, a lonely and windswept spot near Provincetown. Tourist houses on left. Provincetown, Massachusetts. Barnstable County Massacusetts. United States, 1940. Aug. Photograph. https://www.loc.gov/item/2017764679/: 163.

THE LINCOLN

A MODERN-DAY ABOLITIONIST INVESTIGATES
THE POSSIBLE CONNECTION BETWEEN
JOSEPH SMITH, THE BOOK OF MORMON,
AND ABRAHAM LINCOLN

HYPOTHESIS

TIMOTHY BALLARD

About *The Lincoln Hypothesis*

It was a dark time in the history of America. The covenant land had fallen into sin, condoning the evils of slavery and the persecution of religious and ethnic minorities. But there was an answer to the country's woes, and two great leaders—Joseph Smith and Abraham Lincoln—both knew it.

Joseph Smith was killed for his attempts to bring the nation to repentance; Abraham Lincoln lived long enough to play a crucial role in returning the country to its covenant relationship with God. In this fascinating account, author Timothy Ballard shows how that role developed and how Lincoln came to consider himself "a humble instrument in the hands of God."

"As you read," Ballard writes, "you will, like a prosecutor reviewing a case, or like a jury determining a verdict, identify valuable pieces of evidence that can be fully substantiated. You will also identify pieces of evidence that cannot. I ask you to consider all the evidence and weigh it all accordingly. Through this study, many questions regarding the interplay between the restored gospel and the Civil War will be answered. New questions may emerge that will not be so easily answered. Either way, in the end you will find yourself on a most exhilarating investigative journey."

THE
WASHINGTON

A MODERN-DAY INVESTIGATOR EXPLORES
THE POSSIBLE CONNECTION BETWEEN THE
AMERICAN COVENANT, LATTER-DAY TEMPLES,
AND GEORGE WASHINGTON

HYPOTHESIS

TIMOTHY
BALLARD

About *The Washington Hypothesis*

We know that George Washington was a moral man and an
inspiring leader, but did he possibly know more than we suppose?
Was he a national covenant maker like Moses, Abraham, Lehi, or
Captain Moroni? Did he understand that he was fighting for the
liberty of a promised land protected by God, a place where the
Lord's holy temples could be built?

The Washington Hypothesis explores the intriguing evidence
that Washington and the other Founding Fathers knew the Lord
had a greater purpose for America. It takes us on a fascinating
historical journey through the miracles of the Revolutionary War
to the foundational documents of this great nation to the symbolism evident in every corner of the nation's capital. Exploring what
Washington believed and how his beliefs framed his every action,
author Timothy Ballard draws compelling conclusions about the
divinity of that great leader's calling. As we see the evidence of
the Lord's hand in Washington's life and consider what we know
about this promised land, we may discover a much grander design at work in the founding of our nation—and thus a greater
desire to strive to preserve those promised blessings.